KU-298-644

YO' MAMA'S
DISFUNKTIONAL!

Fighting
the Culture Wars
in Urban America

ROBIN D.G. KELLEY

BEACON PRESS · BOSTON

Beacon Press
25 Beacon Street
Boston, Massachusetts 02108-2892
http://www.beacon.org

Beacon Press books
are published under the auspices of
the Unitarian Universalist Association of Congregations.

© 1997 by Robin D.G. Kelley
All rights reserved
Printed in the United States of America

"Horn of Plenty" from *Collected Poems* by Langston Hughes (New York: Alfred A. Knopf, Inc., 1994). Copyright 1994 by Langston Hughes. Reprinted by permission of Alfred A. Knopf, Inc.

"Chocolate City," by George Clinton. Copyright 1975 by Bridgeport Music, Inc. (BMI). Reprinted by permission. All rights reserved.

Chapter 2 appeared in a slightly revised form as "Playing for Keeps: African American Youth in the Postindustrial City," in *The House that Race Built: Black Americans / U.S. Terrain*, ed. Wahneema Lubiano (New York: Random House, 1997), 195–231. Copyright 1997 by Robin D. G. Kelley.

Portions of chapter 5 appeared in a revised form in Robin D. G. Kelley, "The Proletariat Goes to College," *Social Text* 14: 4 (Winter 1996), 37–42. Copyright 1996 by Duke University Press. Reprinted by permission of Duke University Press. All rights reserved.

The epilogue first appeared as "Introduction: Looking B(l)ackward: African American Studies in the Age of Identity Politics," in *Race Consciousness: African-American Studies for the New Century*, eds. Judith Jackson Fossett and Jeffrey A. Tucker (New York: New York University Press, 1997). Copyright 1997 by New York University Press. Reprinted by permission of New York University Press. All rights reserved.

03 02 01 00   8 7 6 5

Text design by [sic]
Composition by Wilsted & Taylor Publishing Services

Library of Congress Cataloging-in-Publication Data

Kelley, Robin D. G.
    Yo' mama's disfunktional! : fighting the culture wars in urban America / Robin D. G. Kelley.
       p.   cm.
    ISBN 0-8070-0940-7 (cloth)
    ISBN 0-8070-0941-5 (paper)
    1. Afro-Americans—Social conditions. 2. Urban poor—United States—Social conditions. 3. Inner cities—United States. 4. Afro-American families—Social conditions. 5. United States—Race relations. 6. Afro-Americans—Civil rights—Government policy. I. Title.
    E185.86.K45   1997
    305.896'073—dc21   97-20067

DATE DUE

			PRINTED IN U.S.A.

Francis Holland School NW1 6XR

WITHDRAWN

T23968

ALSO BY **ROBIN D.G. KELLEY**

Hammer and Hoe:
Alabama Communists during the Great Depression

Race Rebels:
Culture, Politics, and the Black Working Class

Into the Fire:
African Americans Since 1970

DEDICATED TO THE ONLY SANE,
FULLY FUNCTIONAL PERSON I KNOW:
MY MOTHER,
ANANDA SATTWA

CONTENTS

INTRODUCTION

They rung my bell to ask me.
Could I recommend a maid.
I said, yes, your mama.

—LANGSTON HUGHES
"Horn of Plenty"

I grew up in a world in which talking about somebody's mama was
a way of life, an everyday occurrence. For all of us, boys and girls, it
was a kind of game or performance. Whether we called it "capping,"
"snapping," "ranking," "busting," or simply "the dozens," most of
it was ridiculous, surreal humor bearing very little resemblance to
reality: "Your mom's so fat she broke the food chain"; "Your mama's
skin's so ashy she was a stand-in for Casper the Friendly Ghost";
"Your mama's so dumb she thought ring-around-the-collar was a
children's game." More than anything, it was an effort to master the
absurd metaphor, an art form intended to entertain rather than to
damage.

Of course, during those rare moments when our insults moved
beyond wild abstractions and drew on our real-life circumstances,
we had to be prepared for a fight. As rare as those moments were, it
is hard to forget the teary-eyed kids wielding cake cutters (metal

Afro combs) or rocks, the "sucker punch" from behind, the artless refrain of the "F" word shouted in frustrated, chant-like cadences.

You would think that as a kid growing up in this world I could handle any insult, or at least be prepared for any slander tossed in the direction of my mom—or, for that matter, my whole family, my friends, or my friends' families. But when I entered college and began reading the newspaper, monographs, and textbooks on a regular basis, I realized that many academics, journalists, policymakers, and politicians had taken the "dozens" to another level. In all my years of playing the dozens, I have rarely heard vitriol as vicious as the words spouted by Riverside (California) county welfare director Lawrence Townsend: "Every time I see a bag lady on the street, I wonder, 'Was that an A.F.D.C. mother who hit the menopause wall—who can no longer reproduce and get money to support herself?'"[1] I have had kids tell me that my hair was so nappy it looked like a thousand Africans giving the Black Power salute, but never has anyone said to my face that my whole family—especially my mama—was a "tangle of pathology." Senator Daniel Patrick Moynihan has been saying it since 1965 and, like the one about your mama tying a mattress to her back and offering "roadside service," Moynihan's "snap" has been repeated by legions of analysts and politicians, including Dinesh D'Souza, the boy wonder of the far Right. D'Souza has snapped on black people in such a vile manner that his version of the dozens dispenses with all subtlety. In *The End of Racism*, he says in no uncertain terms that African Americans have ushered in "a revival of barbarism in the midst of Western Civilization."[2]

Then again, should we be surprised? It seems like the very people often identified as the inventors and masters of the art of "snapping" are also the prime subjects of a cruel, high-tech game of the dozens that has continued nonstop since the first slave ships embarked from West Africa to the New World. Perhaps "jungle bunny," "darky," "coon," "sapphire," "jezebel," and "mammy" have gone by the wayside, but certain images of the lazy, irresponsible Negro endure in the form of "the underclass," "matriarchy," "welfare queens," "criminals," and "dysfunctional," to name a few. We have been consistently marked as dysfunctional: ironically, dysfunctionality is both the source of the slander directed toward us as well as a source of attraction. Our dysfunctionality fascinates; it is alluring. Black people are different, the true rhythm of the street; the Aunt Jemimah who knows more about white folks than they do; the exotic African; the conjure woman and root doctor; the jazz musician (or basketball player) who plays from his soul rather than his intellect. We have been the thing against which normality, whiteness, and functionality have been defined.

While much of *Yo' Mama's Disfunktional!* critiques the critics, it also attempts to give voice to those urban populations under seige right now. In some respects, the title represents what I imagine the very subjects/objects of reactionary social science and public policy might say if they could speak back to the critics and analysts. Charles Murray, Dinesh D'Souza, even William Julius Wilson would find themselves in a position to have to defend their *own* mamas and their own behavior, not to mention their research. I know that somewhere, sometime in urban America, when an ethnographer, social worker, or sexologist asked a wayward ghetto youth if he had any "illegitimate children," he came back with the classic retort: "Ask your mama." And why not? Some of the claims advanced by people with Ph.D.'s have about as much basis in hard evidence as anything coming out of the dozens, but without the subtlety, irony, and humor. In his defense of Charles Murray and Richard Herrnstein's *The Bell Curve: Intelligence and Class Structure in American Life*, for example, Richard Lynn wrote, "There is one thing the underclass is good at, and that is producing children. These children tend to inherit their parents' poor intelligence and adopt their sociopathic lifestyle, reproducing the cycle of deprivation from generation to generation."[3] Whether we are short on cognitive ability or long on sexual drive, it all adds up to a merciless attack on black mothers specifically, and black families more generally.

I wrote this book quite literally in defense of my own mother and my two sisters, all of whom have made valuable political contributions to the world we inhabit, and all of whom had spent a brief moment of their lives on welfare. It is a defense of my grandmother, a brilliant and proud Jamaican woman who had my brilliant and proud Jamaican mother as an unwed teenager (and both completed their high school education as adults). It is a defense of many, many mothers, daughters, sisters, sons, brothers, and fathers—the nameless masses whom we rarely see beyond the statistics or news footage. It is not the sort of defense that turns the discourse on its head, "flipping the script" in order to paint a noble, unblemished portrait of the black urban poor. Instead, I see this book as a defense of black people's humanity and a condemnation of scholars and policymakers for their inability to see complexity. Part of the book attempts to recognize the importance of pleasure and laughter in people's lives, to see culture and community as more than responses to, or products of, oppression. Hence, when we reflect on the dozens as the book's underlying metaphor, we have to acknowledge the artistry, the fun, the gamesmanship that continues to exist, if not thrive, in a world marked by survival and struggle.

In particular, *Yo' Mama's Disfunktional!* is concerned with the cultural and ideological warfare that continues to rage over black people and the "inner city" as social problems. I am especially interested in how various scholars, activists, policymakers, and displaced urban working people themselves have made sense of the crisis, what solutions they have proposed or strategies they have adopted, and what kinds of social movements have the potential for transforming the city and thus the whole nation.

On another level, *Yo' Mama's Disfunktional!* is an attempt to make sense of the world of my childhood, the vast urban jungles we know euphemistically as the inner city, from the early 1970s to the end of our millennium. Unlike most writers these days, I am not claiming absolute authority or authenticity for having lived there. On the contrary, it is because I did *not* know what happened to our world, to my neighbors, my elders, my peers, our streets, buildings, parks, our health, that I chose not to make this book a memoir. Indeed, if I relied on memory alone I would invariably have more to say about devouring Good & Plentys or melting crayons on the radiator than about economic restructuring, the disappearance of jobs, the resurgence of racism, and the dismantling of the welfare state.

After all, the Temptations opened the 1970s with their hit song "Ball of Confusion," an apt description of the state of the world— particularly the ghetto. Urban rebellions and police-community violence continued to be a source of tension in several cities during the 1970s. The issue of school desegregation was hardly settled, particularly after court-ordered busing was proposed as a solution to integrate public schools. Throughout the country, white opponents of school integration frequently turned to violence to defend all-white schools. And the ghetto schools, like my own P. S. 28 on 155th and St. Nicholas, had their own problems. Besides the whole question of whether black and Latino communities would control their schools, I recall marching around the block with my mom chanting "Overcrowded!" to protest the fact that fifty students were being squeezed into classrooms designed for thirty-five.

Lest we forget, Richard M. Nixon was in the White House, attacking welfare mothers and blaming the black poor for their own poverty. Nixon's domestic advisor, Daniel Patrick Moynihan, passed on a confidential memo proposing that "the time may have come when the issue of race could benefit from a period of 'benign neglect.' "[4] Much of the white middle class agreed. They believed that African Americans received too many government handouts. They were tired of "paying the bill," especially now that racism had allegedly been eliminated with the Civil Rights movement.

Sounds a lot like the nineties, with one exception: twenty-five

years ago black people still had reason to be optimistic. The Civil
Rights movement had made remarkable gains, and many people believed that the Black Power movement might achieve for African
Americans the self-determination they had been seeking for the
past three centuries. The black middle class expanded, as corporate
boardrooms became slightly more integrated and black college-
educated professionals moved to newly built suburban homes. And
there were some stunning victories, especially in the arena of electoral politics. In 1969, 994 black men and 131 black women held
public office; by 1975 the number of black elected officials had
grown to 2,973 men and 530 women. Black politicians won mayoral
races in several major cities, including Los Angeles, Atlanta, New
Orleans, Newark, Philadelphia, and Washington, D.C. Thus, amid
recession, white flight, and rising inner city homicide rates, black
communities marched into the 1970s with at least some hope that
black political power would bring a brighter day. We heard it loudly
and proudly in Parliament's "Chocolate City," the 1975 recording
penned by band leader and musical genius George Clinton:

> There's a lot of chocolate cities around.
> We've got Newark; we've got Gary.
> Somebody told me we got L. A.
> And we're working on Atlanta. . . .
> Hey C. C. [Chocolate City],
> they say you're jive and game and can't be changed.
> On the positive side,
> you're my piece of the rock and I love you C. C.
> Can you dig it?
> We didn't get our forty acres and a mule,
> but we did get you, C. C. . . .
> God Bless C. C. and its Vanilla Suburbs.[5]

We did get our "piece of the rock," but at what cost? For many urban
residents left behind in the nation's "chocolate cities" while the up-

wardly mobile fled to "vanilla suburbs," once the victory parties were over they had a difficult time obtaining city services, affordable housing, or improved schools. In some cases, local politicians consciously tied their fate to big business and growing downtown entrepreneurs. Some black citizens began to question whether having an African American in city hall even made a difference. But those black mayors committed to the communities that put them into office had not counted on massive reductions in federal spending on cities and white and black middle-class flight to the suburbs. The decade of hope was marked by the disappearance of heavy industry, the flight of American corporations to foreign lands and the suburbs, and the displacement of millions of workers across the country. Permanent unemployment and underemployment became a way of life. A few years after the War on Poverty had been declared a victory, the number of black poor grew dramatically. And despite the growing presence of African Americans in political office, affirmative action programs were dismantled, blatant acts of racism began to rise again, and the U.S. economy appeared to be in a permanent crisis.

Actually, it was the working class that experienced the crisis, not the wealthy. For the past sixteen years, at least, we have witnessed a greater concentration of wealth while the living conditions of working people deteriorate—textbook laissez-faire capitalism, to be sure. Certainly the Reagan/Bush revolution ushered in a new era of corporate wealth and callous disregard for the poor. Income inequality is staggering: the richest 1 percent of American families have nearly as much wealth as the bottom 95 percent; between 1980 and 1993, salaries for American CEOs increased by 514 percent while workers' wages rose by 68 percent—well behind inflation. In 1992 the average CEO earned 157 times what the average factory worker earned. And as a result of changes in the tax laws, average workers are paying more to the government while CEOs and their companies are paying less. Sweatshops and the slave labor conditions that accompany them are on the rise again. Corporate profits are reaching record highs, while "downsizing" and capital flight have left millions unemployed. Between 1979 and 1992, the Fortune 500 companies' total labor force dropped from 16.2 million world-wide to 11.8 million. Yet, in 1993, these companies recorded profits of $62.6 billion.[6]

Among other things, *Yo' Mama's Disfunktional!* begins to explain why so many people can believe that barriers to black progress have been removed while conditions for the urban black working class continue to deteriorate. If racism is essentially a thing of the past, as conservatives and many neoliberals now argue, then the failure of the black poor to lift themselves out of poverty has to be found in their behavior or their culture. In short, the problems facing the vast majority of black folk in today's ghettos lie not with government policy or corporate capitalism, but with the people themselves—our criminally minded youth, our deadbeat daddies, and our welfare-dependent mamas. Indeed, it is precisely the prevalence of these kinds of images that allow writers such as Charles Murray and Dinesh D'Souza to be taken seriously in spite of deep and obvious flaws in their scholarship. Stereotypes and sweeping generalizations stand in for serious analysis and complexity. The dozens stand in for fair and impartial intellectual engagement.

I deliberately used the popular phrase *culture wars* in the subtitle of this book because all of these essays, in one way or another, explore the ongoing battle over representations of the black urban condition, as well as the importance of the cultural terrain as a site of struggle. Some readers might find the term *culture wars* inappropriate since it is generally associated with curriculum debates, "political correctness" on college campuses, or the politics of arts and humanities funding. However, there is more to the culture wars than whether or not Cleopatra was black, or if multicultural education constitutes a new form of academic tyranny. The culture wars continue to rage each day in the streets of urban America, in the realm of public policy, in the union halls, and at the workplace. This book is premised on the idea that culture and questions of identity have been at the heart of some of the most intense battles facing African Americans at the end of the century. And as the global economy grows, the terrain of culture becomes even more crucial as a terrain of struggle. Not only has globalization continued to transform black culture, but it has also dramatically changed the nature of work, employment opportunities, class structure, public space, the cultural marketplace, the criminal justice system, political strategies, even intellectual work. The "ghetto" continues to be viewed as the Achilles' heel in American society, the repository of bad values and economic failure, or the source of a vibrant culture of resistance. Depending on who is doing the talking/writing, ghetto residents are either a morally bankrupt underclass or a churchgoing, determined working class living in fear of young riffraff. Whatever the narrative and whoever the source, these cultural and ideological constructions of ghetto life have irrevocably shaped public policy, scholarship, and social movements.

Chapter 1 sets the stage for the cultural construction of the ghetto. Focusing primarily on a group of well-meaning liberal social scientists active during the heyday of ghetto ethnography, I reflect on how their understanding of culture has severely impoverished contemporary debates over the plight of urban African Americans. While some aspects of black expressive cultures might help inner city residents cope with or even resist ghetto conditions, most of the literature ignores what these cultural forms mean for the practitioners. Few scholars acknowledge that what might be at stake here are aesthetics, style, and visceral pleasures that have little to do with racism, poverty, and oppression. Nor do they recognize black urban culture's multicultural roots. Conceiving of black urban culture in the singular opened the door for the invention of the "underclass." Once culture is seen as a static, measurable thing—behavior—that is either part of an old African or slave tradition or a product of dire circumstances, it is not hard to cast black people as pathological products of broken families, broken economies, and/or broken communities.

The next chapter proposes an alternative to the social science approaches I critique in chapter 1. I, too, examine so-called street culture, but through a framework that considers the globalization of capital, the multinational roots of African American culture, and issues related to aesthetics and pleasure. I examine the ways in which some urban youth have turned certain forms of "play" into a source of income or a vocation, and how these kinds of opportunities to escape low-wage labor are gendered. This is also a tale about capitalism's contradictions, for the same global economic structures responsible for expanding poverty and a shrinking labor market also created space for young cultural workers to produce their art and market their talents.

The ironies do not end there. As chapter 3 points out, the same black neoconservatives and conservative nationalists who have dismissed this generation of urban youth are also the biggest proponents of "self-help" as the latest panacea for America's ghettos. A growing number of voices call on black people to break the grip of government dependency and take "personal responsibility" (not coincidentally, the phrase used in the 1996 federal welfare reform bill).

Chapter 3 not only argues for the futility of self-help strategies in the age of global capital and multinational corporations, but also insists that strong government supports and affirmative action are necessary to improve the life chances of African Americans and to challenge a living, vibrant racism. We often forget that state supports have been essential for the creation of suburbia and the success of big capital, and rarely are those subsidies described as "handouts" or "welfare." In defense of the welfare state, I argue that government supports should not be seen simply as entitlements but as a matter of rights.

While the Right blames personal behavior, weak morals, and a pathological culture for the current state of black urban life, a growing posse of white self-proclaimed "progressives" blames the Black Liberation movement, along with other movements seeking to emancipate oppressed ethnic groups, women, and sexual minorities, for destroying the Left. With the implosion of the Left went our only opportunity to challenge three decades of conservative rule and deleterious social policy. Why did this happen? Because, according to critics such as Todd Gitlin, Michael Tomasky, Eric Hobsbawm, and others, the Left has lost touch with its Enlightenment roots, the source of its universalism and radical humanism, and instead has been hijacked by "identity movements" that have led us into a blind alley where universal demands are cast aside in favor of narrow battles around race, ethnicity, gender, and sexuality. Thus, whereas black neocons find inspiration in the late-nineteenth-century ideas of Booker T. Washington, these white neo-Marxists/ liberals reach way back, to the Enlightenment thinkers Jefferson, Locke, and Rousseau. In the name of radical universalism, these guys repackage the old socialist idea that class, unlike race, gender, or ethnicity, constitutes the only basis for "true" progressive politics—one that unites rather than divides.

Chapter 4 takes issue with the neo-Enlightenment Left's vision of emancipation. Besides questioning the relevance of Enlightenment universalism for the twenty-first century, I argue that so-called identity politics has always profoundly shaped labor movements and has been the glue for class solidarity. The Gitlin/Tomasky school of thought fails to see how class is lived through race and gender. Their failure to see social movements focused on race, gender, or sexuality as essential to the emancipation of the whole remains the fundamental stumbling block to building a deep and lasting class-based politics and a new multiracial, grassroots movement in our crisis-ridden cities.

Despite the pronouncements of neo-Enlightenment liberals

or neoconservative Negroes, new multiracial working-class movements *are* emerging in cities across the country. Chapter 5 surveys a
few of the key movements and attempts to assess their impact on
the current and future political landscape. Focusing on several black
and multiracial grassroots movements at work and in urban communities, I suggest that struggles against class-based racism are lay-
ing the basis for new emancipatory social movements that have the
potential to transform the nation.

After demonstrating the importance of identity and culture in
the key political and economic struggles of our time, I end the book
with a parody that explores the limitations of identity politics in
some of the scholarship coming out of African American studies.
Based loosely on Edward Bellamy's 1887 classic *Looking Backward*,
the final essay imagines where Black Studies might be 100 years
from now and creates an imaginary dialogue between the represen-
tatives of various schools of thought. While cautioning against
trends that overly romanticize the African past, ignore political
economy and the state, or engage in unnecessary moralizing, the
parody also imagines what life and scholarship might be like if the
neoconservative (and liberal) social scientists working on the urban
underclass had their way. Whatever one might think about the various battles taking place within the realm of Black Studies, it should
be clear to all that these battles have profound implications for dealing with race, the urban crisis, and the culture wars that continue to
rage in the streets, the workplace, and the groves of academe.

In writing this book, I not only set out to defend my mom and other
victims of racist and sexist social science, social policy, and social
disinvestment, but also to make the case that women and men like
my mom—working or not—can and must save us all. The hope and
future of America lie with the very multicolored working class that
for so long has been seen as the problem rather than the solution.
The new "wretched of the earth" are rebuilding the labor move-

ment, reinventing civil rights, and reconfiguring scholarship in ways that radically challenge the status quo. I don't expect many victories in the near future, but if we believe that our cities are worth saving and the world is worth remaking, we need to look in different places with new eyes. This book is but one tiny, incomplete step toward clearing the dust so that we might see more clearly.

CHAPTER ONE

LOOKINGFOR THE"REAL" NIGGA:

Social Scientists
Construct the Ghetto

Perhaps the supreme irony of black Ameri-can existence is how broadly black people debate the question of cultural identity among themselves while getting branded as a cultural monolith by those who would deny us the complexity and complexion of a community, let alone a nation. If Afro-Americans have never settled for the racist reductions imposed upon them—from chattel slaves to cinematic stereotype to so-ciological myth—it's because the black collective conscious not only knew better but also knew more than enough ethnic diver-sity to subsume these fictions.

——GREG TATE,
Flyboy in the Buttermilk

The biggest difference between us and white folks is that we know when we are playing.

——ALBERTA ROBERTS, QUOTED IN
JOHN LANGSTON GWALTNEY, *Drylongso*

"I think this anthropology is just another way to call me a nigger." So observed Othman Sullivan, one of many informants in John Langston Gwaltney's classic study of black culture, *Drylongso*.[1] Perhaps a kinder, gentler way to put it is that anthropology, not unlike most urban social science, has played a key role in marking "blackness" and defining black culture to the "outside" world. Beginning with Robert Park and his protégés to the War on Poverty-inspired ethnographers, a battery of social scientists have significantly shaped the current dialogue on black urban culture. Today sociologists, anthropologists, political scientists, and economists compete for huge grants from Ford, Rockefeller, Sage, and other foundations to measure everything measurable in order to get a handle on the newest internal threat to civilization. With the discovery of the so-called underclass, terms like *nihilistic, dysfunctional,* and *pathological* have become the most common adjectives to describe contemporary black urban culture. The question they often pose, to use Mr. Othman Sullivan's words, is what *kind* of "niggers" populate the inner cities?

Unfortunately, too much of this rapidly expanding literature on the underclass provides less an understanding of the complexity of people's lives and cultures than a bad blaxploitation film or an Ernie Barnes painting. Many social scientists are not only quick to generalize about the black urban poor on the basis of a few "representative" examples, but more often than not, they do not let the natives speak. A major part of the problem is the way in which many mainstream social scientists studying the underclass define *culture*. Relying on a narrowly conceived definition of culture, most of the underclass literature uses *behavior* and *culture* interchangeably.

My purpose, then, is to offer some reflections on how the culture concept employed by social scientists has severely impoverished contemporary debates over the plight of urban African Americans and contributed to the construction of the ghetto as a reservoir of pathologies and bad cultural values. Much of this literature not only conflates behavior with culture, but when social scientists explore "expressive" cultural forms or what has been called "popular culture" (such as language, music, and style), most reduce it to expressions of pathology, compensatory behavior, or creative "coping mechanisms" to deal with racism and poverty. While some aspects of black expressive cultures certainly help inner city residents deal with and even resist ghetto conditions, most of the literature ignores what these cultural forms mean for the practitioners. Few scholars acknowledge that what might also be at stake here are aesthetics, style, and pleasure. Nor do they recognize black urban culture's hybridity and internal differences. Given the common belief that inner city communities are more isolated than ever before and have completely alien values, the notion that there is one discrete, identifiable black urban culture carries a great deal of weight. By conceiving black urban culture in the singular, interpreters unwittingly reduce their subjects to cardboard typologies who fit neatly into their own definition of the "underclass" and render invisible a wide array of complex cultural forms and practices.

"IT'S JUST A GHETTO THANG":
THE PROBLEM OF AUTHENTICITY AND
THE ETHNOGRAPHIC IMAGINATION

A few years ago Mercer Sullivan decried the disappearance of "culture" from the study of urban poverty, attributing its demise to the fact that "overly vague notions of the culture of poverty brought disrepute to the culture concept as a tool for understanding the effects of the concentration of poverty among cultural minorities."[2] In some respects, Sullivan is right: the conservatives who maintain that persistent poverty in the inner city is the result of the behavior of the poor, the product of some cultural deficiency, have garnered so much opposition from many liberals and radicals that few scholars are willing even to discuss culture. Instead, opponents of the "culture of poverty" idea tend to focus on structural transformations in the U.S. economy, labor force composition, and resultant changes in marriage patterns to explain the underclass.[3]

However, when viewed from another perspective, culture never really disappeared from the underclass debate.[4] On the contrary, it has been as central to the work of liberal structuralists and radical Marxists as it has been to that of the conservative culturalists. While culturalists insist that the behavior of the urban poor explains their poverty, the structuralists argue that the economy explains their behavior as well as their poverty.[5] For all their differences, there is general agreement that a common, debased culture is what defines the "underclass," what makes it a threat to the future of America. Most interpreters of the "underclass" treat behavior as not only a synonym for culture but also as the determinant for class. In simple terms, what makes the "underclass" a class is members' common behavior—not their income, their poverty level, or the kind of work they do. It is a definition of class driven more by moral panic than by systematic analysis. A cursory look at the literature reveals that there is no consensus as to precisely what behaviors define the underclass. Some scholars, like William Julius Wilson, have offered a more spatial definition of the underclass by focusing on areas of "concentrated poverty," but obvious problems result when observers discover the wide range of behavior and attitudes in, say, a single city block. What happens to the concept when we find people with jobs engaging in illicit activities and some jobless people depending on church charity? Or married employed fathers who spend virtually no time with their kids and jobless unwed fathers participating and sharing in child care responsibilities? How does the concept of underclass behavior hold up to Kathryn Edin's findings that many so-called welfare-dependent women must also work for wages in order to make ends meet?[6] More importantly, how do we fit criminals (many first-time offenders), welfare recipients, single mothers, absent fathers, alcohol and drug abusers, and gun-toting youth all into one "class"?

When we try to apply the same principles to people with higher

(margin note, handwritten) Statistics how should be computed?

incomes, who are presumed to be "functional" and "normative," we ultimately expose the absurdity of it all. Political scientist Charles Henry offers the following description of pathological behavior for the very folks the underclass is supposed to emulate. This tangle of deviant behavior, which he calls the "culture of wealth," is characterized by a "rejection or denial of physical attributes" leading to "hazardous sessions in tanning parlors" and frequent trips to weight-loss salons; rootlessness; antisocial behavior; and "an inability to make practical decisions" evidenced by their tendency to own several homes, frequent private social and dining clubs, and by their vast amount of unnecessary and socially useless possessions. "Finally," Henry adds, "the culture of the rich is engulfed in a web of crime, sexism, and poor health. Drug use and white collar crime are rampant, according to every available index. . . . In sum, this group is engaged in a permanent cycle of divorce, forced child separations through boarding schools, and rampant materialism that leads to the dreaded Monte Carlo syndrome. Before they can be helped they must close tax loopholes, end subsidies, and stop buying influence."[7]

As absurd as Henry's satirical reformulation of the culture of poverty might appear, this very instrumentalist way of understanding culture is deeply rooted even in the more liberal social science approaches to urban poverty. In the mid- to late 1960s, a group of progressive social scientists, mostly ethnographers, challenged the more conservative culture-of-poverty arguments and insisted that black culture was itself a necessary adaptation to racism and poverty, a set of coping mechanisms that grew out of the struggle for material and psychic survival.[8] Ironically, while this work consciously sought to recast ghetto dwellers as active agents rather than passive victims, it has nonetheless reinforced monolithic interpretations of black urban culture and significantly shaped current articulations of the culture concept in social science approaches to poverty.

With the zeal of colonial missionaries, these liberal and often radical ethnographers (mostly white men) set out to explore the newly discovered concrete jungles. Inspired by the politics of the 1960s and mandated by Lyndon Johnson's War on Poverty, a veritable army of anthropologists, sociologists, linguists, and social psychologists set up camp in America's ghettos. In the Harlem and Washington Heights communities where I grew up in the mid- to late 1960s, even our liberal white teachers who were committed to making us into functional members of society turned out to be foot soldiers in the new ethnographic army. With the overnight success of published collections of inner city children's writings like *The Me Nobody Knows* and Caroline Mirthes's *Can't You Hear Me Talking to You?*, writing about the intimate details of our home life seemed like our most important assignment.[9] (And we made the most of it by enriching our mundane narratives with stories from *Mod Squad, Hawaii Five-O,* and *Speed Racer.*)

Of course, I do not believe for a minute that most of our teachers gave us these kinds of exercises hoping to one day appear on the *Merv Griffin Show.* But, in retrospect at least, the explosion of interest in the inner city cannot be easily divorced from the marketplace. Although these social scientists came to mine what they believed was *the* "authentic Negro culture," there was real gold in them thar ghettos since white America's fascination with the pathological urban poor translated into massive book sales.

Unfortunately, most social scientists believed they knew what "authentic Negro culture" was before they entered the field. The "real Negroes" were the young jobless men hanging out on the corner passing the bottle, the brothers with the nastiest verbal repertoire, the pimps and hustlers, and the single mothers who raised streetwise kids who began cursing before they could walk. Of course, there were other characters, like the men and women who went to work every day in foundries, hospitals, nursing homes, private homes, police stations, sanitation departments, banks, garment factories, assembly plants, pawn shops, construction sites, loading docks, storefront churches, telephone companies, grocery and department stores, public transit, restaurants, welfare offices, recreation centers; or the street vendors, the cab drivers, the bus drivers, the ice cream truck drivers, the seamstresses, the numerologists and fortune tellers, the folks who protected or cleaned downtown buildings all night long. These are the kinds of people who lived in my neighborhood in West Harlem during the early 1970s, but they rarely found their way into the ethnographic text. And when they did show up, social scientists tended to reduce them to typologies—"lames," "strivers," "mainstreamers," "achievers," or "revolutionaries."[10]

Perhaps these urban dwellers were not as interesting, as the hard-core ghetto poor, or more likely, they stood at the margins of a perceived or invented "authentic" Negro society. A noteworthy exception is John Langston Gwaltney's remarkable book, *Drylongso: A Self-Portrait of Black America* (1981). Based on interviews conducted during the 1970s with black working-class residents in several Northeastern cities, *Drylongso* is one of the few works on urban African Americans by an African American anthropologist that appeared during the height of ghetto ethnography. Because Gwaltney is blind, he could not rely on the traditional methods of observation and interepretation. Instead—and this is the book's strength—he allowed his informants to speak for themselves about what *they* see and do. They interpret their own communities, African American culture, white society, racism, politics and the state, and the very discipline in which Gwaltney was trained—anthropology. What the book reveals is that the natives are aware that anthropologists are constructing them, and they saw in Gwaltney—who relied primarily on family and friends as informants—an opportunity to speak back. One, a woman he calls Elva Noble, said to him: "I'm not trying to tell you your job, but if you ever do write a book about us, then I hope you really do write about things the way they really are. I guess that depends on you to some extent but you know that there are more of us who are going to work every day than there are like the people who are git'n over."[11] While his definition of a "core black culture" may strike some as essentialist, it emphasizes diversity and tolerance for diversity. Gwaltney acknowledges the stylistic uniqueness of African American culture, yet he shows that the central facet of this core culture is the deep-rooted sense of community, common history, and collective recognition that there is indeed an African American culture and a "black" way of doing things. Regardless of the origins of a particular recipe, or the roots of a particular religion or Christian denomination, the cook and the congregation have no problem identifying these distinct practices and institutions as "black."

Few ghetto ethnographers have understood or developed Gwaltney's insights into African American urban culture. Whereas Gwaltney's notion of a core culture incorporates a diverse and contradictory range of practices, attitudes, and relationships that are dynamic, historically situated, and ethnically hybrid, social scientists of his generation and after—especially those at the forefront of poverty studies—treat culture as if it were a set of behaviors. They assume that there is one identifiable ghetto culture, and what they observed was *it*. These assumptions, which continue to shape much current social science and most mass media representations of the "inner city," can be partly attributed to the way ethnographers are trained in the West. As James Clifford observed, anthropologists studying non-Western societies are not only compelled to describe the communities under interrogation as completely foreign to their own society, but if a community is to be worthy of study as a group it must posses an identifiable, homogeneous culture. I think, in principle at least, the same holds true for interpretations of black urban America. Ethnographers can argue that inner city residents, as a "foreign" culture, do not share "mainstream" values. Social scientists do not treat behavior as situational, an individual response to a specific set of circumstances; rather, inner city residents act according to their own unique cultural "norms."[12]

For many of these ethnographers, the defining characteristic of African American urban culture was relations between men and women. Even Charles Keil, whose *Urban Blues* is one of the few ethnographic texts from that period to not only examine aesthetics and form in black culture but take "strong exception to the view that lower-class Negro life style and its characteristic rituals and expressive roles are the products of overcompensation for masculine self-doubt," nonetheless concludes that "the battle of the sexes" is precisely what characterizes African American urban culture.[13] Expressive cultures, then, were not only constructed as adaptive, functioning primarily to cope with the horrible conditions of ghetto life, but were conceived largely as expressions of masculinity. In fact, the linking of men with expressive cultures was so pervasive that the pioneering ethnographies focusing on African American women and girls—notably the work of Joyce Ladner and Carol Stack—do not explore this realm, whether in mixed-gender groupings or all-female groups. They concentrated more on sex roles, relationships, and family survival rather than expressive cultures.[14]

Two illuminating examples are the debate over the concept of "soul" and the verbal art form known to most academics as "the dozens." In the ethnographic imagination, "soul" and "the dozens" were both examples par excellence of authentic black urban culture as well as vehicles for expressing black masculinity. The bias toward expressive male culture must be understood within a particular historical and political context. In the midst of urban rebellions, the masculinist rhetoric of black nationalism, the controversy over the Moynihan report, and the uncritical linking of "agency" and resistance with men, black men took center stage in poverty research.[15]

Soul was so critical to the social science discourse on the adaptive culture of the black urban poor that Lee Rainwater edited an entire book about it, and Ulf Hannerz structured his study of Washington, D.C. on it.[16] According to these authors, *soul* is the expressive lifestyle of black men adapting to economic and political marginality. This one word supposedly embraces the entire range of "Negro lower class culture"; it constitutes "essential Negroness." Only authentic Negroes had soul. In defining *soul*, Hannerz reduces aesthetics, style, and the dynamic struggle over identity to a set of coping mechanisms. Among his many attempts to define *soul*, he insists that it is tied to the instability of black male-female relationships. He deduced evidence for this from his findings that "success with the opposite sex is a focal concern in lower-class Negro life," and the fact that a good deal of popular black music—soul music— was preoccupied with courting or losing a lover.[17]

Being "cool" is an indispensable component of soul; it is also regarded by these ethnographers as a peculiarly black expression of masculinity. Indeed, the entire discussion of cool centers entirely on black men. Cool as an aesthetic, as a style, as an art form expressed through language and the body, is simply not dealt with. Cool, not surprisingly, is merely another mechanism to cope with racism and poverty. According to Lee Rainwater and David Schulz, it is nothing more than a survival technique intended to "make yourself interesting and attractive to others so that you are better able to manipulate their behavior along lines that will provide some immediate gratification." To achieve cool simply entails learning to lie and putting up a front of competence and success. But like a lot of adaptive strategies, cool is self-limiting. While it helps young black males maintain an image of being "in control," according to David Schulz, it can also make "intimate relationships" more difficult to achieve.[18]

Hannerz reluctantly admits that no matter how hard he tried, none of the "authentic ghetto inhabitants" he had come across could define *soul*. He was certain that soul was "essentially Negro," but concluded that it really could not be defined, for to do that would be to undermine its meaning: it is something one possesses, a ticket into the "in crowd." If you need a definition you do not know what it means. It's a black (male) thang; you'll never understand. But Hannerz obviously felt confident enough to venture his own definition, based on his understanding of African American culture, that *soul* was little more than a survival strategy to cope with the harsh realities of the ghetto. Moreover, he felt empowered to determine which black people had the right to claim the mantle of authenticity: when LeRoi Jones and Lerone Bennett offered their interpretation of soul, Hannerz rejected their definitions, in part because they were not, in his words, "authentic Negroes."[19]

By constructing the black urban world as a single culture whose function is merely to survive the ghetto, Rainwater, Hannerz, and most of their colleagues at the time ultimately collapsed a wide range of historically specific cultural practices and forms and searched for a (*the*) concept that could bring them all together. Such an interpretation of culture makes it impossible for Hannerz and others to see soul not as a thing but as a discourse through which African Americans, at a particular historical moment, claimed ownership of the symbols and practices of their own imagined community. This is why, even at the height of the Black Power movement, African American urban culture could be so fluid, hybrid, and multinational. In Harlem in the 1970s, Nehru suits were as popular and as "black" as dashikis, and martial arts films placed Bruce Lee among a pantheon of black heroes that included Walt Frazier and John Shaft. As debates over the black aesthetic raged, the concept of soul was an assertion that there are "black ways" of doing things, even if those ways are contested and the boundaries around what is "black" are fluid. How it manifests itself and how it shifts is less important than the fact that the boundaries exist in the first place. At the very least, *soul* was a euphemism or a creative way of identifying what many believed was a black aesthetic or black style, and it was a synonym for black itself or a way to talk about being black without reference to color, which is why people of other ethnic groups could have soul.

Soul in the 1960s and early 1970s was also about transformation. It was almost never conceived by African Americans as an innate, genetically derived feature of black life, for it represented a shedding of the old "Negro" ways and an embrace of "Black" power and pride. The most visible signifier of soul was undoubtedly the Afro. More than any other element of style, the Afro put the issue of hair squarely on the black political agenda, where it has been ever since. The current debates over hair and its relationship to political consciousness really have their roots in the Afro. Not surprisingly, social scientists at the time viewed the Afro through the limited lens of Black Power politics, urban uprisings, and an overarching discourse of authenticity. And given their almost exclusive interest in young men, their perspective on the Afro was strongly influenced by the rhetoric and iconography of a movement that flouted black masculinity. Yet, once we look beyond the presumably male-occupied ghetto streets that dominated the ethnographic imagination at the time, the story of the Afro's origins and meaning complicates the link to soul culture.

First, the Afro powerfully demonstrates the degree to which soul was deeply implicated in the marketplace. What passed as "authentic" ghetto culture was as much a product of market forces and the commercial appropriation of urban styles as experience and individual creativity. And very few black urban residents/consumers viewed their own participation in the marketplace as undermining their own authenticity as bearers of black culture. Even before the Afro reached its height of popularity, the hair care industry stepped in and began producing a vast array of chemicals to make one's "natural" more natural. One could pick up Raveen Hair Sheen, Afro Sheen, Ultra Sheen, Head Start vitamin and mineral capsules, to name a few. The Clairol Corporation (whose CEO supported the Philadelphia Black Power Conference in 1967) did not hesitate to enter the "natural" business.[20] Listen to this Clairol ad published in *Essence Magazine* (November 1970):

> No matter what they say . . . Nature Can't Do It Alone! Nothing pretties up a face like a beautiful head of hair, but even hair that's born this beautiful needs a little help along the way. . . . A little brightening, a little heightening of color, a little extra sheen to liven up the look. And because that wonderful natural look is still the most wanted look . . . the most fashionable, the most satisfying look you can have at any age . . . anything you do must look natural, natural, natural. And this indeed is the art of Miss Clairol.

Depending on the particular style, the Afro could require almost as much maintenance as chemically straightened hair. And for those women (and some men) whose hair simply would not cooperate or who wanted the flexibility to shift from straight to nappy, there was always the Afro wig. For nine or ten dollars, one could purchase a variety of different wig styles, ranging from the "Soul-Light Freedom" wigs to the "Honey Bee Afro Shag," made from cleverly labeled synthetic materials such as "Afrylic" or "Afrilon."[21]

Secondly, the Afro's roots really go back to the bourgeois high fashion circles in the late 1950s. The Afro was seen by the black and white elite as a kind of new female exotica. Even though its intention, among some circles at least, was to achieve healthier hair and express solidarity with newly independent African nations, the Afro entered public consciousness as a mod fashion statement that was not only palatable to bourgeois whites but, in some circles, celebrated. There were people like Lois Liberty Jones, a consultant, beauty culturist, and lecturer, who claimed to have pioneered the natural as early as 1952! She originated "Coiffures Aframericana" concepts of hair styling which she practiced in Harlem for several years from the early 1960s.[22] More importantly, it was the early, not the late, 1960s, when performers like Odetta, Miriam Makeba, Abby Lincoln, Nina Simone, and the artist Margaret Burroughs began wearing the "au naturelle" style—medium to short Afros. Writer Andrea Benton Rushing has vivid memories of seeing Odetta at the Village Gate long before Black Power entered the national lexicon. "I was mesmerized by her stunning frame," she recalled, "in its short kinky halo. She had a regal poise and power that I had never seen in a 'Negro' (as we called ourselves back then) woman before—no matter how naturally 'good' or diligently straightened her hair was." Many other black women in New York, particularly those who ran in the interracial world of Manhattan sophisticates, were first introduced to the natural through high fashion models in au naturelle shows, which were the rage at the time.[23]

Helen Hayes King, associate editor of *Jet*, came in contact with the au naturelle style at an art show in New York, in the late 1950s. A couple of years later, she heard Abby Lincoln speak about her own decision to go natural at one of these shows and, with prompting from her husband, decided to go forth to adopt the 'fro. Ironically, one of the few salons in Chicago specializing in the au naturelle look was run by a white male hairdresser in the exclusive Northside community. He actually lectured King on the virtues of natural hair: "I don't know why Negro women with delicate hair like yours burn and process all the life out of it. . . . If you'd just wash it, oil it and take care of it, it would be so much healthier. . . . I don't know how all this straightening foolishness started anyhow." When she returned home to the Southside, however, instead of compliments she received strange looks from her neighbors. Despite criticism and ridicule by her co-workers and friends, she stuck with her au naturelle, not because she was trying to make a political statement or demonstrate her solidarity with African independence movements. "I'm not so involved in the neo-African aspects of the 'au naturelle' look," she wrote, "nor in the get-back-to-your-heritage bit." Her explanation was simple: the style was chic and elegant and in the end she was pleased with the feel of her hair. It is fitting to note that most of the compliments came from whites.[24]

What is also interesting about King's narrative is that it appeared in the context of a debate with Nigerian writer Theresa Ogunbiyi over whether black women should straighten their hair or not, which appeared in a 1963 issue of *Negro Digest*. In particular, Ogunbiyi defended the right of a Lagos firm to forbid employees to plait their hair; women were required to wear straight hair. She rejected the idea that straightening hair destroys national custom and heritage: "I think we carry this national pride a bit too far at times, even to the detriment of our country's progress." Her point was that breaking with tradition *is* progress, especially since Western dress and hairstyles are more comfortable and easier to work in. "When I wear the Yoruba costume, I find that I spend more time than I can afford, re-tying the headtie and the bulky wrapper round my waist. And have you tried typing in an 'Agbada'? I am all for nationalisation but give it to me with some comfort and improvement."[25]

Andrea Benton Rushing's story is a slight variation on King's experience. She, too, was a premature natural hair advocate. When she stepped out of the house sporting her first Afro, perhaps inspired by Odetta or prompted by plain curiosity, her "relatives thought I'd lost my mind and, of course, my teachers at Juilliard stole sideways looks at me and talked about the importance of appearance in auditions and concerts." Yet, while the white Juilliard faculty and her closest family members found the new style strange and inappropriate, brothers on the block in her New York City neighborhood greeted her with praise: " 'Looking good, sister,' 'Watch out, African queen!' " She, too, found it ironic that middle-class African woman on the continent chose to straighten their hair. During a trip to Ghana years later, she recalled the irony of having her Afro braided in an Accra beauty parlor while "three Ghanaians (two Akan-speaking government workers and one Ewe microbiologist) . . . were having their chemically-straightened hair washed, set, combed out, and sprayed in place."[26]

No matter what spurred on the style or who adopted it, however, the political implications of the au naturelle could not be avoided. After all, the biggest early proponents of the style tended to be women artists whose work identified with the black freedom movement and African liberation. In some respects, women such as Abby Lincoln, Odetta, and Nina Simone were part of what might be called black bohemia. They participated in a larger community—based mostly in New York—of poets, writers, musicians of the 1950s, for whom the emancipation of their own artistic form coincided with the African freedom movement. *Ebony, Jet,* and *Sepia* magazines were covering Africa, and African publications such as *Drum* were being read by those ex-Negroes in the States who could get their hands on it. The Civil Rights movement, the struggle against apartheid in South Africa, and the emergence of newly independent African nations found a voice in recordings by various jazz artists, including Randy Weston's *Uhuru Afrika,* Max Roach's *We Insist: Freedom Now Suite* (featuring Abby Lincoln, Roach's wife), Art Blakey's "Message from Kenya" and "Ritual," and John Coltrane's "Liberia," "Dahomey Dance," and "Africa." Revolutionary political movements, combined with revolutionary experiments in artistic creation—the simultaneous embrace and rejection of tradition—forged the strongest physical and imaginary links between Africa and the diaspora.[27] Thus, it is not surprising that Harold Cruse, in one of his seminal essays on the coming of the new black nationalism, anticipated the importance of the style revolution and the place of the au naturelle in it. As early as 1962, Cruse predicted that in the coming years "Afro-Americans . . . will undoubtedly make a lot of noise in militant demonstrations, cultivate beards and sport their hair in various degrees of la mode au naturel, and tend to be cultish with African- and Arab-style dress."[28]

Of course, he was right. By the mid-1960s, however, the Afro was no longer associated with downtown chic but with uptown rebellion. It was sported by rock-throwing black males and black-leathered militants armed to the teeth. Thus, once associated with feminine chic, the Afro suddenly became the symbol of black manhood, the death of the "Negro" and birth of the militant, virulent Black man.[29] The new politics, combined with media representations of Afro-coifed black militants, profoundly shaped the ethnographic imagination. As new narratives were created to explain the symbolic significance of the natural style, women were rendered invisible. The erasure of women, I would argue, was not limited to histories of style politics but to ghetto ethnography in general.

The masculinism of soul in contemporary ghetto ethnography has survived to this day, despite the last quarter-century of incisive black feminist scholarship. The ethnographic and sociological search for soul has made a comeback recently under a new name: the "cool pose." In a recent book, Richard Majors and Janet Mancini Bilson have recycled the arguments of Lee Rainwater, Ulf Hannerz, Elliot Liebow, and David Schulz, and have suggested that the "cool pose" captures the essence of young black male expressive culture. Like earlier constructors of soul, they too believe that the "cool pose" is an adaptive strategy to cope with the particular forms of racism and oppression black males face in America. "Cool pose is a ritualized form of masculinity that entails behaviors, scripts, physical posturing, impression management, and carefully crafted performances that deliver a single, critical message: pride, strength, and control." Echoing earlier works, the cool pose is also a double-edged sword since it allegedly undermines potential intimacy with females.[30] By playing down the aesthetics of cool and reducing the cool pose to a response by heterosexual black males to racism, intraracial violence, and poverty, the authors not only reinforce the idea that there is an essential black urban culture created by the oppressive conditions of the ghetto but ignore manifestations of the cool pose in the public "performances" of black women, gay black men, and the African American middle class.

A more tangible example of black urban expressive culture that seemed to captivate social scientists in the 1960s is "the dozens." Yet, in spite of the amount of ink devoted to the subject, it has also been perhaps the most misinterpreted cultural form coming out of African American communities. Called at various times in various places "capping," "sounding," "ranking," "bagging," or "dissing," virtually all leading anthropologists, sociologists, and linguists agree that it is a black male form of "ritual insult," a verbal contest involving any number of young black men who compete by talking about each other's mama. There is less agreement, however, about how to interpret the sociological and psychological significance of the dozens. In keeping with the dominant social science interpretations of the culture concept, so-called ritual insults among urban black youth were either another adaptive strategy or an example of social pathology.

The amazing thing about the sociological and ethnographic scholarship on the dozens, from John Dollard's ruminations in 1939 to the more recent misreadings by Roger Lane and Carl Nightingale, is the consistency with which it repeats the same errors. For one, the almost universal assertion that the dozens is a "ritual" empowers the ethnographer to select what appears to be more formalized verbal exchanges (e.g., rhyming couplets) and ascribe to them greater "authenticity" than other forms of playful conversation. In fact, by framing the dozens as ritual, most scholars have come to believe that it is first and foremost a "contest" with rules, players, and mental scorecards rather than the daily banter of many (not all) young African Americans. Anyone who has lived and survived the dozens (or whatever name you want to call it) cannot imagine turning to one's friends and announcing, "Hey, let's go outside and play the dozens." Furthermore, the very use of the term *ritual* to describe everyday speech reinforces the exoticization of black urban populations, constructing them as Others whose investment in this cultural tradition is much deeper than trying to get a laugh.[31]

These problems, however, are tied to larger ones. For example, white ethnographers seemed oblivious to the fact that their very presence shaped what they observed. Asking their subjects to "play the dozens" while an interloper records the "session" with a tape recorder and notepad has the effect of creating a ritual performance for the sake of an audience, of turning spontaneous, improvised verbal exchanges into a formal practice. More significantly, ethnographers have tailor-made their own interpretation of the dozens by selecting what they believe were the most authentic sites for such verbal duels—street corners, pool halls, bars, and parks. In other words, they sought out male spaces rather than predominantly female and mixed-gender spaces to record the dozens. It is no wonder that practically all commentators on the dozens have concluded that it is a boy thing. The fact is, evidence suggests that young women engaged in these kinds of verbal exchanges as much as their male counterparts, both with men and between women. And they were no less profane. By not searching out other mixed-gender and female spaces such as school buses, cafeterias, kitchen tables, beauty salons, and house parties, ethnographers have overstated the extent to which the dozens were the sole property of men.[32]

Folklorist Roger Abrahams, who pioneered the study of the dozens in his book on black vernacular folklore "from the streets of Philadelphia," is one of the few scholars to appreciate the pleasure and aesthetics of such verbal play. Nevertheless, he argues that one of the primary functions of the dozens is to compensate for a lack of masculinity caused by too many absent fathers and domineering mothers, which is why the main target of insults is an "opponent's" mother. "By exhibiting his wit, by creating new and vital folkloric expression, [the dozens player] is able to effect a temporary release from anxiety for both himself and his audience. By creating playgrounds for playing out aggressions, he achieves a kind of mascu-

line identity for himself and his group in a basically hostile environment."[33] David Schulz offers an even more specific interpretation of
the dozens as a form of masculine expression in an environment
dominated by dysfunctional families. He writes: "Playing the dozens occurs at the point when the boy is about to enter puberty and
suffer his greatest rejection from his mother as a result of his becoming a man. The dozens enables him to develop a defense against
this rejection and provides a vehicle for his transition into the ma-
nipulative world of the street dominated by masculine values expressed in gang life." It then serves as a "ritualized exorcism" that
allows men to break from maternal dominance and "establish their
own image of male superiority celebrated in street life."[34]

Allow me to propose an alternative reading of the dozens. The
goal of the dozens and related verbal games is deceptively simple: to
get a laugh. The pleasure of the dozens is not the viciousness of the
insult but the humor, the creative pun, the outrageous metaphor.
Contrary to popular belief, mothers are not the sole target; the subjects include fathers, grandparents, brothers, sisters, cousins,
friends, food, skin color, smell, and hairstyles. I am not suggesting
that "your mama" is unimportant in the whole structure of these
verbal exchanges. Nor am I suggesting that the emphasis on "your
mama" has absolutely nothing to do with the ways in which patriarchy is discursively reproduced. However, we need to understand
that "your mama" in this context is almost never living, literal, or
even metaphoric. "Your mama" is a generic reference, a code signal-
ing that the dozens have begun—it signifies a shift in speech. "Your
mama" is also a mutable, nameless body of a shared imagination
that can be constructed and reconstructed in a thousand different
shapes, sizes, colors, and circumstances. The emphasis on "your
mama" in most interpretations of the dozens has more to do with
the peculiar preoccupation of social science with Negro family
structure than anything else. Besides, in many cases the target is
immaterial; your mama, your daddy, your greasy-headed granny are

merely vehicles through which the speaker tries to elicit a laugh and display her skills. In retrospect, this seems obvious, but amid the complicated readings of masculine overcompensation and ritual performance, only a handful of writers of the period—most of whom were African Americans with no affiliation with the academy—recognized the centrality of humor. One was Howard Seals, who self-published a pamphlet on the dozens in 1969 titled *You Ain't Thuh Man Yuh Mamma Wuz*. In an effort to put to rest all the sociological overinterpretation, Seals explains: "The emotional tone to be maintained is that of hilariously, outrageously funny bantering."[35] Compare Seals's comment with linguist William Labov, who, while recognizing the humor, ultimately turns laughter into part of the ritual and thus reinforces the process of Othering:

> The primary mark of positive evaluation is laughter. We can rate the effectiveness of a sound in a group session by the number of members of the audience who laugh.
> A really successful sound will be evaluated by overt comments ... the most common forms are: "Oh!," "Oh shit!" "God damn!," or "Oh lord!" By far the most common is "Oh shit!" The intonation is important; when approval is to be signalled the vowel of each word is quite long, with a high sustained initial pitch, and a slow-falling pitch contour.[36]

Without a concept of, or even an interest in, aesthetics, style, and the visceral pleasures of cultural forms, it should not be surprising that most social scientists explained black urban culture in terms of coping mechanisms, rituals, or oppositional responses to racism. And trapped by an essentialist interpretation of culture, they continue to look for that elusive "authentic" ghetto sensibility, the true, honest, unbridled, pure cultural practices that capture the raw, ruffneck "reality" of urban life. Today, that reality is rap. While studies of rap and Hip Hop culture have been useful in terms of nudging contemporary poverty studies to pay attention to expressive cultures, they have not done much to advance the culture concept in social science. Like its progenitor, the dozens, rap or Hip Hop has been subject to incredible misconception and overinterpretation. Despite the brilliant writing of cultural critics like Tricia Rose, Greg Tate, George Lipsitz, Brian Cross, James Spady, dream hampton, Seth Fernando, Jonathan Scott, Juan Flores, Toure, and others, a number of scholars have returned to or revised the interpretive frameworks developed by the previous generation of ethnographers.[37]

For example, in a very recent book on poor black youth in postwar Philadelphia, Carl Nightingale suggests that the presumed loss of oral traditions like toasting (long, often profane vernacular narrative poetry performed orally) and the dozens, and the rise of rap music and similar commercialized expressive cultures partly explains the increase in violence among young black males. The former, he argues, has played a positive role in curbing violence while the latter is responsible for heightening aggression. He thus calls on young black men to return to these earlier, presumably precommercial cultural forms to vent emotions. Nightingale advocates resurrecting the ring shout, drumming, singing the blues, even toasting, to express black male pain and vulnerability.

The suggestion that rap music has undermined black cultural integrity is made even more forcefully in a recent article by Andre Craddock-Willis. He criticizes nearly all rap artists—especially hard-core gangsta rappers—for not knowing the "majesty" of the blues. The Left, he insists, "must work to gently push these artists to understand the tradition whose shoulders they stand on, and encourage them to comprehend struggle, sacrifice, vision and dedication—the cornerstones for the Black musical tradition."[38] (A tradition, by the way, that includes the great Jelly Roll Morton, whose 1938 recording of "Make Me a Pallet on the Floor" included lines like: "Come here you sweet bitch, give me that pussy, let me get in your drawers/I'm gonna make you think you fuckin' with Santa Claus."[39])

On the flip side are authors who insist that rap music is fundamentally the authentic, unmediated voice of ghetto youth. Tommy Lott's recent essay, "Marooned in America: Black Urban Youth Culture and Social Pathology," offers a powerful critique of neoconservative culture-of-poverty theories and challenges assumptions that the culture of the so-called underclass is pathological, but he nevertheless reduces expressive culture to a coping strategy to deal with the terror of street life. For Lott, the Hip Hop nation is the true voice of the black lumpenproletariat whose descriptions of street life are the real thing. "As inhabitants of extreme-poverty neighborhoods," he writes, "many rap artists and their audiences are entrenched in a street life filled with crime, drugs, and violence. Being criminal-minded and having street values are much more suitable for living in their environment." Of course, most rap music is not about a nihilistic street life but about rocking the mike, and the vast majority of rap artists (like most inner city youth) were not entrenched in the tangled web of crime and violence. Yet, he is convinced that Hip Hop narratives of ghetto life "can only come from one's experiences on the streets. Although, at its worst, this knowledge is manifested through egotistical sexual boasting, the core meaning of the rapper's use of the term 'knowledge' is to be *politically* astute, that is, to have a full understanding of the conditions under which black urban youth must survive."[40]

By not acknowledging the deep visceral pleasures black youth derive from making and consuming culture, the stylistic and aesthetic conventions that render the form and performance more attractive than the message, these authors reduce expressive culture to a political text to be read like a less sophisticated version of *The Nation* or *Radical America*. But what counts more than the story is the "storytelling"—an emcee's verbal facility on the mic, the creative and often hilarious use of puns, metaphors, similes, not to mention the ability to kick some serious slang (or what we might call linguistic inventiveness). As microphone fiend Rakim might put it, the function of Hip Hop is to "move the crowd." For all the implicit and explicit politics of rap lyrics, Hip Hop must be understood as a sonic force more than anything else.

Despite their good intentions, ignoring aesthetics enables these authors not only to dismiss "egotistical sexual boasting" as simply a weakness in political ideology but also to mistakenly interpret narratives of everyday life as descriptions of personal experience rather than a revision of older traditions of black vernacular poetry and/or appropriations from mainstream popular culture. To begin with rap music as a mirror image of daily life ignores the influences of urban toasts and published "pimp narratives," which became popular during the late 1960s and early 1970s. In many instances the characters are almost identical, and on occasion rap artists pay tribute to toasting by lyrically "sampling" these early pimp narratives.[41]

Moreover, the assumption that rappers are merely street journalists does not allow for the playfulness and storytelling that is so central to Hip Hop specifically, and black vernacular culture generally. For example, violent lyrics in rap music are rarely meant to be literal. Rather, they are more often than not metaphors to challenge competitors on the microphone. The mic becomes a Tech-9 or AK-47, imagined drive-bys occur from the stage, flowing lyrics become hollow-point shells. Classic examples are Ice Cube's "Jackin' for Beats," a humorous song that describes sampling other artists and producers as outright armed robbery, and Ice T's "Pulse of the Rhyme" or "Grand Larceny" (which brags about stealing a show).[42] Moreover, exaggerated and invented boasts of criminal acts should sometimes be regarded as part of a larger set of signifying practices. Growing out of a much older set of cultural practices, these masculinist narratives are essentially verbal duels over who is the "baddest." They are not meant as literal descriptions of violence and aggression, but connote the playful use of language itself.[43]

Of course, the line between rap music's gritty realism, storytelling, and straight-up signifyin(g) is not always clear to listeners, nor is it supposed to be. Hip Hop, particularly gangsta rap, also attracts listeners for whom the "ghetto" is a place of adventure, unbridled violence, erotic fantasy, and/or an imaginary alternative to suburban boredom. White music critic John Leland, who claimed that Ice Cube's turn toward social criticism "killed rap music," praised the group NWA because they "dealt in evil as fantasy: killing cops, smoking hos, filling quiet nights with a flurry of senseless buckshot." This kind of voyeurism partly explains NWA's huge white following and why their album *Efil4zaggin* shot to the top of the charts as soon as it was released. As one critic put it, "In reality, NWA have more in common with a Charles Bronson movie than a PBS documentary on the plight of the inner-cities." NWA members have even admitted that some of their recent songs were not representations of reality "in the hood" but inspired by popular films like *Innocent Man* starring Tom Selleck, and *Tango and Cash*.[44]

Claims to have located the authentic voice of black ghetto youth are certainly not unique. Several scholars insist that Hip Hop is the pure, unadulterated voice of a ghetto that has grown increasingly isolated from "mainstream" society. Missing from this formulation is rap music's incredible hybridity. From the outset, rap music embraced a variety of styles and cultural forms, from reggae and salsa to heavy metal and jazz. Hip Hop's hybridity reflected, in part, the increasingly international character of America's inner cities resulting from immigration, demographic change, and new forms of information, as well as the inventive employment of technology in creating rap music. By using two turntables, and later digital samplers, deejays played different records, isolated the "break beats" or what they identified as the funkiest part of a song, and boldly mixed a wide range of different music and musical genres to create new music. And despite the fact that many of the pioneering deejays, rappers, and break dancers were African American, West Indian, and Puerto Rican and strongly identified with the African diaspora, rap artists wrecked all the boundaries between "black" and "white" music. Deejay Afrika Islam remembers vividly the time when Hip

Hop and punk united for a moment and got busy at the New Wave clubs in New York during the early 1980s. Even before the punk rockers sought a relationship with uptown Hip Hop deejays, Afrika Islam recalls, in the Bronx they were already playing "everything from Aerosmith's 'Walk This Way' to Dunk and the Blazers." Grand Master Caz, whose lyrics were stolen by the Sugarhill Gang and ended up in *Rapper's Delight* (the first successful rap record in history), grew up in the Bronx listening to soft rock and mainstream pop music. As he explained in an interview, "Yo, I'd bug you out if I told you who I used to listen to. I used to listen to Barry Manilow, Neil Diamond, and Simon and Garfunkel. I grew up listening to that. WABC. That's why a lot of the stuff that my group did, a lot of routines that we're famous for all come from all white boy songs."[45]

If you saw a picture of Caz, this statement would seem incongruous. He looks the part of an authentic black male, a real ruffneck, hoodie, "G," nigga, criminal, menace. And yet, he is a product of a hybrid existence, willing to openly talk about Simon and Garfunkel in a book that I could only purchase from a Nation of Islam booth on 125th Street in Harlem. He is also the first to call what he does "black music," structured noise for which the beat, no matter where it is taken from, is everything. Moreover, like the breakers who danced to his rhymes, the kids who built his speakers, the deejay who spun the records, Caz takes credit for his creativity, his artistry, his "work." This is the "black urban culture" which has remained so elusive to social science; it is the thing, or rather the process, that defies concepts like "coping strategy," "adaptative," "authentic," "nihilistic," and "pathological."

REVISING THE CULTURE CONCEPT:
HYBRIDITY, STYLE, AND AESTHETICS
IN BLACK URBAN CULTURE

Aside from the tendency to ignore expressive/popular cultural forms, and limit the category of culture to (so-called dysfunctional) behavior, the biggest problem with the way social scientists employ the culture concept in their studies of the black urban poor is their inability to see what it all means *to the participants and practitioners.* In other words, they do not consider what Clinton (George, that is) calls the "pleasure principle." If I may use a metaphor here, rather than hear the singer they analyze the lyrics; rather than hear the drum they study the song title. Black music, creativity and experimentation in language, that walk, that talk, that style, must also be understood as sources of visceral and psychic pleasure. Though they may also reflect and speak to the political and social world of inner city communities, expressive cultures are not simply mirrors of social life or expressions of conflicts, pathos, and anxieties.

Paul Willis's concept of "symbolic creativity" provides one way out of the impasse created by such a limited concept of culture. As Willis argues, constructing an identity, communicating with others, and achieving pleasure are all part of symbolic creativity—it is literally the labor of creating art in everyday life. Despite his distrust of and vehement opposition to "aesthetics," he realizes that, in most cases, the explicit meaning or intention of a particular cultural form is not the thing that makes it attractive. The appeal of popular music, for example, is more than lyrical: "Songs bear meaning and allow symbolic work not just as speech acts, but also as structures of sound with unique rhythms, textures and forms. Thus, it is not always what is sung, but the *way* it is sung, within particular conventions or musical genres which gives a piece of music its communicative power and meaning."[46] Indeed, words like *soul* and *funk* were efforts to come up with a language to talk about that visceral element in music, even if they did ultimately evolve into market categories. Over two decades ago, black novelist Cecil Brown brilliantly captured this "thing," this symbolic creativity, the pleasure principle, soul, or whatever you want to call it. Writing about the godfather of soul, James Brown, he argued that his lyrics are less important than how they are uttered, where they are placed rhythmically, and "how he makes it sound." "What, for instance, does 'Mother Popcorn' mean? But what difference does it make when you're dancing to it, when you are feeling it, when you are it and it you (possession). It's nothing and everything at once; it is what black (hoodoo) people who never studied art in school mean by art."[47]

Yet to say it is a "black" thing doesn't mean it is made up entirely of black things. As Greg Tate makes clear in his recent collection of essays, *Flyboy in the Buttermilk*, and in the epigraph to this chapter, interpreters of the African American experience—in our case social scientists—must bear a large share of the responsibility for turning ghetto residents into an undifferentiated mass. We can no longer ignore the fact that information technology, new forms of mass communication, and immigration have made the rest of the world more accessible to inner city residents than ever before.[48] Contemporary black urban culture is a hybrid that draws on Afro-diasporic traditions, popular culture, the vernacular of previous generations of Southern and Northern black folk, new and old technologies, and a whole lot of imagination. Once again, James Clifford's ruminations on the "predicament of culture" are useful for exposing the predicament of social science. He writes: "To tell . . . local histories of cultural survival and emergence, we need to resist deep-seated habits of mind and systems of authenticity. We need to be suspicious of an almost-automatic tendency to relegate non-Western (read: black) peoples and objects to the pasts of an increasingly homogeneous humanity."[49]

CHAPTER TWO

LOOKING TO GET PAID:

How Some Black Youth Put Culture to Work

I don't like to dream about gettin paid, so I
Dig into the books of the rhymes that I made. . . .
——ERIC B AND RAKIM,
"Paid in Full"

If you can run ball for 6–7 hours, you have already
established your ability to work.
——JAMES SPADY, "Running Ball"

Graffiti writing for the unemployed black ghetto kid
may have developed because there is little else to do but street
wisdom tells you to turn it to your advantage. The rap insists on
self-realisation but on your own terms, to be unafraid of estab-
lished channels, but to use them on your own terms, i.e., rip
them off.

——ATLANTA AND ALEXANDER,
"Wild Style: Graffiti Painting"

Nike, Reebok, L. A. Gear, and other athletic shoe conglomerates have profited enormously from postindustrial decline. TV commercials and print ads romanticize the crumbling urban spaces in
which African American youth must play, and in so doing they have
created a vast market for overpriced sneakers. These televisual representations of "street ball" are quite remarkable; marked by chain-
link fences, concrete playgrounds, bent and rusted netless hoops,
graffiti-scrawled walls, and empty buildings, they have created a
world where young black males do nothing *but* play.

And yet, representations of the ghetto as a space of play and
pleasure amid violence and deterioration are more than simply
products of the corporate imagination. Inner city public parks and
school facilities *are* falling apart or disappearing at an alarming rate.
The writings of "aerosol artists" *have* altered concrete walls, abandoned buildings, and public transportation; some have created masterpieces amidst urban rubble, and most have highlighted the rubble by "tagging" public structures with signs and signatures. Play
areas—like much of the inner city—have become increasingly fortified, caged in by steel fences, wrought iron gates, padlocks, and razor ribbon wire. The most striking element in this postindustrial
urban spectacle are the people who occupy these urban spaces.
Parks and schoolyards are full of brown bodies of various hues
whose lack of employment has left them with plenty of time to
"play." In other words, while obscuring poverty, unemployment,
racism, and rising police repression, commercial representations of
the contemporary "concrete jungles" powerfully underscore the
link between urban decline, joblessness, and the erosion of recreational spaces in the inner city. At the same time, they highlight the
historic development of "leisure" time for the urban working class
and, therefore, offer commodities to help fill that time. The difference between the creation and commodification of urban leisure at
the turn of the century and now, however, is that opportunities for

wage labor have virtually disappeared and the bodies of the displaced workers are overwhelmingly black and brown.

In this chapter I hope to offer some suggestive observations
about the relationship between the rise of permanent unemployment, the transformation of public space, and the changing mean-
ings and practices of play for African American urban youth. The
approach I take challenges the way in which work and leisure have
been dichotomized in studies of the U.S. working class. In much of
this literature, play is seen as an escape from work, something that
takes place on the weekends or evenings in distinctive spaces set
aside for leisure. Indeed, these leisure spaces constitute the flip side
of work for, as Paul Gilroy puts it, the body "is here celebrated as an
instrument of pleasure rather than an instrument of labor."[1] What I
am suggesting, however, is that the pursuit of leisure, pleasure, and
creative expression is *labor*, and that some African American urban
youth have tried to turn that labor into cold hard cash. Thus, play has
increasingly become, for some, more than an expression of stylistic
innovation, gender identities, and/or racial and class anger—increasingly it is viewed as a way to survive economic crisis or a means
to upward mobility. Having stated the essential outlines of my argument, however, let me add a few clarifications and caveats. First, I
am in no way suggesting that this kind of self-commodification of
play is emancipatory, revolutionary, or even resistive. Rather, it com-
prises a range of strategies within capitalism—some quite entrepreneurial, in fact—intended to enable working-class urban youth to
avoid dead-end, low-wage labor while devoting their energies to creative and pleasurable pursuits. These strategies do not undermine
capitalism; profits generated by the most successful ventures simply buttress capital and illustrate, once again, its amazing resilience
and elasticity, even when the commodities themselves offer ideological challenges to its basic premise. Furthermore, these strategies
do not necessarily improve the position of the entire black commu-

nity, nor are they intended to. On the contrary, in some instances they might have negative consequences for African Americans—that is, through the circulation of representations that ultimately undergird racist ideologies, or "success" narratives that let racism off the hook by demonstrating that "hard work" in the realm of sports or entertainment is all one needs to escape the ghetto. Second, I am not suggesting that all or even most youth engaged in these forms of play are trying to turn their efforts and skills into a commodity. Nor am I suggesting that the self-commodification of "play-labor" is unique to the black community—though the structural position of working-class African Americans in the political and cultural economy of the U.S. terrain lends itself to these kinds of opportunities. In a nation with few employment opportunities for African Americans and a white consumer market eager to be entertained by the Other, blacks have historically occupied a central place in the popular culture industry. Thus, while the postindustrial city has created a different set of opportunities and limitations on black youths' efforts to turn play into a means to escape wage labor, what I discuss below has a much older trajectory.

Economic restructuring leading to permanent unemployment; the shrinking of city services; the rising number of abandoned buildings; the militarization of inner city streets; and the decline of parks, youth programs, and public schools altered the terrain of play and creative expression for black youth. The loss of manufacturing jobs was accompanied by expansion of low-wage "service" jobs—retail clerks, janitors, maids, data processors, security guards, waitresses, and cooks, which tend to be part-time and offer limited health or retirement benefits. By Reagan's second term, over one-third of black families earned incomes below the poverty line. For black teenagers, the unemployment rate increased from 38.9 to 43.6 percent under Reagan. And in Midwestern cities—once the industrial heartland—black teenage unemployment rates ranged from 50 to 70 percent in 1985.[2] Federal and state job programs for inner city youth were also wiped out at an alarming rate. In California, both the Neighborhood Youth Corps and the Comprehensive Employment and Training Act (CETA) were dismantled, and the Jobs Corps and Los Angeles Summer Job Program have been cut back substantially.[3]

Massive joblessness contributed to the expansion of the underground economy, and young people, not surprisingly, are among its biggest employees. The invention and marketing of new, cheaper drugs (PCP, crack, and synthetic drugs) combined with a growing fear of crime and violence, the transformation of policing through the use of new technologies, and the erosion of youth programs and recreational facilities have had a profound impact on public life. When the crack economy made its presence felt in poor black communities in Los Angeles, for instance, street violence intensified as various gangs and groups of peddlers battled for control over markets. Because of its unusually high crime rate, Los Angeles gained the dubious distinction of having the largest urban prison population in the country. Yet, in spite of the violence and financial vulnerability that went along with peddling crack, for many black youngsters it was the most viable economic option.[4]

While the rise in crime and the ascendance of the crack economy, however, might have put money into some people's pockets, for the majority it meant greater police repression. Black working-class communities in Los Angeles were turned into war zones during the mid- to late 1980s. Police helicopters, complex electronic surveillance, even small tanks armed with battering rams became part of this increasingly militarized urban landscape. Housing projects, such as Imperial Courts, were renovated along the lines of minimum security prisons and equipped with fortified fencing and a Los Angeles Police Department substation. Imperial Courts residents were suddenly required to carry identity cards and visitors were routinely searched. As popular media coverage of the inner city linked drugs and violence to black youth, young African Americans in Los Angeles and elsewhere were subject to increasing police harassment and, in some cases, feared by older residents.[5]

In trying to make sense of the intensification of violence and crime in the inner city during the past two decades, we must resist the tendency to romanticize the past, to recall a golden age of urban public life free of violence and conflict. At the turn of the century, for example, bloody turf wars were common among European immigrant youth. Recalling his youth on the Lower East Side of Manhattan, Communist writer and activist Mike Gold wrote:

> The East Side, for children, was a world plunged in eternal war. It was suicide to walk into the next block. Each block was a separate nation, and when a strange boy appeared, the patriots swarmed. . . . The beating was as cruel and bloody as that of grown-ups; no mercy was shown. I have had three holes in my head, and many black eyes and puffed lips from our street wars. We did it to others, they did it to us. It was patriotism, though what difference there was between one East Side block and another is now hard to see.[6]

In addition to Jewish and Italian gang violence, historian Cary Goodman points out that some of the most vicious fights that erupted in the Lower East Side during this era took place between socialists and anarchists. Likewise, in Philadelphia during the 1950s, gangs fought with zip guns and switchblades, which resulted in even more deaths and serious injuries than the turn-of-the-century street wars.[7]

The difference between then and now is not the levels of violence or crime (indeed, few criminologists are willing to admit that the crime rate in predominantly white turn-of-the-century cities was often higher than it is now). Rather, it is a combination of the growing importance of street gangs in the urban political economy and the dramatic improvement in technology that is different. Taking advantage of the gaping hole left by the disappearance of a viable local economy, some gangs have become businesses, distributors of illegal and *legal* goods and services, and they generally define their markets by territory. The very technological revolutions that enable them to connect up with international cartels, expand their ventures, or maintain contact with one another (through reasonably priced pagers, laptop computers, and hand-held fax machines) have also increased the stakes by facilitating greater investment diversity and territorial reach.[8]

More importantly, the proliferation of inexpensive and powerful semi-automatic weapons is what distinguishes the 1990s from the 1950s, or for that matter, from the 1890s. The National Rifle Association (NRA), the nation's largest lobby against gun control, played a major role in ensuring the availability of firearms. Backed by huge weapons manufacturers and armed with one of the wealthiest political action committees in the country (its annual budget is close to $30 million and in the 1992 elections it contributed $1.7 million to House and Senate candidates), the NRA has fought tenaciously against bans on the kinds of automatic assault weapons that are appearing more frequently in inner city communities. Under Reagan, whose presidential campaign received strong backing from the NRA, the regulatory power of the Bureau of Alcohol, Tobacco, and Firearms (ATF) was weakened considerably. By the mid-1980s, obtaining a license to sell guns became so easy that potential dealers needed only to pay a mere thirty-dollar fee and undergo an unusually casual background check. According to one report, "the ATF's background checks were once so lax that the agency even issued licenses to dogs." Ironically, the *fear* of crime partly explains the success of the NRA lobby and their closest allies, gun manufacturers and distributors. During the past decade, the gun industry has banked on crime fears to sell its products, focusing attention less on the hunting market and more on citizens' desire to protect themselves and their property. After a sales slump in the early 1980s, gun sellers not only expanded their marketing strategy to women and

teens but brought back cheap semi-automatic pistols, which are frequently used in street crimes. In the end, however, middle-class
families concerned about crime, not criminals, are the primary consumers of handguns. In 1992 alone, estimated sales of firearms to-
taled more than $774 million.[9]

The fear of crime has also spawned new developments in late-
twentieth-century urban architecture. The design of the built environment has had a profound impact on how public space is defended and protected, which in turn shapes the way people interact
with one another. The work of Camilo José Vergara and Mike Davis
powerfully illustrates the degree to which cities are built and conceived as fortifications against the presumed criminality and chaos
of the streets. Vergara writes:

> Buildings grow claws and spikes, their entrances acquire metal
> plates, their roofs get fenced in. . . . Even in areas where statistics
> show a decrease in major crime, fortification continues to esca-
> late, and as it does, ghettos lose their coherence. Neighborhoods
> are replaced by a random assortment of isolated bunkers, struc-
> tures that increasingly resemble jails or power stations, their in-
> teriors effectively separated from the outside. . . . In brick and
> cinderblock and sharpened metal, inequality takes material
> form.[10]

Recession and Reagan-era budget cuts, combined with the militarization of urban life, have devastated inner city public recreational
facilities and altered the landscape of play significantly. Beginning
in the 1970s, a wave of public recreational service employees were
either furloughed, discharged, or allowed to retire without replace-
ment; the service and maintenance of parks and playgrounds was
cut back substantially; many facilities were eliminated or simply de-
teriorated; and the hours of operation were drastically reduced. During the mid-1970s, for instance, Cleveland's recreation department
had to close down almost $50 million dollars worth of facilities. In
New York City, municipal appropriations for parks dropped by more

than $40 million between 1974 and 1980—a sixty-percent cut in real dollars. Staff cutbacks were even more drastic: between the late 1960s and 1979, the number of park employees dropped from almost 6,100 to 2,600. To make matters worse, a growing number of public schoolyards in inner city communities have become inaccessible during after-school hours.[11]

More recently, we have witnessed a growing number of semipublic/private play spaces like "people's parks" which require a key (such as the playground in Greenwich Village that services residents of New York University–owned apartments) and highly sophisticated indoor play areas that charge admission. The growth of these privatized spaces has reinforced a class-segregated play world and created yet another opportunity for investors to profit from the general fear of crime and violence. Thus, in the shadows of Central Park, Frederick Law Olmsted's great urban vision of class integration and public sociability, high-tech indoor playgrounds such as WonderCamp, Discovery Zone, and PlaySpace charge admission to eager middle- and upper-class children whose parents want a safe play environment. Protection from the outside is emphasized; at PlaySpace, for example, young workers are expected to size up potential customers before "buzzing" them in. While these play areas are occasionally patronized by poor and working-class black children, the fact that most of these indoor camps/playgrounds are built in well-to-do neighborhoods and charge an admission fee ranging between five and nine dollars prohibits poor families from making frequent visits.[12]

Privatization has also adversely affected public parks. Parks directors in several big cities, notably New York, have turned to "public-private partnerships" and begun to charge "user fees" in order to make ends meet. New York City's Department of Parks and Recreation has already transferred zoos, skating rinks, and parking lots to private operators, and there has been discussion of contracting out recreational and maintenance services to private companies. Moreover, during the 1980s, the city and state used tax abatements as a way of encouraging private developers to build parks and plazas, which usually manifest themselves as highly surveilled "arcades, interior atriums, and festival marketplaces attached to office and condominium towers." The move toward private ownership of public space is powerfully captured in a plaque located on a plaza in midtown Manhattan: "PUBLIC SPACE, Owned and Maintained by AT&T."[13]

Of course, I do not want to exaggerate the impact of the disappearance of public play areas on urban youth. In New York, for example, the sidewalks and streets have long been a desirable place to play, not just for children but for adults as well. In the immigrant working-class neighborhoods of the Lower East Side during the early twentieth century, parents preferred to be within hearing distance of their children, and the streets were often crowded with kids. Scenes of dozens of Jewish and Italian kids surrounding an open fire hydrant on a hot summer day in the 1920s are not much different from scenes in Harlem in the early 1970s. Young and old kids have constantly carved out space on the sidewalk for jacks, craps, double dutch, hopscotch, and handball, and the streets have been used as stickball diamonds that incorporate existing landmarks (such as cars and fire hydrants) as bases. Moreover, since 1909, the New York Police Athletic League has run an annual program whereby it blocks off traffic through selected streets during the summer in order to create more safe places to play.[14]

But as the streets become increasingly dangerous, or are perceived to be so, more and more young children are confined indoors, limited to backyards, or (for those who can afford it) shuttled to the city's proliferating "discovery zones." For inner city families, the threat of drive-bys has turned porches and front doors, which once spilled out onto sidewalks and streets as extensions of play areas, into fortified entrances with iron "screen" doors that lock from the inside. Sadly, the increasingly common practice of placing iron gates over windows and doors is partly responsible for a rise in fire-related deaths in urban black communities.

The simultaneous decline in employment opportunities; public leisure spaces for young people; and overly crowded, poorly funded public schools and youth programs simply expanded an urban landscape in which black teenagers—the throwaways of a new, mobile capitalism—became an even larger, more permanent (and in the minds of many, more menacing) presence in parks and on street corners. The growing numbers of young brown bodies engaged in "play" rather than work (from street-corner bantering, to "malling" [hanging out at shopping malls], to basketball) have contributed to popular constructions of the "underclass" as a threat and shaped urban police practices. The invention of terms such as *wilding*, as Houston Baker points out, reveal a discourse of black male youth out of control, rampaging teenagers free of the disciplinary strictures of school, work, and prison.[15]

I want to argue that many of these young bodies are not merely idle bystanders. They are not uniformly devoid of ambition or a work ethic. Increasingly, young people have tried to turn play into an alternative to unfulfilling wage labor. Basketball, for black males at least, not only embodies dreams of success and possible escape from the ghetto. In a growing number of communities pickup games are played for money much like cards or pool. While it is true that some boys and young men see basketball as a quick (though *never* easy) means to success and riches, it is ludicrous to believe that everyone on the court shares the same aspirations.[16] In the context of a game with competition, it becomes clear very quickly who can play and who cannot. Most participants are not deluding themselves into believing that it is an escape from the ghetto; rather, they derive some kind of pleasure from it. But for that small minority who hold onto the dream and are encouraged, the work ethic begins quite early and they usually work harder than most turn-of-the-century child wage workers. As cultural critic James Spady observes in the epigraph to this chapter, running ball all day long is evidence of a work ethic. Besides, black working-class men and their families see themselves as having fewer career options than whites, so sports have been more of an imagined possibility than becoming a highly educated professional—"it was *the* career option rather than *a* career option," writes Michael Messner.[17] Nowhere is this better illustrated than in the highly acclaimed documentary film *Hoop Dreams*. Charting the tragic lives of Arthur Agee and William Gates, two young talents from the South Side of Chicago who were recruited by a white suburban Catholic high school to play ball, the filmmakers capture the degree to which many black working-class families have invested their hopes and aspirations in the game of basketball.[18]

Not surprisingly, the vast majority are disappointed. Of the half-million high school basketball players in the United States, only 14,000 (2.8 percent) play college ball, and only twenty-five of those (.005 percent) make it to the National Basketball Association. More generally, only 6 or 7 percent of high school athletes ever play college sports; roughly 8 percent of draft-eligible college football and basketball players are drafted by the pros, and only 2 percent ever sign a contract. The chances of attaining professional status in sports are approximately 4 in 100,000 for white men, 2 in 100,000 for black men, and 3 in 1,000,000 for U.S.-born Latinos.[19]

Practically all scholars agree that young women and girls have had even fewer opportunities to engage in either work or play. They have less access to public spaces, are often responsible for attending to household duties, and are policed by family members, authorities, and boys themselves from the "dangers" of the streets. Aside from the gender division of labor that frees many boys and men from child care responsibilities and housecleaning, the fear of violence and teen pregnancy has led parents to cloister girls even more. Thus, when they do spend much of their play time in the public spaces of the city, parent-imposed curfews and other pressures limit their time outside the household.

Controlling women's access to public space is just part of the story. Because sports, street gambling, hanging out in parks and street corners, and other forms of play are central to the construction of masculinity, boys, young men, and authority figures erect strict gender boundaries to keep women out. In fact, one might argue that play is at least as, if not more, important than work in shaping gender identities. After all, our sense of maleness and femaleness is made in childhood, and the limits, boundaries, and contestations in the world of play constitute key moments in the creation and shaping of gender identity.[20] And given the transformation of the labor market in the age of multinational capital, the gendering and gender policing of play has enormous implications. With the extension of a service-based economy (often gendered as feminized or servile labor) and the rise of permanent unemployment, work no longer seems to be a primary factor in the construction of masculinity—if it ever was.

The policing of these boundaries has a material element as well; it ultimately helps reproduce gender inequalities by denying or limiting women's access to the most potentially profitable forms of creative leisure. Of course, girls and young women do participate in mixed-gender play, and some even earn the right to participate in the men's world of play. For instance, women do play basketball, occasionally with the fellas, but they have fewer opportunities for pickup games, to participate in organized street leagues, or to dream that honing one's skills could land a college scholarship or trip to the pros. Yet, despite the policing of gender boundaries, which tends to become more rigid when children reach preadolescence, girls find forms of homosocial play and pleasure which they defend and protect. And like boys' games and mixed-gender play in declining urban centers, modern social reformers have occasionally tried to turn these forms into "supervised play" as a way to build self-esteem, discipline, and the work ethic (though these virtues were allegedly instilled in young girls through "domestic science" programs). The most fascinating example is the Double Dutch League of New York, originally founded in 1973 by the Police Athletic League (PAL) and later sponsored by McDonald's restaurant. Girls were organized into teams that competed at Lincoln Center for scholarship money and other prizes. Some of the crews, like the Jazzy Jumpers and the Ebonnettes, became fairly big in New York and nationally.[21]

Double dutch is a very old jump-rope game in which participants skip over two ropes spinning in opposite directions. Although it is not exclusive to African American youth, it has been a cultural mainstay among black urban girls for decades. Double dutch is not a competitive sport; rather, it is a highly stylized performance accompanied by (frequently profane) songs and rhymes and can involve three or more girls. Two girls turn the rope (though boys occasionally participate as turners, especially if they are under big sister's supervision) while one or sometimes two participants "jump in."[22] The good jumpers perform improvised acrobatic feats or complicated body movements as a way of stylizing and individualizing the performance. What is particularly interesting about the Double Dutch League is the degree to which its male founders, like its president David Walker, saw the game in terms of the peculiar needs and interests of girls. Walker explained that he had been thinking about activities for girls, especially after failing to attract many girls to his bicycling program. Walker explained, "When I heard the expression double dutch about a thousand bulbs lit in my mind. I started realizing it was an activity that girls really related to. . . . Mothers did it when they were kids. . . . See the relationship—mother—clothesline—daughter." Moreover, he believed it was an important activity for controlling inner city girls and teaching them the benefits of competition. Once PAL and other groups began institutionalizing double dutch, the jumpers who participated in these formal contests found the improvisational character of the game sharply circumscribed. Within the PAL-sponsored contests and demonstrations, moves became highly formalized and choreographed, despite the fact that League organizers encouraged innovation. Contestants were judged on speed and accuracy—criteria that simply were less important on the streets. The organizers even tried to sever its inner city linkages by referring to double dutch as "street ballet" and by practically eliminating the verbal component so essential to double dutch. Few girls participated in these tournaments, in part because there was little incentive. The financial promise of basketball (which could still be played without supervision) was missing in double dutch.[23]

Even more than sports and various schoolyard games, forms of "play" that fall outside the pale of recreation—visual art, dance, and music—offered black urban youth more immediate opportunities for entrepreneurship and greater freedom from unfulfilling wage labor. Performance and visual arts, in particular, powerfully dramatize how young people have turned the labor of play into a commodity, not only to escape wage work but to invest their time and energy in creative expression, or what ethnographer and cultural theorist Paul Willis calls "symbolic creativity." As Willis argues, constructing an identity, communicating with others, and achieving pleasure constitute the labor of creating art in everyday life. Hence, it is in the realm of symbolic creativity that the boundaries between work and play are perhaps most blurred, especially as these forms become commodified.[24]

The struggle to carve out a kind of liminal space between work and play, labor and performance, is hardly new. Today in the streets of New Orleans, children as young as five years old maintain a tradition of street performance, playing "second line" jazz in makeshift marching bands through the French Quarter. And the subway stops and downtown sidewalks of New York; Washington, D.C.; Atlanta; Oakland; and elsewhere are filled with young black musicians of mixed talent trying to make a living through their craft. Perhaps the most famous young black "street musician" is Larry Wright, a talented percussionist who milked a plastic bucket and a pair of drumsticks for every timbre and tonality imaginable. He began performing on street corners in New York City as an adolescent, earning change from passersby who found his complex polyrhythms appealing. His mother encouraged Larry to pursue his art, which ultimately earned him acceptance into New York's highly competitive High School for the Performing Arts. When he was still only fifteen, two filmmakers "discovered" him and made a half-hour video about his life and music that put his name in circulation—and the rest, as they say, is history. After an appearance in the film *Green Card*, a Levi's commercial shot by Spike Lee, and a Mariah Carey video, his example spawned a number of imitators throughout the country. I have seen kids in front of the Pavilion (an eatery and shopping center on Pennsylvania Avenue in Washington, D.C.) with white buckets and sticks trying to reproduce his sound.[25]

While street performance is as old as cities themselves, new technologies and the peculiar circumstances of postindustrial decline have given rise to new cultural forms that are even more directly a product of grassroots entrepreneurship and urban youth's struggle over public space. These forms demanded specific skills, technical knowledge, and often complicated support systems that provided employment and investment opportunities for nonperformers. The most obvious example is Hip Hop culture, a broad cultural movement that emerged in the South Bronx during the 1970s. But even before the Hip Hop scene blew up in New York City as an alternative vocation for black and Latino kids, the slums of Washington, D.C., became a source of both musical inspiration and entrepreneurial imagination. Out of D.C.'s black ghettos emerged a highly percussive music called Go-Go, which indirectly influenced the direction of East Coast Hip Hop. Originating in the late 1960s, when Go-Go guru Charles Brown formed a dynamic band called the Soul Stirrers, Go-Go had always been a distinctive Washington,

D.C., style. The bands tended to be large—sometimes a dozen pieces—and were characterized by heavy funk bass, horns, rhythm guitar, and various percussion instruments—from snares, congas, and cow bells to found objects. Like Hip Hop and other black Atlantic musical traditions, Go-Go music places a premium on sustaining the rhythm and getting the dancers involved in the performance through call and response. Just as Hip Hop deejays keep the dancers on the floor by playing a seamless array of break beats, Go-Go bands play continuously, linking different songs by using a relentless back beat and bass guitar to string the music together into an intense performance that could last an hour or more.[26]

Go-Go groups like Trouble Funk, E.U. (Experience Unlimited), Redds and the Boys, Go-Go Allstarz, Mass Extension, and the appropriately named Junkyard Band were products of high school and junior high inner city music programs. Some band members met at high school marching band competitions or were involved in summer youth projects intended to get kids off the streets. As black D.C. artist and activist Malik Edwards remembers, "It was just kids trying to play their music, bands trying to outjam each other. E.U. came out of the Valley Green Courtesy Patrol summer project, which got them some instruments through the community center and a place to practice." Performing on cheap, often battered instruments, young Go-Go musicians created a distinctive "pot-and-pan" sound. "The sound was created out of inefficient instruments, just anything they could do to make an instrument," recalls Go-Go promoter Maxx Kidd.[27] Yet, these artists still made the most popular music in the District, sometimes performing to capacity dance crowds in school gyms, parks, recreation centers, empty warehouses, rented hotel ballrooms, and a vast array of "Go-Go's" (clubs) in the neighborhood.

With few exceptions, no one really got rich off of Go-Go. Throughout the 1970s, neither radio stations nor the record industry took an interest in this new urban music. Despite the initial lack of commercial interest, Go-Go gave up-and-coming musicians a space to learn their craft, perform for audiences, make a little money on the side, and an opportunity for creative expression. Ironically, it is precisely because the early Go-Go scene remained free of major corporate investment that it spawned a fairly lucrative underground economy for inner city youth who sold bootleg tapes, made posters, organized dances, made and repaired musical instruments, and indirectly benefited from the fact that black working-class consumers spent their money on local entertainment.[28] Unfortunately, just as Go-Go began building an international following and the record industry took a greater interest in the mid-1980s, its popularity in D. C. began to decline. Moreover, it never achieved the kind of following Hip Hop enjoyed; after hit songs by E.U., Trouble Funk, and Charles Brown, the big studios lost interest in Go-Go soon thereafter. There is still a vibrant Go-Go scene in Washington, but it is only a fraction of what it was a decade ago.

Hip Hop, on the other hand, was more than music; it embraced an array of cultural forms that included graffiti art and break dancing as well as rap music. Because each of these forms generated different kinds of opportunities and imposed different sorts of limitations, we must examine them separately. We might begin with the oldest—and perhaps least lucrative—component of Hip Hop culture: graffiti. Of course, various forms of wall writing go back centuries, from political slogans and gang markings to romantic declarations. But the aerosol art movement is substantially different. Calling themselves writers, graffiti artists, aerosol artists, and subterranean guerrilla artists, many of the young pioneers of this art form treated their work as a skilled craft and believed they were engaged in worthwhile labor. During the 1970s, some graffiti artists sold their services to local merchants and community organizations, and a handful enjoyed fleeting success in the Soho art scene.

Subway trains provided the most popular canvases. They enabled the artist to literally circulate his or her work through the city.

Moreover, many young people thought of themselves as waging war against the Metropolitan Transit Authority (MTA). They felt the Transit police were repressive, the fares were too high, and trains assigned to poor communities like Harlem and the South Bronx were inferior. Writers often "bombed" the interiors of trains with "tags"—quickly executed and highly stylized signatures, often made with fat markers rather than spray cans. Outside the trains they created "masterpieces," elaborate works carefully conceived and designed ahead of time. Good writers not only had to be skilled artists, but because they were breaking the law by defacing property, they had to work quickly and quietly. They often executed their work in complete darkness, sometimes beginning around 2:00 or 3:00 A.M. The threat of arrest was constant, as was the potential of being seriously injured by a moving train or the electrified third rail. Most artists protected themselves by working in crews rather than as lone individuals. From the outset women writers like Lady Pink, Charmin, and Lady Heart were part of these crews and most worked alongside male artists, though female writers had to battle male sexism and protect themselves from possible sexual assault while executing their work.[29]

By the early 1970s, graffiti writing became a widely debated and discussed phenomenon, becoming the subject of several dramatic and documentary films. Although this partly explains the mainstream art world's fleeting interest in aerosol art, the fact is that graffiti writers themselves took the first initiative. Through organizations such as United Graffiti Artists (UGA) and the Nation of Graffiti Artists (NOGA), some of the leading artists attempted to collectively market their work and establish ties to art dealers and downtown galleries. Launched in 1972, UGA's initial mission was to redirect graffiti into socially acceptable avenues and to get black and Puerto Rican kids off the street. Very quickly, however, it became a primary vehicle for exposing a fairly exclusive group of aerosol artists to galleries and dealers. A year after its founding, the

UGA exhibited graffiti on canvases at the Razor Gallery in SoHo (downtown Manhattan). The paintings were priced between $200 and $3,000, and several of the pieces sold.[30] NOGA artists also enjoyed a few fleeting successes in the mid-1970s. Unlike UGA, which had a small membership of selected artists, NOGA was founded as a community youth artists' collective open to just about everyone. With the assistance of former dancer and entrepreneur Jack Pelsinger and graphic artist and gallery manager Livi French, two veterans of the New York arts scene, NOGA arranged several exhibits in public venues throughout the city. They could not command as much as the UGA artists for their work; NOGA writers rarely sold canvases for more than $300 and 25 percent of their proceeds went back to the organization to pay for supplies. Because they were not regarded as legitimate artists, institutions that hired them to paint large-scale murals frequently saw no need to pay them. Author Craig Castleman relates one such incident in which Prospect Hospital in the Bronx commissioned NOGA artists to produce a mural:

> When the mural was complete, Jacob Freedman, director and owner of the hospital, thanked the artists and had the mural rolled and taken into the hospital. He then started back to his office. At that point, Jack [Pelsinger] related, "I asked him for the money. 'What money?' he said. 'The money for the artists!' He acted like he didn't understand. It was like he was saying 'What! Pay kids for painting a mural for my hospital!' Well, I kept after him and finally he coughed up a hundred dollars. A hundred dollars for a mural that had taken all day to complete."[31]

While UGA members demanded higher prices, in some ways they did not fare much better in terms of earning respect as legitimate artists. Those who tried to branch out beyond graffiti were often discouraged, and gallery and museum directors who invited them to show their work tended to treat them in an incredibly disrespectful manner. After arranging a show at the Chicago Museum of Science and Industry in 1974, museum staff not only refused to help them hang their own show but put the artists up at the YMCA rather than a nearby hotel.[32]

In any event, the American and European art world's fascination with aerosol artists did not last long, and it was largely limited to male writers since "high art" critics viewed graffiti as the embodiment of an aggressive masculine street culture. (Many of the artists also promoted this image; the UGA, for example, systematically denied women membership.) The only writers who made it big were Jean Michel Basquiat and a white artist named Keith Haring, both of whom have since died. To most veteran writers, Basquiat and Haring were peripheral to the graffiti scene since neither had done a train piece.[33] Nevertheless, the overnight success of these major artists, especially Basquiat, gave hope to some writers that the visual arts might offer a lucrative alternative to low-wage labor and an opportunity to live off of their own creativity. And for some writers, hard work and talent paid off. St. Maurice, a veteran writer from Staten Island whose parents were artists, pursued his art professionally and eventually opened a framing shop. All twelve original members of UGA went on to either college or art school. Most of them became professional artists.[34]

Writers most committed to the genre, however, wanted to get paid but were unwilling to "sell out." Despite a strong desire to make money from their work and to become full-time artists, few writers wholeheartedly embraced the downtown art scene. As Lady Pink explained it: "Painting on canvas or a gallery's walls removes the element of risk, of getting one's name around, of interaction with one's peers and one's potential younger rivals. The pieces in galleries cease to be graffiti because they have been removed from the cultural context that gives graffiti the reason for being, a voice of the ghetto."[35]

And as the risks increased, the number of masterpieces in the public sphere slowly dwindled, and with them went the excitement of the downtown art world. By the late 1970s, the city launched a fairly successful (and very expensive) war against subway graffiti. In 1977, the MTA began spending $400,000 per year cleaning the trains with petroleum hydroxide and huge buffing machines. They also protected the train yards with attack dogs and 24 million dollars' worth of new fencing topped with ribbon wire, a razor-sharp form of barbed wire that ensnares and shreds the body or object attempting to cross it. Ironically, while the MTA largely succeeded in keeping the trains graffiti free, aerosol art exploded throughout other city spaces and has spread throughout the world during the 1980s and 1990s. Tagging can be found in virtually every urban landscape, and masterpieces continue to pop up on the sides of housing projects, schoolyards, abandoned buildings and plants, under bridges, and inside tunnels that service commuter trains. Furthermore, writers have developed vehicles in which to circulate their work—mainly 'zines devoted exclusively to graffiti and independently produced videos.[36]

Why does aerosol art lose its value as soon as it is removed from its site of origin—the urban jungle? On the surface, the answer seems obvious: it is regarded by artists and critics as more authentic when it is produced illegally and can simultaneously deface property while conveying a message. Yet, when we compare graffiti with basketball, it is interesting to note that the latter does not lose its street credentials once individuals take their skills into more bourgeois, institutionalized contexts. Indeed, stories of black college players who were "discovered" on the playgrounds of some horrific metropolitan ghetto have become stock narratives among sportscasters and columnists. By contrast, once a piece of aerosol art enters the hallowed space of a museum or gallery, it is instantly dismissed as inauthentic or constructed for viewers as an extreme example of "outsider art." The different responses to sports and graffiti, I believe, are linked to the very nature of sports as a spectacle of performing bodies. The physicality of certain sports (like basketball); the eroticizing and racializing of the bodies participating in these spectacles; and the tendency to invest those bodies with the hopes, dreams, and aspirations of a mythic, heroic working class keep most popular, commercialized team sports at a safe distance from the world of high culture. Visual arts are a different story; it is precisely the similarities in form and technique (not to mention aesthetics) that push graffiti uncomfortably close to the official realm of modern art. And as residents of newly gentrified communities know, policing becomes more intense when the threat is in close proximity. Moreover, when the creative product is the body itself rather than a painting, a sculpture, a book, or even a musical score, it is rendered as less cerebral or cognitive and thus, inadvertently, devalued. It is not ironic, for example, that the media paid as much attention to Jean Michel Basquiat's physical appearance as to his paintings.[37]

As aerosol art was pushed further underground, rap music emerged from the underground with a vengeance. Young West Indian, African American, and Puerto Rican deejays and emcees in the South Bronx plugged their sound systems into public outlets and organized dance parties in schoolyards and parks, partly as a means to make money. A whole underground economy emerged, which ranged from printing and selling T-shirts advertising crews (Hip Hop groups), to building speakers, reconfiguring turntables, buying and selling records and bootleg tapes, even to selling food and drink at these outdoor events.[38] The real money, however, was in promoting, deejaying, and rapping. In fact, production and performance of Hip Hop music not only required musical knowledge but skills in electronics and audio technology. It is not an accident, for instance, that most pioneering Hip Hop deejays and graffiti artists had attended trade and vocational schools. Others got their start deejaying for house parties, a practice particularly common in Los Angeles. Los Angeles Hip Hop deejay G-Bone recalls, "I got out of high school, working at Fox Hills [mall I] must have been making minimum wage, about three dollars then, we came up with the DJ idea . . . we started buyin' records from Music Plus with our whole paycheques. . . . All we had was two speakers, Acculab speakers and a home amp with tubes and a Radio Shack mixer that didn't have crossfaders. They made it with buttons."[39] Calling themselves Ultrawave Productions, they started out making $60 a gig before muscling out another neighborhood deejay company (Baldwin Hills Productions) for clients. Then their fee shot up to $150. Young rappers and deejays also made money by selling homemade tapes on the streets or through local record shops willing to carry them. Toddy Tee's hit song "Batteram" started out as a street tape, and Oakland rapper Too Short sold homemade tapes for several years before getting a record contract.

Serious deejays invested the money they made doing dances and house parties in better equipment. Dr. Dre, formerly of the now defunct rap group Niggas With Attitude (NWA), used the money he made deejaying in high school to set up a four-track recording studio above his mother's garage in Compton, California. "That's how I learned how to use the board and everything. From the four track I advanced to the eight track and then fucking around in a little demo studio we had, using the money we had from DJing we bought a few things for a little twelve track studio." After selling street tapes for a while, he finally put his music on vinyl—before he got a record contract. Dre remembers, "We was just sellin' 'em out the trunk, trying to make money, we sold close to ten thousand records right out the car before we got signed."[40]

Break dancing, like rap music, apparently emerged in the South Bronx during the 1970s. The word *break* refers to "break beats"—fragments of a song that dancers enjoyed most and that the deejay would isolate and play over and over by using two turntables. The breakers were sometimes called "B-boys" or "B-girls" for short. Thanks to popular films such as *Flashdance*, most people have some familiarity with break dancing—the head and backspins, the jerky body movements of the "Electric Boogie" and the "Egyptian."[41] Per-

formed by men and women, sometimes in "crews" that did choreographed and "freestyle" moves before audiences and often in competition with other crews, breaking involved incredible body
contortions and acrobatic feats. What many outsiders take for
granted, however, is the extent to which moves like spinning on
one's hand or head requires an enormous amount of practice and
body conditioning. Besides rigorous physical preparation, break-
dancers constantly risked injury, particularly since they generally
performed on the streets and sidewalks. Some placed a flattened
cardboard box between themselves and the hard concrete, but it was
not enough to protect them from serious injuries ranging from
stress fractures and scrotal contusions to brain hemorrhaging.
Training and discipline were of utmost importance if dancers
wanted to avoid injury. One particularly dangerous move was the
"suicide," where the dancer does a front flip and lands on his/her
back. As Dee-rock of The Furious Rockers put it, "It can be dangerous. . . . If you don't learn right, you'll kill yourself."[42]

Perhaps more than most dance crazes, breaking ultimately became a contest over public space. It was a style performed in malls,
hallways, and especially city streets. Historian and cultural critic
Tricia Rose explains:

> Streets were preferred practice spaces for a couple of reasons. In-
> door community spaces in economically oppressed areas are
> rare, and those that are available are not usually big enough to ac-
> commodate large groups performing acrobatic dances. In addi-
> tion, some indoor spaces had other drawbacks. One of the break-
> ers with whom I spoke pointed out that the Police Athletic
> League [of New York], which did have gymnasium-size space,
> was avoided because it was used as a means of community sur-
> veillance for the police. Whenever local police were looking for a
> suspect, kids hanging out in the PAL were questioned.

But, despite the fantasy scenes of dancers taking to the streets in
films like *Fame* and *Flashdance*, breakers did not go unmolested.
There were several cases in which break-dancers were arrested for

disturbing the peace or "attracting undesirable crowds" in public spaces such as shopping malls.[43]

One of the main reasons break-dancers performed in public was simply to make money. Like practitioners of sports, graffiti, and rap music, break-dancers were not only willing to work within the marketplace, but actively promoted the commodification of the form as an alternative to dead-end wage labor. The Furious Rockers, a predominantly Puerto Rican group from Brooklyn, were typical of most crews—at first. They began performing at Coney Island amusement park for nickels and dimes, carrying only a boom box and a flattened cardboard box, and within months graduated to local gigs in New York public schools. Then they got a real break: choreographer Rosanne Hoare "discovered" them and arranged appearances on NBC's *Today* show and in Gene Kelly's film *That's Dancing.*[44]

While most break-dancers continued to hustle coins and dollar bills for their street-corner performances, the overnight success of the style itself and its rapid appropriation by advertising firms, professional dance schools, and the entertainment industry raised the stakes considerably. It suggested to young practitioners that break dancing was worth pursuing professionally. Some, like Rock Steady Crew, appeared in several movies that focus on Hip Hop culture, including *Beat Street, Breaking,* and *Wild Style.* Burger King, Panasonic, Pepsi, and Coca Cola have all used break-dancers in their commercials. All of these "breaks" left a deep imprint on young up-and-coming breakers that their craft might lead them out of the ghetto and into a worthwhile career and financial security.[45] But as one of the pioneers of break dancing, Rock Steady Crew's Crazy Legs, put it, "We got ripped off by so many people." As inner city black and Puerto Rican youth who lacked professional status within the entertainment industry, they were frequently hired by downtown clubs to perform for their elite clientele and paid virtually nothing. Indeed, the very fact that The Furious Rockers even had an agent was rare. The film industry did not do much better, either paying break-dancers less than union scale or hiring professional dancers to learn the moves so as to bypass the problem of hiring nonunion labor. Besides, like most dance trends, breaking declined almost as rapidly as it came into style.[46]

Perhaps because break dancing was both a skill that could be learned by professional dancers and a component of Hip Hop that was ultimately subordinated to rap music—serving more or less as a colorful backdrop to the emcee and deejay—breakers had far fewer opportunities to market their skills. Besides, breaking was introduced to the wider consumer audience without the overwhelming emphasis on the ghetto origins of the performers that one finds in rap and graffiti. Television shows like *Star Search* promoted suburban white preteens performing the most clichéd routines that combined breaking and gymnastics. I might add that Hip Hop culture in particular and dance and visual arts in general simply lack the institutional reward structures one finds in college and professional sports. The chances of landing a college scholarship or getting commercial endorsements (unless one is marketing malt liquor to underage drinkers) on the basis of one's skills as an emcee, break-dancer, or aerosol artist are slim indeed. Rap music is the only potential moneymaker, and the most successful artists usually earn a fraction of what star athletes make. Given the wider range of financial opportunities available in sports, is it any wonder that athletics (including basketball) continue to be the most multiracial realm of "play-labor" and the most intensely defended as a "color-blind" site of cultural practice?

None of these realms of play-labor, however, claim to be "gender-blind." Participants in and advocates for sports, Hip Hop, and Go-Go erect gender boundaries to maintain male hegemony in the areas of production, promotion, and performance. Of course, music and the arts offered women more opportunities for entry than the highly masculinized and sex-segregated world of sports. Women not only persevered to become respected graffiti artists in spite of the pressures against them; they had also been part of the rap scene since its inception. At the same time, gender boundaries within Hip Hop were vigilantly policed at all levels of production. Young men often discouraged or ridiculed women emcees; such women were often denied access to technology, ignored, or pressured by gender conventions to stay out of a cultural form identified as rough, profane, and male. Indeed, one might argue that rap music's misogyny is partly a function of efforts of male Hip Hop artists to keep it a masculine space. On the other hand, because the record industry markets rap as a profane, masculine street music, selling the bodies of the performers is as important as producing the music. Perhaps this explains why, during the formative years of rap music, it was easier for women to get on the mic at a local place like the Hevalo Club in the Bronx than to secure a record contract. Hip Hop, like other contemporary popular music, has become a highly visual genre that depends on video representations to authenticate the performer's ghetto roots and rough exterior. In a world of larger-than-life B-boys surrounded by a chaotic urban backdrop, there are few spaces for women outside the realm of hypermasculinity. Sometimes women rappers might challenge hypermasculine constructions of Hip Hop, but rarely do they step outside of those constructions. While there is something strangely empowering about women being able to occupy that profane, phallocentric space through which to express their own voices, it nonetheless sets limits on women's participation and ensures male dominance in the Hip Hop industry.[47]

On the other hand, women have been essential to the Hip Hop and Go-Go scene as consumers and participants. The pioneering deejays made their money by throwing parties, either in small underground clubs or at outdoor events. In order to ensure women's presence at these heterosocial affairs, gender differences shaped admissions policies substantially. Because women do not have the same access to cash wages, or unfettered movement through public space, they were often subsidized at these gatherings (ladies' night was almost every night; many house parties in California charged men and admitted women free). This should not be surprising since men depend on the presence of women for their own pleasure in the context of heterosexual exchange.

Indeed, it is in the world of sexuality that young men, more than young women, become consumers in the urban marketplace. In this complicated arena of public play, sex is one of the few realms of pleasure in which young women could make money. By exploring how young women have tried to turn the commodification of their own bodies and sexuality into "pleasure and profit" for themselves, however, I am not arguing that heterosexual relations are merely extensions of the marketplace. I am not suggesting that black working-class urban youth have no genuine loving relationships, even when economic transactions are involved. Rather, I am merely suggesting that because black women have less access than black men to public space, employment opportunities, entrepreneurial opportunities, and the most lucrative cultural opportunities, it has a profound impact on their daily social relations. For poor young black women, sex is one of the few "hustles" they have since virtually every other avenue is closed to them.

Sex, whether it is sexual intercourse or public expressions of sexuality, is a very complicated issue to think about in terms of the kinds of entrepreneurial activities I have outlined thus far. It is equally complicated when we consider the fact that sex is almost never performed or experienced in a context of pure pleasure. It carries with it the potential for deep emotional ties, scars, and/or obligations (such as fidelity, devotion, possession, agreed-upon codes of public behavior) between partners. Sex, therefore, is not simply another game or performance. Although all forms of play operate within discrete relations of power (indeed, the very notion of "leveling the playing field" acknowledges deep power relations in sports itself), the ideological and emotional currents that shape sexual encounters foreground the issue of power. Sex, after all, is neither competition nor an expression of aesthetic value, though in practice it might contain elements of both. For example, heterosexual courtship for men is often highly competitive, analogous to hunters competing for game which they display as a way of demonstrating their prowess. The physical attractiveness of the prey also enhances the hunter's claims of prowess. Although consensual sexual intercourse itself may contain elements of competition and value an aesthetic of form, *ideally* it is people enjoying and partaking in the erotic, sensual pleasures of the body—someone else's and/or their own. *Realistically*, I think it is safe to say, sex involves control and manipulation, not just physically and emotionally but discursively.

When we examine the commodification of sex in relation to our argument about how displaced urban youth turn forms of "play" into paid labor, discursive constructions of sex as a source of power become extremely important. These discourses powerfully reproduce a gender hierarchy in which professionalization ultimately increases the value of men's sexuality while devaluing women's sexuality. The pimp, whose very survival depends on the commodification of sex and the private ownership of women's bodies, is considered a heroic figure rich in sexual prowess. On the other hand, when women presumably use sex as a lever to obtain nice things or even decent treatment they are labelled "hos," "gold diggers," and "skeezers." It is a discourse that absolves men of responsibility, erasing their own participation in the sexual transaction. While women are constructed as possessing extraordinary sexual powers, when they do employ their sexuality as an exchange value, their prowess and worth are sharply downgraded. The contrast with other forms of play-labor I have discussed is striking. Unlike sports and most aspects of Hip Hop culture (with the possible exception of aerosol art), when a woman's sexual exercises remain just "play" and are not widely circulated, they are more highly valued. If she turns "professional" and earns money and becomes more highly circulated, she loses "value."[48]

The most unambiguous example of the professionalization of sex is obviously prostitution. The word *prostitution*, however, carries enormous moral connotations and focuses attention solely on the woman rather than the men who are equally involved in the transaction, both as consumers and employers. Few female prostitutes describe their work as creative or fulfilling in the same way that graffiti artists, athletes, or musicians do. And, in most cases, it is not autonomous work but an exploitive wage relationship—piece work is perhaps a better description. Because streets are dominated and controlled by men, prostitutes often require protection; even if they are not assaulted, the fear of assault is constantly circulated. Most importantly, women turn to prostitution for the money.[49]

On the other hand, when discussing prostitution in a heterosexual context, we run the risk of stripping women of any agency or removing from the transaction the issue of female desire. For instance, while prostitution offers women a means of income, we must consider the extent to which anonymous sex is a source of pleasure. Furthermore, in light of the ways in which black women's sexual expression or participation in popular amusements (especially in heterosocial public places) has been constrained historically, black women's involvement in the pleasure industry might be seen as both typical and transgressive. Typical in that black women's bodies have historically been exploited as sites of male pleasure and embodiments of lasciviousness; transgressive in that women were able to break the straitjacket of what historian Evelyn Brooks Higginbotham calls the "politics of respectability" in exchange for the possibility of female pleasure. It is also potentially empowering since it turns labor not associated with wage work—sexual play and intercourse—into income.[50]

One young Harlem woman, simply identified as "Margo," who turned to prostitution as early as fifteen, took pleasure in the fact that she could earn an average of $200 per customer for doing something she enjoyed—having sex. As the product of an abusive home and grinding poverty, Margo sold her body as a means of survival. At the same time, by describing prostitution as her "pastime" rather than her job, she indirectly illustrated the pleasure she sometimes derived from the transaction: "If a guy approached me and said I was beautiful and asked how much would it cost him to have me, I would tell him whatever came to my mind. If he looked well dressed and clean I would say $200, $300, $400. It depended on my mood. If I was real horny, I would react quicker but that didn't mean the price went down. I would just choose someone who I thought was good looking. Someone who I thought would be pleasant to fuck."[51]

Sex, in Margo's view, was undoubtedly labor, but it was unlike the wage relationships that dominate the labor market. Besides, she found a way to bypass a pimp and work for herself, which meant that she kept all of her earnings. "It was sort of like getting your cake and eating it too," she pointed out. "You wake up, eat, sleep, you don't punch no clocks, you don't conform to no rules and regulations or courtesy to co-workers, customers, bosses, clients, patients, staff, etc. Best of all, you don't pay taxes either."[52]

Margo's world is hardly ideal and it certainly does not challenge the structures of capitalism. On the contrary, her decisions are driven somewhat by capitalist principles: namely, reducing labor expenditures and maximizing profit. However, she is resisting what would otherwise be her fate in an increasingly service-oriented, low-wage economy with shrinking opportunities for working-class ghetto residents. She exercises some control over her labor time, retains the full fee for her services, and often enjoys the work she performs. For her, sex is both work she can earn money from and play she can enjoy.

All of these examples, in their own unique way, reveal the dia-

lectical links between work and play within the context of capitalism. Although the concept of play in the modern era is inextricably
tied to the creation of leisure time as a form of consumption and re-
cuperation for wage workers in capitalist political economy, play is a
form of agency that is generally regarded as pleasurable activities
that take place in "free" time. Play undeniably requires labor, but it
is usually thought to be creative and fulfilling to those involved; it is
autonomous from the world of work. In a postindustrial economy
with fewer opportunities for wage work that might be financially or
even psychologically fulfilling, art and performance—forms of labor not always seen as labor—become increasingly visible as options to joblessness and low-wage service work. Of course, the
opportunities that music, sports, visual arts, and sex offer as alternative roads to upward mobility are actually quite limited. Nevertheless, these arenas have provided young people with a wider range
of options for survival, space for creative expression, and at least a
modicum of control over their own labor. In other words, neither an
entrepreneurial spirit nor a work ethic is lacking in many of these
inner city youths. Indeed, the terms *work* and *play* themselves presume a binarism that simply does not do justice to the meaning of
labor, for they obscure the degree to which young people attempt to
turn a realm of consumption (leisure time/play time) into a site of
production. Their efforts are clearly within the spirit of laissez faire,
but the definition of *profit* is not limited to monetary gain; equally
important are the visceral pleasures of the form, the aesthetic quality of the product, the victory, the praise.

Of course, turning the labor of play into a commodity is hardly
new. What is new, however, are the particular cultural forms that
have emerged in this era and the structural context of the postindustrial urban political economy. As I have argued, the decline of recreational facilities and accessible play spaces for inner city youths has
coincided with the transformation of a criminal justice system in
which reform is clearly no longer on the agenda. Today, policing

the inner city is geared toward the corralling and managing of a young, displaced, and by most estimates permanently unemployed, black working-class population. Ironically, while city and state expenditures on parks and recreation dwindle and the corporate sector invests in more class-segregated, forbidding "public" play spaces, a growing number of voices have called for a return to supervised play in order to get kids "off the streets" and instill them with discipline and a strong work ethic. The movement sounds strikingly similar to Progressive Era efforts to replace what appeared to be disorganized street life with middle-class norms and behavior.[53] Not surprisingly, the introduction of an old idea to solve relatively new problems is in keeping with the new conservative agenda of the current Republican-dominated Congress under the leadership of Newt Gingrich. (Ironically, whereas the Republicans' "Contract with America"—a highly publicized commitment to sharply limit government and pass a broad plank of extremely conservative legislation—emphasizes "family values," crime, and personal safety, they have deeply cut expenditures on recreation and urban development. Instead of supervised play, Gingrich and his followers have favored forms of incarceration, from longer prison sentences to orphanages for children whose parents are deemed incompetent. Suddenly, supervised play seems like the liberal answer to "juvenile delinquency.")

While the movement for organized play has plenty of virtues, I hope we do not make the same mistakes of a century ago; more social control will do little to unleash and develop the creative capacities of black urban youth. Rather than try to change the person through rigid regimentation and supervised play, we need to change the streets themselves, the built environment, the economy, and the racist discourse that dominates popular perceptions of black youth. The presence of large numbers of African American and Latino youth together in parks, schoolyards, subway stations, or on street corners does not necessarily mean they are conspiring to rob somebody. Nor does it mean they are leading a life of idleness.

Finally, in the struggles of urban youths for survival and pleasure inside capitalism, capitalism has become both their greatest friend and greatest foe. It has the capacity to create spaces for their entrepreneurial imaginations and their "symbolic work," to allow them to turn something of a profit, and to permit them to hone their skills and imagine getting paid. At the same time, it is also responsible for a shrinking labor market, the militarization of urban space, and the circulation of the very representations of race that generate terror in all of us at the sight of young black men and yet compels most of America to want to wear their shoes.

CHAPTER THREE

BACK**WARD:** **LOOKING**

The Limits
of Self-Help Ideology

*For white people who both deny racism
and see a heavy dose of the Horatio Alger myth as the answer
to blacks' problems, how sweet it must be when a black person
stands in a public place and condemns as slothful and unambi-
tious those blacks who are not making it. Whites eagerly embrace black conservatives' homilies to self-help, however grossly
unrealistic such messages are in an economy where millions,
white as well as black, are unemployed and, more important,
in one where racial discrimination in the workplace is as vicious (if less obvious) than it was when employers posted signs
"no negras need apply."*

— DERRICK BELL,
Faces at the Bottom of the Well

I recently came across an old poster an-
nouncing the first meeting of the Black Women's United Front to be
held in Detroit in January 1975. The gathering was organized by the

Congress of Afrikan People, the group founded by writer/activist
Amiri Baraka which, at the time, was shifting from cultural nation-
alism to Marxist-Leninism. The top of the poster read: "ABOLI-
TION OF EVERY POSSIBILITY OF OPPRESSION & EXPLOI-
TATION, That Is Our Slogan!" "Join with us to build an anti-racist,
anti-capitalist, anti-imperialist BLACK WOMEN'S UNITED
FRONT to join the struggle of the working masses." Beneath that
were drawings of black women on the march, holding up picket
signs that read: "Free and Public Education," "Public Housing—
Low Cost," "Fight Inflation, High Prices, Unemployment,"
"Shorter Work Day," "Child Care for Working Mothers," "Free
Medical Care," "Stop Killer Cops."[1]

I couldn't help but get a little teary eyed and nostalgic looking
at that poster—after all, these were the kinds of struggles that
shaped my own political awakening. I remember back in 1984,
when we organized "Survivalfest," a march of close to 10,000
people in downtown Los Angeles during the Olympics to demand
jobs, peace, a moratorium on military spending, and an increase in
welfare spending. None of us were ashamed of our demands. None
of us thought we were asking for a handout. But given today's political climate, demanding that the state provide free medical care and
child care for working mothers, an expansion in welfare spending,
or a shorter work week would be quickly dismissed as the ravings of
an unreconstructed liberal or a communist who had not heard that
the Berlin Wall had fallen.

We have come so far since those halcyon days when we believed
that government entitlements needed no justification. Indeed, let
us compare this poster with Minister Farrakhan's call for the Million Man March—regarded by some as the most important black
mass "action" of the nineties. Whereas these black women believed
that capitalism and racist/sexist social policy were responsible for
their conditions, and therefore placed demands on the state to provide fundamental services—decent housing, jobs, and child care—

Farrakhan argued that the problem plaguing black America is its overreliance on government and its failure to take "personal responsibility." Personal responsibility, if you will recall, was the Million Man March's central theme, and the original call for the march essentially let the government off the hook. The hundreds of thousands of men who took the "Million Man March Pledge" promised to strive toward personal improvement and "to build business, build houses, build hospitals, and to enter international trade." Not surprisingly, some of the most glowing endorsements of the march came from the Right. Linda Chavez and Newt Gingrich praised the gathering. Dinesh D'Souza could hardly contain his enthusiasm: "When hundreds of thousands of black men gather on the Mall in Washington to emphasize atonement, self-help, entrepreneurship, strong families, and taking responsibility for their actions, the world is changing and there are grounds for hope."[2]

Although Farrakhan is nowhere close to declaring the end of racism, we have moved a long, long way since the Black Women's United Front over twenty years ago. Sadly, I run into too many young people who do not have a sense of what is possible, a vision of what this country could become. Rather, they accept the current arrangements as an immutable given, and figure out how best to survive within them. They not only see laissez-faire capitalism as the only possible road to freedom, but they regard the Nation of Islam as the most radical alternative to mainstream integrationist politics. More damaging, however, is the current wave of antistatism emerging in African American communities. In the current popular discourse, state supports are frequently treated as damaging to the economy and people's psyche. I hear too many black people describe the state as if it is "the white man." Of course, antistatism is hardly unique to black people; on the contrary, antistatism goes hand in hand with laissez-faire and right-wing institutions such as the Heritage Foundation, the American Enterprise Institute, and the like, which have helped disseminate and popularize an ideology of self-help that is hostile to the state. The difference, however, is that few African Americans nowadays express a sense of entitlement—that they have a right to state supports as taxpaying citizens. Rather, they see "self-help" in terms of breaking dependency, getting out from under "the white man."

I am convinced that we need to get that sense of entitlement back. Call me old-fashioned, but opposing strong government supports in favor of some romantic notion of self-reliance is tantamount to relinquishing our citizenship. Let us not forget that government policies, not black people's moral failings, are largely responsible for the current crisis. The Reagan/Bush revolution dismantled state protections for the poor, working people, people of color, and the environment; it expanded the urban police state; and it assembled a judiciary clearly more concerned with protecting capital than protecting the rights of ordinary citizens. Attacks on affirmative action and welfare have undermined our claims to state resources as citizens. Institutions created to enforce Title VII of the Civil Rights Act of 1964 and police workplace discrimination, most notably the Civil Rights Commission, the Office of Federal Contracts and Compliance Programs, the Equal Employment Opportunity Commission, and the Civil Rights Division of the Justice Department, have been stripped of any notable power. The appointment of conservative justices under Reagan, and later Bush, led to major reversals in laws pertaining to equal rights and affirmative action. In several landmark cases during the 1988–89 term, the Court severely limited some key civil rights statutes that protected African Americans from discrimination at the workplace, in schools, and at the polls. More recently, in *Hopwood v. State of Texas* (1996), the Court of Appeals for the Fifth Circuit Court decided to prohibit the use of race-based admissions criteria to achieve diversity at the University of Texas Law School. Think of the implications: this decision opens the door for the elimination of all college and university programs designed to increase minority representation. Indeed, *Hop-*

wood helped legitimize Proposition 209 (the so-called California Civil Rights Initiative, CCRI), which will effectively dismantle all state affirmative action programs in California. CCRI's recent passage is merely a foreboding of what is to come.[3]

What three decades ago were seen as rights are now cast as a burden or drain on the state, or (in the case of affirmative action) discrimination against white guys. This free-market ideology has helped make government downsizing more palatable. In addition to the erosion of municipal and state tax bases due to capital flight and suburban tax revolts, major urban governments suffered huge cutbacks, which further resulted in the shrinking of urban labor markets. The federal government cut funds for cities and for poor people and reduced guarantees for benefits and services. Perhaps the most draconian measure of the late twentieth century is the welfare reform bill, signed not by a Republican president but by a self-proclaimed liberal Democrat: Bill Clinton. (It is more than a bit ironic that the welfare reform bill Clinton signed into law was called the "Personal Responsibility and Work Opportunity Reconciliation Act of 1996.") Among other things, the act replaces entitlements to Aid to Families with Dependent Children (AFDC) with state block grants, denies benefits to *legal* immigrants, and cuts funding for low-income programs, such as food stamps, Supplemental Security Income (SSI)—a program that targets the elderly and disabled poor—by $55 billion over the next six years.

The main purpose of the law is to force welfare recipients into an extremely low-wage labor market without concern for the needs of children. Under the new law, for example, recipients whose youngest child is more than a year old must do some form of paid or unpaid work after twenty-four months of receiving benefits, or lose their benefits altogether. By the year 2002, states are required to have 50 percent of single parents receiving cash assistance in work programs. Unfortunately, in order to meet their quota, it is easier for states to drop people from the rolls than try to employ them all.

And those required to work who fail to find jobs within two months of receiving assistance must enroll in a mandatory "workfare" program. The Personal Responsibility Act does not include higher education in its definition of work or "training programs"; rather, welfare recipients will be limited to vocational programs approved by the state. To make matters worse, anyone convicted of a drug felony cannot receive direct aid or welfare *for life*. Unemployed adults between eighteen and fifty with no children will be limited to just three months of food stamps in any three-year period, which essentially means that the only safety net available to them would be unemployment insurance. Altogether, welfare reform will leave some 3.5 million children without any means of support. Moreover, we must consider the startling fact that approximately 60 percent of mothers on welfare have been battered; this means that the increased use of time limits might unintentionally force women back into abusive relationships in order to survive.[4]

Short of a massive expansion of decent paying jobs to absorb the women and men being thrown off the welfare rolls, the end result will only be more misery and exploitation under the guise of "workfare." In New York City in 1996, about 30,000 welfare recipients employed by the Work Experience Program (WEP) earned biweekly "wages" as low as $68.50 in cash and $60 in food stamps. At twenty-six hours a week, the jobs range from street sweeping to transporting corpses in city hospitals. Most WEP workers are single, childless recipients of Home Relief, who under 1994 state law must work for their benefit checks. But with federal welfare reform an increasing number of mothers receiving funds through the Temporary Assistance to Needy Families Block Grants (TANF)—which replaces AFDC under the Personal Responsibility Act—will be added to the workfare rolls. By some estimates, under the new reforms at least 70,000 recipients will be added to the city's workfare programs.[5]

The consequences for labor are potentially disastrous. Workfare undermines union-scale wages and creates an ultracheap, superexploited workforce without the basic protections that ordinary workers have. Indeed, in New York City the MTA has already begun to hire workfare workers to clean the subway trains at below-union wages. Furthermore, federal and state labor laws have made it difficult, if not impossible, for WEP workers to organize collectively and fight back. They are not entitled to bargain as a group under federal laws, nor do they come under the jurisdiction of the National Labor Relations Board, which essentially means that they cannot hold union elections under federal law. The conditions of work and the treatment they have received from regular employees leaves much to be desired. Street cleaners often have to work without gloves, and the chances for advancement within a job are slim to none. To add insult to injury, a sign hangs over the rest room in the New York City Sanitation Department building that reads, "No WEP Workers Allowed."[6]

WEP workers have attempted to organize themselves and fight back. They have sought strategies that would increase wages and benefits to union scale, improve the conditions of work, and expand rather than reduce job training programs. A group of WEP workers, in fact, approached various advocacy organizations, including Community Voices Heard, the Fifth Avenue Committee based in Brooklyn, and the Urban Justice Center in Manhattan, and they have received support from a few unions, such as Local 1180 of the Communications Workers of America and the progressive wing of the transit workers' union. In a few instances, they fought back and won. At City University of New York, for example, new WEP work requirements had forced thousands of students to leave school to accept sanitation and park jobs away from campus. As a result of political mobilization, activists forced the state legislature to pass a bill allowing for on-campus work sites.[7]

Whether we call it "personal responsibility" or "individual initiative," good old-fashioned "self-help" has become, once again, the new panacea for the black poor. Of course, African Americans have a rich tradition of "self-help" that, one could argue, is rooted in movements for social change. As Dorothy Height, longtime president of the National Council of Negro Women, pointed out several years ago: "The civil rights movement of the 1950s and 1960s was perhaps the most extraordinary example of a mass 'self-help' movement in American history: self-help mounted under grave conditions to throw off the yoke of American apartheid."[8] But for the most part, self-help has been (and continues to be) defined along the lines Booker T. Washington established at the turn of the century. Ideally, the Washingtonian vision of self-help meant building black enterprise on the presumption that black business can employ black people and provide them with consumer goods. However, self-help was more than an economic strategy to combat Jim Crow. Rather, its proponents believed that the failings of the black poor could be attributed to moral deficiencies such as the lack of a work ethic, frugality, and thrift. Self-help was as much about moral uplift and instilling the virtues of hard work as it was about "buying black." Thus, in the tradition of Garveyism even more than Booker T., the Nation of Islam (NOI) combines black enterprise, social conservatism, and racial militancy to create an attractive self-help philosophy. During its heyday, the NOI's philosophy of self-help and moral uplift even impressed black conservative George Schuyler, New York editor of the *Pittsburgh Courier*, who praised the NOI for its values and moral standards. "Mr. Muhammad may be a rogue and a charlatan," wrote Schuyler in 1959, "but when anybody can get tens of thousands of Negroes to practice economic solidarity, respect their women, alter their atrocious diet, give up liquor, stop crime, juvenile delinquency and adultery, he is doing more for the Negro's welfare than any current Negro leader I know."[9]

On the other hand, the NOI was never your typical black bourgeois uplift organization; it has always maintained ties to black working-class communities. The NOI has a long tradition of reaching out to wayward youth and the "down and out," and it has sustained a fairly antagonistic stance toward the rising black middle class. Indeed, as historian C. Eric Lincoln pointed out in his pioneering study of the Nation, *The Black Muslims in America* (1961), most NOI recruits "do not typically identify with the strivers of the black middle class. They tend to live comfortably, but frugally. The Movement continues to emphasize its affiliation with the working class."[10] Although many converts discovered the Nation as prisoners, ex-hustlers, or jobless wanderers, the NOI's highly structured and disciplined environment instilled a strong work ethic into its congregation. Muhammad's followers worked, and worked very hard, but the majority lived in the ghettos of North America and made barely enough to tithe.

During the 1960s, even after Malcolm X's assassination, the NOI had its radical flashes. *Muhammad Speaks*, the Nation's national newspaper, hired several black leftists (some non-Muslims) on its staff, and it was one of the few publications paying attention to international issues and sympathetically covering ghetto rebellions.[11] However, the NOI has undergone a dramatic change after the death of Elijah Muhammad in 1975. As soon as Wallace D. Muhammad, Elijah's son, took over the leadership of the NOI, he denounced his father's earlier teachings that the white man was the devil and that white people were created by an evil black scientist. Wallace, a respected Muslim scholar who had studied Arabic in Egypt, adopted an orthodox approach to Islam, changing the name of the organization to the "World Community of al-Islam in the West." He even invited whites to join the group. In 1978, Louis Farrakhan, a devoted follower of Elijah Muhammad, broke from the World Community and re-established the old NOI under Elijah's original tenets. Under Farrakhan's leadership, the reconstituted

Nation of Islam attracted a huge following among young people, many of whom were in search of solutions to joblessness, drug addiction, and the inability of poor African Americans to effect change in the political structure. Ironically, the Nation, for the most part, continued to distance itself from direct political participation and support a fairly conservative agenda. Its policies centered on self-help, the creation of black business, and the maintenance of traditional relations between men and women. Although women are exalted in Farrakhan's teachings, he insists nonetheless that women should take primary responsibility for the home and child rearing.[12]

Through its economic wing, People Organized and Working for Economic Rebirth (POWER), the NOI has tried to create a nationwide cooperative of black businesses so that consumers and entrepreneurs can coordinate a massive "buy black" campaign. POWER has also introduced its own products, from soaps and shampoos to various food items, which it markets through black stores or street-corner vendors. By encouraging young, jobless African Americans to sell POWER products, they sought to create alternatives to crime and drug dealing and instill in them a sense of entrepreneurship. As Farrakhan himself explained,

> This productivity of black people will cause us to address our own unemployment concerns. It will enable us to rebuild a stable black family life. It will drastically reduce the involvement of black people in crime and drugs. . . . It would make the streets of the cities of America safer for all. And at the core it would strengthen America, for the condition of black people in America makes us the Achilles heel of this nation.[13]

In many ways, the basic premise behind POWER differs little from the ideas being advocated by black neoconservatives rooted in Republican Party politics and hostile to the NOI. First, Farrakhan tends to agree that African Americans, not policies pursued by the state and by corporate America, are the problem. Second, there is an implicit presumption in both their arguments that unemployment can be addressed outside of policies and structural conditions that created unemployment in the first place. Third, they both believe that certain forms of government assistance—mainly welfare—damage black families by creating dependency, eroding a work ethic, and destroying self-esteem. As Adolph Reed put it, Farrakhan

> weds a radical oppositional style to a program that proposes private and individual responses to social problems; he endorses moral repressiveness; he asserts racial essentialism; he affirms male authority; and he lauds bootstrap capitalism. . . . His focus on self-help and moral revitalization is profoundly reactionary and meshes perfectly with the victim-blaming orthodoxy of the Reagan/Bush era.[14]

However, Farrakhan's understanding of the political implications of black self-help departs from the neoconservatives. For him and the NOI as a whole, economic strength is a source of political power—a position outlined by the advocates of Black Power in the late 1960s and articulated in Stokely Carmichael's and Charles Hamilton's classic 1967 text, *Black Power: The Politics of Liberation in America*. Exactly twenty years after the publication of *Black Power*, Farrakhan told an audience in Washington, D.C.,

> Don't tell me that that's your tax dollar. Shutup, they don't treat you like a tax paying citizen. They treat you like a piece of property, and that is all that Black people have been in America, something to be used. And now that you have no more utility, you and I are facing death in America, because the Black man and woman have become obsolete. We respect our managers of white enterprise, but I think that if we become economically strong our mayors would be more responsive to our needs.[15]

The NOI under Farrakhan has also defended the gains of the Civil Rights movement and generally came out in support of affirmative action programs. The black neoconservatives (or "negrocons" as I like to call them), on the other hand, have placed much of the blame for the current state of affairs on racial preferences. Neoconservative economist Thomas Sowell, for example, has insisted that the problem of poor African Americans can be attributed to a lack of moral values and a work ethic. For Sowell, the social policy implications are clear: welfare and affirmative action policies must be eliminated since they undermine middle-class values of hard work and thrift, and make African Americans dependent on government assistance. Black Harvard economist Glen Loury made similar arguments (though recently he has had an epiphany of sorts, admitting that racism is a major stumbling block to black progress).[16] Loury has argued that racial preferences and equal opportunity legislation are worthless since the problems of the black poor are largely products of weak cultural values, broken families, and irresponsible parenting. Other leading negrocons include Ward Connerly, the conservative black businessman who came up with the "California Civil Rights Initiative"; Robert L. Woodson, head of the National Center for Neighborhood Enterprise; Wendell Wilkie Gunn, assistant treasurer of Pepsi-Cola Corporation; Art Fletcher, former director of the United Negro College Fund; Samuel Pierce, secretary of housing and urban development under Reagan; writer Shelby Steele; Roy Innis, of the Congress on Racial Equality; black journalist Tony Brown; and political scientist Charles V. Hamilton. I can also point to the recent group of black right-wing radio talk show hosts, such as Armstrong Williams, Ken Hamblin, Star Parker, Earl Jackson, and Republican presidential candidate Alan Keyes.[17]

Amazingly, most of these negrocons have couched their opposition to affirmative action and welfare in terms of Dr. Martin Luther King, Jr.'s dream for a "color-blind" society. In other words, they have seized the language of the Civil Rights movement and turned it on its head. Robert Woodson joined several other negrocons in a 1994 Heritage Foundation-sponsored seminar entitled "The Conservative Virtues of Martin Luther King," in which he argued that affirmative action betrayed King's dream of seeing people valued for the content of their character rather than the color of their skin. Likewise, the so-called Institute of Justice under the leadership of Clint Bolick has consistently supported anti–civil rights legislation in the name of civil rights. In particular, Bolick helped draft the Dole-Canady measure making it illegal for the federal government to use race and gender preferences in hiring or contracting. Other movements that have appropriated the language of civil rights for conservative ends include the Campaign for a Color-Blind America, Landmark Legal Foundation, and the Center for New Black Leadership. All of these groups invoke the rhetoric of equality and opportunity to justify dismantling race-based programs. In the words of Edward Blum, chair of the Campaign for a Color-Blind America, "The great civil rights legal briefs that were written in the 1950s articulated a vision of America in which race does not play a role. That's the direction that these new conservative civil rights organizations are moving."[18]

Finally, it is more than a bit ironic that these avid defenders of self-help are themselves caught in a web of financial dependency. The same negrocons who lecture the poor on the dangers of dependency and why they need to earn their own way are engaged in their own battle royale for government and private foundation money to support their work and lifestyle. After all, Booker T. himself depended more heavily on gifts and grants from the Carnegie Foundation, Rosenwald Fund, and Phelps Stokes for his budget than on the meager wages of Southern black folk. Today the major source of financial support for this group of black neoconservative thinkers are the right-wing think tanks, including the Lynde and Harry Bradley Foundation (which helped finance Charles Murray and Richard Herrnstein's *The Bell Curve*), the John M. Olin Foundation (which is a major donor for the American Enterprise Institute), the Sarah Scaife Foundation, the Earhart Foundation, and the Adolph Coors Foundation.[19]

PUBLIC FICTIONS:
STATE INTERVENTION AND
THE MYTH OF LAISSEZ FAIRE

Besides making dubious, unfounded claims about the black poor's moral weaknesses or the cultural impact of government supports, the negrocons often begin with the premise that self-help and state supports are mutually exclusive. Indeed, government assistance of any kind—including affirmative action—is generally defined as the opposite of self-help (unless one is talking about government subsidies to industry or tax breaks for the wealthy). Their arguments betray an incredibly naive faith in the free market to do the work of creating equality. Proponents of black capitalism as the most effective (if not the only) form of self-help, they presume that profits derived from black enterprise will trickle down to the poor without any system to redistribute wealth. Moreover, they take for granted that the "free market" actually operates free of racism and that the playing field is even—which is why they have called for "color-blind" policies, completely rejecting any race-based entitlements or special privileges. The clamor for "color-blind" social policy not only delegitimizes race-based explanations for inequality but it camouflages the racist underpinnings of much contemporary political discourse. *Welfare mothers, criminals,* and the *underclass* are the most recent code words for black people. Each of these terms reflect a growing "common sense" that black behavior—whether we call it nihilism, a culture of poverty, or plain irresponsibility—is the source of urban poverty and violence and a drain on our national resources. "When welfare reformers devise remedies for maternal irresponsibility," writes law professor and activist Dorothy Roberts, "they have Black single mothers in mind. . . . The image of the lazy

Black welfare queen who breeds children to fatten her allowance shapes public attitudes about welfare policy."[20]

Calls for color blindness and laissez-faire economic strategies also camouflage the critical role the state has played in reproducing inequality and creating an *uneven* playing field. Tax laws and social welfare, retirement, and housing policies have impaired the ability of African Americans to accumulate assets while facilitating white access to wealth. For most people the key to wealth accumulation is home ownership. White homeowners in the post–World War II era enjoyed a dramatic rise in property values, which served as the basis for the baby boom generation's upward mobility. The return on their investment enabled them to pass on wealth as well as educational opportunities to their children.

For most black folk, however, segregation shut off much of the post–World War II housing market. To compound matters, Federal Housing Administration (FHA) policies of giving mixed and African American neighborhoods lower ratings, racial discrimination by lending institutions, redlining, white flight—you name it—put black folks at a disadvantage in the housing market. In St. Louis, for example, between 1943 and 1960, suburban home buyers received six times more loan money than those in the city, which was becoming increasingly black. In 1966, because of their growing black and Puerto Rican populations, Camden and Paterson, New Jersey, received no FHA mortgages. Too many families who were "movin' on up" were forced to pay above-market prices in a market that was quickly devalued by their very presence. In addition to real estate redlining, a massive study of 10 million applications to savings and loan associations between 1983 and 1988 revealed that the rejection rate for blacks was more than twice that of whites, and that high-income African Americans were rejected more than low-income whites. This pattern continued well into the 1990s. Unpublished data from the Federal Reserve in 1991 showed that income had little to do with the high rejection rate of blacks. The Manufacturers Hanover Trust Company of New York, for instance, turned down 43 percent of its mortgage applications from high-income blacks compared with 18 percent from high-income whites. Similarly, in Houston the NCNB Bank of Texas turned down 36 percent of its middle-income black applicants compared with 13 percent of middle-income whites.[21]

As a result, by 1988 63.8 percent of whites owned their homes compared to 41.6 percent of African Americans. And according to the 1987 Survey of Income and Program Participation data, the median home value among blacks was $31,000 compared to $45,000 for white owners. The lower black home values not only reduce gross equity but make it difficult for African Americans to use their residences as collateral for obtaining loans for other investments, such as college or business.[22]

Race impacts zoning laws as well, and can have devastating results: One study released in 1987 estimated that three out of five African Americans live dangerously close to abandoned toxic waste sites and commercial hazardous waste landfills. A 1992 study concluded that polluters based in minority areas are treated less severely by government agencies than those in largely white communities. Also, federally sponsored toxic cleanup programs, according to the report, take longer and are less thorough in minority neighborhoods. Government policies generate racial inequality in other ways as well. We can point to the billions spent for highways, water, and sewage facilities for white suburban communities while inner city infrastructures crumbled. Besides, many of these highways paved over poor and working-class black communities, causing displacement.[23]

Of course, urban renewal's destruction of black neighborhoods did not take place without a fight. While community activists during the 1960s could not stop these projects, their efforts—buttressed by urban rebellions—resulted in an increase in federal spending on cities. These monies had a positive impact overall, funding the creation of community and educational programs and public housing. But just as jobs began to disappear, so did federal funding, particularly after Reagan took office. In addition to closing down the Neighborhood Self-Help and Planning Assistance program, which allotted $55 million to assist inner cities in 1981, Reagan reduced grants and aid to cities to a fraction of what it had been under Nixon. City governments were forced to cut their budgets as well, leading to massive layoffs of low- and midlevel municipal workers. Since African Americans held many of these government jobs, they were hardest hit by these cutbacks. To make matters worse, many major cities experienced a "tax revolt" from suburban communities that no longer wanted their property taxes to fund urban schools or city services. Some communities simply tried to secede from the city and form their own autonomous municipal governments; others successfully passed legislation that substantially reduced the amount of taxes they had to pay. Despite an eroding tax base, the cuts continued. The Urban Development Action Grant program's budget dropped from $675 million in 1981 to $216 million in 1988; the Department of Housing and Urban Development's housing program budget declined from $55.7 billion in 1980 to $15.2 billion in 1987. This does not include cutbacks in public education, health care, and other social services, or take into account the resultant strain the cuts put on the criminal justice system, whose administrative costs continue to skyrocket since it is now placed in the position of dealing with most social problems.[24]

The slow and uneven development of black entrepreneurship also explains the failure on the part of the black middle class to accumulate wealth. It has nothing to do with a poor work ethic or an inability to defer gratification. Contrary to the current wave of nostalgia for the "good old days" before integration, recent research shows that segregation actually hindered black entrepreneurship by limiting its potential market. State and local policies under segregation restricted black economic activity, and successful black-owned businesses were often subject to violence and intimidation. In the end, few black entrepreneurs of the Jim Crow era have been able to accumulate sufficient assets to pass on to future generations. Thus the impediments to black business and black home ownership have sharply curtailed the intergenerational transfer of wealth among African Americans. As Melvin Oliver and Thomas Shapiro point out in *Black Wealth/White Wealth*, "Nearly three-quarters of all black children, 1.8 times the rate for whites, grow up in households possessing no financial assets. Nine in ten black children come of age in households that lack sufficient financial reserves to endure three months of no income at the poverty line, about four times the rate for whites."[25]

What is important to recognize here is that middle-class and affluent white Americans have benefited from certain kinds of "affirmative action" under a different name, i.e., government supports and subsidies, and that in virtually every Western country the state is employed to reduce poverty and create equality of opportunity and monitor discrimination. The fact is, we do not have a free-market economy and never completely had a free-market economy. Many of the problems minority workers and students face, and many of the benefits white workers and students receive, are not merely the product of thrift and hard work in a free-market economy but outcomes determined largely by government policy.

In other words, instead of avoiding the state, we need to recognize it as an extremely important site of struggle—one we cannot afford to ignore. Take affirmative action, for example. One place where affirmative action policies made a difference was the public sector, and that was largely a product of political struggle; by 1970, more than half of black college-educated men and 60 percent of black college-educated women were public employees. They were even paid more in the public sector—blacks earned 85 percent of the income of white workers of the same age and education. But the gains were made at the very moment when public sector jobs were declining, along with wages, as a result of cuts in federal and state programs. After a steady 5 percent growth, after blacks were hired the public sector only grew at a rate of 3 percent, then even slower at 1.3 percent. Between 1980 and 1991, public employment showed virtually no growth, the workforce remaining constant at 2.9 million. And since 1994, government employees have experienced significant downsizing—and guess who is first to go?[26]

The reality is, all the self-help in the world will not eliminate poverty or create the number of good jobs needed to employ the African American community. Multinational corporations control 70 percent of world trade, and about one-third of world trade consists of transfers within the 350 largest global corporations. Rather than merely exploit Third World labor to extract or cultivate raw materials, increasingly we have witnessed the export of whole production processes as corporations seek to take advantage of cheaper labor, relatively lower taxes, and a deregulated environment. This, of course, combined with technological developments and the problem of overproduction, led to an enormous number of plant closures. Well-paying jobs made possible by decades of union struggle disappeared. By 1979, for example, 94 percent of the profits of the Ford Motor Company and 63 percent of the profits from Coca-Cola came from overseas operations. Between 1973 and 1980, at least 4 million U.S. jobs were lost to firms moving to foreign countries. And during the decade of the 1970s, at least 32 million jobs were lost as a result of shutdowns, relocations, and scaling back operations.[27]

Moreover, the economy we are dealing with is not only global and transnational but depends on state intervention to help keep it afloat—a state, by the way, we fund with our tax dollars. Besides a battery of tax breaks and subsidies, some corporations earn huge profits by selling goods and services to the state itself. The most absurd example is the current trend toward the privatization of the welfare state. In 1996, for example, Lockheed Martin bid aggressively for contracts to take over welfare operations in several states.

Ross Perot's company, Electronic Data Systems, makes millions providing computer management services for welfare administrations in thirty states. Author and welfare rights activist Betty Reid Mandell states:

> Small corporations are already in the welfare business. Curtis & Associates "supplements its successful welfare-to-work jobs clubs with accessories like 'motivational fortune cookies' at $3.99 a dozen. A sample message is, 'The way to control your future is to work hard today.' " Maximus Inc., a consulting company in McLean, Va., did $100 million in business this year, including $7 million in welfare-to-work programs in Boston, two California counties and Fairfax, Va.[28]

There is big money in the welfare business to be sure, but the corporate share is much greater than what the poor receive.

Perhaps the fastest growing "private sector" industry whose fortunes are tied to the corporate welfare state is the prison business. After all, prison construction and maintenance is a costly venture: a 1993 report issued by the Edna McConnell Clark Foundation shows that the construction of state facilities costs an average of $54,209 per bed, while the per-bed cost for federal facilities runs about $78,000. These figures do not account for financing costs—interest, debt service. With the world's second highest imprisonment rate of 1.3 million people, the country shells out about $27 billion annually. The basic maintenance of prisoners, not counting prison construction, costs almost $25,000 per head (in a maximum security prison, the cost can be as high as $100,000)—more than the tuition at most Ivy League universities, and more than three times what many welfare recipients receive in the way of transfer payments.[29]

While taxpayers have borne much of the burden of paying for our sprawling prison system, during the past decade several private firms have actually stood to gain. For-profit prisons have been making a comeback since 1984, when the federal government contracted the Corrections Corporation of America (CCA) to operate an immigrant detention center in Houston, Texas. The Reagan administration had essentially reversed a sixty-year-old policy that outlawed for-profit prisons because of prison-labor abuses in the South. CCA, based in Nashville, Tennessee, is currently the leading private prison conglomerate. It registered $207 million in revenues in 1995 and controls almost half of the privatized prison beds in the country. CCA's stock has risen through the roof, with shares doubling in 1996. Wackenhut Corrections is now the second largest private incarceration company in the country; so successful that it made *Forbes* magazine's "200 Best Small Companies" list. Since 1994, Wackenhut's stock price has risen by 800 percent.[30]

Beyond the actual construction and maintenance of prisons, subsidiary industries—from food products to furniture to medical care—made huge profits selling goods and services to prisons. Michael Kroll, author of *The Fortress Economy: The Economic Role of the U.S. Prison System*, discovered that "San Quentin offers more than 250 products for prisoners to purchase, from cupcakes and fried pies to perm-cream relaxers and pinup calendars. In 1984, Unicor, the federal prison industries, earned a net profit of $18 million on $210 million in sales." Furthermore, prisoners proved to be not only a new source of consumers but a reservoir of cheap labor. In South Bay, Florida, for example, Wackenhut Corrections built a new prison whose inmates will be employed in a variety of occupations, including telemarketing, light manufacturing, and textiles. The starting wages and benefits packages are so low that the Wackenhut facility drastically underbid Florida's state prisons.[31]

By the close of 1997, the United States will boast at least 102 for-profit private prisons, each receiving some form of federal subsidy with limited federal protection of prisoners' rights or prison conditions. As one observer put it recently, "The pressure to deliver both government savings and corporate profits, however, has led to overall industry operating margins of 2 to 4 percent. This worries some market analysts—and civil libertarians—who point out that as maintenance costs rise over time, corporations may resort to overcrowding or cost cutting to remain in the black."[32]

The double entendre here is telling. It is precisely the Willie Hortons of the world, the pervasive images of the black criminal raping, pillaging, "wilding," emptying bullets into the houses of innocent children, and selling crack to the sons and daughters of suburbia, that have justified if not fueled the massive expansion of the prison-industrial complex. Indeed, it is the image that convinced Boston's Charles Stuart that he could kill his wife and get away with it by blaming a black assailant; the image that persuaded Susan Smith of South Carolina that she could drown her children and escape punishment by saying a black man forced her out of her car and took off. It is the image that Reagan, Bush, and Clinton used to attract white swing voters. Despite this pervasive stereotype, the fact of the matter is that violent crime in general, and crimes committed by African Americans in particular, have declined steadily since the mid-1970s. The percentage of black arrests for robbery, burglary, larceny, and aggravated assault actually decreased from 1988 to 1992. And yet, since 1980 the number of African Americans in prison has tripled. Between 1979 and 1992, the percentage of African Americans admitted to state and federal prisons grew from 39 percent to 54 percent. In 1990, for every 100,000 African Americans, 1,860 were in jail or prison; for whites the ratio was 289 out of every 100,000.[33]

How do we explain the disparity, especially if the overall crime rate has declined? Part of the reason is that black felons are generally given longer sentences than whites for the same crime. Although racial disparities in sentencing have been documented since the turn of the century, the dramatic shift that took place during the 1980s can be attributed to the "war on drugs" declared by the Reagan and Bush administrations, especially the ten-year mandatory sentence for possession of crack cocaine. The results are staggering:

in 1980, drug offenders constituted 22 percent of federal prison admissions; in 1988 39 percent; 1990 42 percent; by 1992 58 percent of all federal prisoners were drug offenders. Despite indicators that African Americans have lower drug and alcohol use rates than whites, the war on drugs was declared against the black poor. This war was visible, crack cocaine was linked to criminality, and it was politically advantageous for the Right to lay claim to a "law and order" stance. Under mandatory crack cocaine sentencing laws, the sentences are 100 times more severe for crack than for powder cocaine. Because crack is much cheaper than powder cocaine and more pervasive in poor urban communities, it is not surprising that 91 percent of those sentenced for federal crack offenses were black while only 3 percent were white. Yet studies show that whites constitute a higher proportion of crack users: 2.4 million (64.4 percent) for whites compared to 990,000 (26.6 percent) blacks, and 384,000 (9.2 percent) Latinos.[34]

It is not an accident, then, that the move toward privatizing prisons coincides with a massive increase in the prison population during the mid-1980s. Under Reagan and Bush, the state helped generate an explosion in the prison population and brought in private industry to try to resolve it. Ultimately, corporate interests were the real benefactors of the shift from welfare to jailfare. One particularly startling statistic in support of this point is the fact that 70 percent of all prison space being utilized today was built since 1985.[35]

We cannot afford to be embarrassed or afraid to demand massive social investment. After all, it is our money. And according to a study by Melvin Oliver and Thomas Shapiro, systematic discrimination has cost the black community an estimated $89 million. Creating good jobs, rebuilding schools and homes, improving the health of communities—in short, reversing a couple of centuries of deleterious social policy—costs a lot of money. We can afford it, if our country is willing to divert funds from war (foreign and domestic), substantially reduce the work week without cutting wages, and start forcing rich people and corporations to pay their fair share of taxes. Whether we ever create a state that puts working people's needs before corporations will depend on which vision of society we embrace. A well-paying, fulfilling job and a strong "safety net" in troubled times should be a basic right, not a handout or an entitlement. Janet McCrae, a black woman interviewed by anthropologist John Langston Gwaltney two decades ago, put it best: "I have worked and paid taxes since I was seventeen, so I think that the country should help me if I can't get work or if I can't work. That's what a decent country should do for everybody in the country!"[37]

Decent countries are made, not born. While atonement, personal responsibility, and self-transformation are vitally important to our collective spiritual well-being, political struggles do matter. By political struggle, I do not mean simply registering voters and selecting candidates. I am referring to a social movement with a radical democratic vision, a way of imagining and remaking the world in a manner we have never seen. I am immediately reminded of the efforts to reconstruct America in the aftermath of the Civil War, perhaps the world's shining example of what democracy could have become. Imagine what the entire world would look like had the federal government fully empowered ex-slaves, allowed them to keep their guns and the vote, handed over the land on which they worked and allowed them to organize production on their own terms, and dismantled the master class (after all, they were war criminals). The death of Reconstruction was a tragedy not only for black people but for American democracy as a whole. "Democracy died save in the hearts of black folk," W. E. B. Du Bois told us in *Black Reconstruction in America*.[38]

Democracy did continue to live in the hearts of black folk and other folk in the United States and the world. The problem, of course, was that the triumph of capitalism in America meant that the guarantee of good public services, humane housing, safety, security, support during hard times, and power over decision making was never a right. It always comes back to the bottom line: profits before people. And in a system like this, all the personal industriousness in the world will not necessarily result in a decent income if there are no jobs available, no requirements to pay a living wage, or no recognition that raising children is work. On the other hand, if we ever regarded the United Nations General Assembly as a governing body of a higher order, perhaps we can sue the state for violation of the "Universal Declaration of Human Rights" adopted back in 1948. According to this document, now half a century old, everyone has the right to work, earn equal pay for equal work, join trade unions, and receive "just and favorable remuneration" that would enable working people and their families to live in comfort and dignity. Moreover, whether one works or not, everyone "has the right to a standard of living adequate for the health and well-being of himself [herself] and of his [her] family, including food, clothing, housing, and medical care and necessary social services and the right to security in the event of unemployment, sickness, disability, widowhood, old age, or other lack of livelihood in circumstances beyond his [her] control."[39]

Meanwhile, whether we dust off the "Universal Declaration of Human Rights" or line up behind one of the more recent initiatives calling for a guaranteed "living wage," we must never lose sight of the bigger picture. We are more than workers and consumers; indeed, we are more than bodies in need of food, clothes, shelter. We are humanity, complex and multi-, the victims and shapers of the world we inhabit. Our oppressions are not always visible or tangible, but are serious and painful nonetheless. For this reason, we should consider reviving that slogan from the Black Women's United Front: "ABOLITION OF EVERY POSSIBILITY OF OPPRESSION & EXPLOITATION."

CHAPTER FOUR

LOOKING
EXTREMELY
BACKWARD:

Why the Enlightenment
Will Only Lead Us into the Dark

You cannot link arms under a universalist banner when you can't find your name on it.

—MARTIN DUBERMAN,
"Bring Back the Enlightenment"

If we are to keep the enormity of the forces aligned against us from establishing a false hierarchy of oppression, we must school ourselves to recognize that any attack against Blacks, any attack against women, is an attack against all of us who recognize that our interests are not being served by the systems we support. Each one of us here is a link in the connection between antipoor legislation, gay shootings, the burning of synagogues, street harrassment, attacks against women, and resurgent violence against Black people.

—AUDRE LORDE, "Learning from the 60s"

The beauty of the line "Abolition of Every Possibility of Oppression and Exploitation" is that it resists hierarchies. It refuses to privilege class over race, or race over gender, or sexuality over class, race, or gender. Yet, it seems like every time I invoke that line some holier-than-thou radical accuses me of left-wing utopianism. Apparently, in the age of defeat simply imagining a movement fighting to radically transform society is seen as a descent into utopianism— a horrible crime to those embroiled in the realpolitik of restoring the welfare state, building union membership, and providing minimal health care for the poor. Worse, to insist that the fight for women's studies on college campuses or the battle against racist representations in popular culture is as important as the "class struggle" (whatever that means) is to fall into the identity trap.

Welcome to the left-wing version of P. C. circus, where a handful of mostly forty-something white guys have courageously stood up to multiculturalism and "identity politics" in the name of Marx, Engels, or Thomas Jefferson. Usually renegades from the New Left, the most notable figures here are Todd Gitlin (*Twilight of Our Common Dreams: Why America is Wracked by Culture Wars*) and Michael Tomasky (*Left for Dead: The Life, Death and Possible Resurrection of Progressive Politics in America*), though some of their ideas have been echoed by the likes of Richard Rorty, Jim Sleeper, Eric Hobsbawm, and others.[1] Their main concern is that "class" has dropped out of our analytical vocabulary, swallowed up by a proliferation of "identities." It is precisely the disappearance of "class," they argue, that explains why the Left remains small, divided, and parochial, entrenched for better or worse in the groves of academe. To put it bluntly, class is the one universal category that unites us all and can lift us out of the dismal swamp of identity politics.[2]

Tomasky and Gitlin, in particular, set out to explain why the Left failed to mobilize a mass-based response to the rise of the Right. Their explanation: "The Left" has lost touch with its Enlightenment roots, the source of its universalism and radical humanism, and instead has been hijacked by a "multicultural Left" wedded to "iden-

tity politics," which has led us all into a cul-de-sac of ethnic particu-
larism, race consciousness, sexual politics, and radical feminism.
Much of the blame falls on the shoulders of women, gays and lesbians, and colored people for the fracturing of the American Left,
abandoning honest class struggle, and alienating white men who
could be allies but will not because of the terrible treatment meted
out to them by the loud minority. Universal categories such as class
have fallen before the narrow, particularistic mantras of the radical
chic: race, gender, sexuality, and disability. Indeed, in Tomasky and
Gitlin's view class is not just another identity; it transcends identity.
If the Left wants to save itself, we must abandon our ever shrinking
identity niches for the realm of majoritarian thinking. After all, we
are told, the majority of Americans are white and heterosexual and
have little interest in radical feminism, minority discourse, and
struggles centered on sexual identity.

In some ways, I can sympathize with these guys about the limitations of identity politics. While the growing interest in the politics
of identity has extended our analytical scope to overlooked or trivialized cultural spheres and expanded our understanding of intellectual history, in *some* circles it has also tended to limit discussions of
power to cultural politics. And while so-called identity politics has
always profoundly shaped labor movements and—even more than
vague, abstract notions of class unity—has been the glue for class
solidarity, by the same token it has also become a noose around the
necks of oppressed people, as in the case of white racism or certain
variants of black nationalism.

On the other hand, we have to recognize that the backlash
against so-called identity politics is also deeply personal, reflecting a
tragic sense of loss or irrelevance experienced by some of these critics. Indeed, Gitlin feels personally victimized by identity movements because, in his words, they cast the "Straight White Male" as
the "common enemy." Even when white guys are not seen as "an
oppressor, the white male is a blank, made to feel he lacks roots, culture, substance." Similarly, British Marxist critic David Harris, in

his polemic against cultural studies titled *From Class Struggle to the Politics of Pleasure*, whined about cultural studies' obsession with black people and women (race and gender). He took it personally: "I find myself invisible, relegated to a 'natural' substratum, untheorised, an empty signifier, a mere 'Other' against which more glamorous identities are defined." If this isn't identity politics, I don't know what is.[3]

White male angst notwithstanding, whatever cul-de-sacs we might have entered, the Gitlin/Tomasky model will not lead us out. These critics assume that the universal humanism they find so endearing and radical can be easily separated from the historical context of its making; indeed, that it is precisely what can undo the racism and modern imperialism it helped to justify. The racialism of the West, slavery, imperialism, the destruction of indigenous cultures in the name of "progress," are treated as aberrations, coincidences, or not treated at all. They insist that these historical developments do not render the Enlightenment's radical universalism any less radical, and those who take up this critique are simply rejecting Enlightenment philosophers because they are "dead white males." Their uncritical defense of the Enlightenment (which includes a strange tendency to collapse Marx, Locke, and Jefferson into the same category), betrays an unwillingness to take ideas seriously, let alone history. Gitlin certainly acknowledges these contradictions inherent in Enlightenment philosophy as well as the historical context of slavery, racism, and colonialism. But in an intellectual sleight of hand he brackets these contradictions, reduces a huge body of complex, historically specific ideas to transhistorical abstractions (which he uses selectively to make his case against identity politics), and then presumes that Enlightenment thought constitutes the central reservoir of ideas for the very identity movements he critiques:

> The Enlightenment is not to be discarded because Voltaire was anti-Semitic or Hume, Kant, Hegel, and Jefferson racist, but rather further enlightened—for it equips us with the tools with

which to refute the anti-Semitism of a Voltaire and the racism of the others. . . . In none of these cases was bigotry at the core of the man's intellectual system; it reflected the routine white prejudice of the time. The Enlightenment is self-correcting. The corrective to darkness is more light.[4]

Good liberalism, to be sure, but its analytical insight leaves much to be desired. To pose the question as pro or con, keep the Enlightenment or discard it, sidesteps fundamental questions such as the legacy of eighteenth-century social thought for modern conceptions of race or the philosophical underpinnings of racial slavery in an age when free labor and free-market ideology triumphed. For example, while racialist ideas can be traced to ancient thought and forms of domination internal to Europe, the Enlightenment also ushered in a transformation in Western thinking about race. How could it not? After all, as many, many commentators since the French Revolution have observed, the expansion of slavery and genocidal wars against non-European peoples took place alongside, and by some accounts made possible, bourgeois democratic revolutions that gave birth (in the West) to the concept that liberty and freedom are inalienable rights. This contradiction is fundamental to Enlightenment philosophy, notions of progress, and developments in scientific thinking. As the work of George Mosse, David Theo Goldberg, Cedric Robinson, and many others have demonstrated, modern racism is one of the "gifts" of the Enlightenment. It is not an accident that during the eighteenth century modern science moved toward classification as one of its primary endeavors, turning to aesthetic criteria derived from ancient Greece as the source of measurement. These Enlightenment scientists—in some respects, the founders of modern anthropology—began to associate outward, physical signs of "beauty" with inner rationality, piety, intelligence, and harmony. Thus a century before social Darwinism we see scientific justifications for racial hierarchy and domination. Christian Meiners's influential book *Outline of the History of Mankind* (1785) put it bluntly: "One of the chief characteristics of tribes and peoples is the beauty or ugliness of the whole body or of the face." At the same time, the idealization of the so-called primitive (the noble savage) espoused by several seventeenth-century travel writers as well as Rousseau began to give way to notions of European superiority vis-à-vis Africans and Native Americans. Non-Europeans were unambiguously classified as representing a lower stage of human development. The primitive mind was constructed as the very opposite of Reason: atavistic, regressive, barbaric. Again, science provided a rationale for racial hierarchies. Climatic theories explaining the origins of racial difference were called into question by Enlightenment thinkers who proposed the radical idea that Africans, Asians, and "Indians" originated from different species. Voltaire certainly made this claim, as did Scottish jurist Lord Kames in his *Sketches of the History of Man* (1774), and Charles White in his celebrated *An Account of the Regular Gradation in Man* (1799). Enlightenment thought not only opened the door for future arguments about the inherent inferiority of different "races," but also sharply limited the definition of *humanity*. Thus, at the very moment when a discourse of universal humanism was finding voice in the bourgeois democratic revolutions of the era, colored people and Europeans rendered marginal to civilization (such as Jews and Irish) were being written out of the family of "Man." (Is this why the Haitian Revolution is still not considered one of the most important revolutions of the bourgeois democratic era?)[5]

Besides assuming that the "universal" is truly "self-evident," the neo-Enlightenment Left cannot conceive of movements led by African Americans, women, Latinos, or gays and lesbians speaking for the whole or even embracing radical humanism. The implications are frightening: the only people who can speak the language of universalism are white men (since they have no investment in identity politics beyond certain white working-class ethnic movements) and women and colored people who have *transcended or rejected* the politics of identity. Moreover, they either do not understand or refuse to acknowledge that class is lived through race and gender. There is no universal class identity, just as there is no universal racial or gender or sexual identity. The idea that race, gender, and sexuality are particular whereas class is universal not only presumes that class struggle is some sort of race- and gender-neutral terrain but takes for granted that movements focused on race, gender, or sexuality necessarily undermine class unity and, by definition, cannot be emancipatory for the whole.

Don't get me wrong. I am not defending "identity politics" over the struggle to build a world we have never seen before—a world free of market forces and all the terrible things that go with them. Rather, I have trouble with these critics' characterization of race, gender, and sexuality as narrow identity politics while class is regarded as some transcendent, universal category that rises above these other identities. Indeed, Gitlin calls the first three "birthrights," and despite an obligatory nod to Anthony Appiah, he fails to treat these categories as social constructs that have enormous consequences for how class is lived. Along with these so-called identities come regimes of oppression. Are churches being burned because black people are alienating white folks? Is this why the Justice Department focuses much of its investigation on black congregations rather than on white supremacist groups? Is pro–Proposition 187 sentiment [a California initiative denying immigrants' basic rights] and callousness toward immigrants the result of Mexican and Central American immigrants' refusal to be "inclusive"?

I find the neo-Enlightenment position incredibly problematic given what we know of the history of class struggle in the United States.[6] These writers' arguments rest not on a serious analysis of the social movements they lump together under the heading "identity politics," but on caricature, stereotypes, omissions, innuendo, and historical analysis that borders on comical at times. Indeed, these movements are rarely ever named and their positions never spelled out in any detail. Yet, despite the lack of depth and scholarly rigor as well as an overreliance on personal impressions, their arguments seem to be winning over a broad section of high-profile liberals/leftists who believe the time has come for us to "transcend" all this race and gender stuff and get to the matter at hand: class warfare against the bosses. During the recent labor teach-in at Columbia University, for example, both Betty Friedan and Richard Rorty, taking a page from Gitlin's book, told the audience that the time had come to graduate from narrow identity movements to the bigger picture. It was as if antiracist and antisexist struggles were not fundamental to the struggles of working people across race and gender lines, or worse, that they had been essentially resolved and were no longer pressing problems.[7]

Although their books have been widely reviewed, we have yet to subject the neo-Enlightenment position to a serious political critique. I don't know how many times I have been told, "Don't attack them, they're on our side!" Besides the obvious analogy to the issue of the Left's stance toward Clinton, I am always inclined to repeat Tonto's response to the Lone Ranger: "What do you mean, 'we'?" Of course, to say "we" invites accusations of identity politics, of identifying with colored people at the expense of the poor Lone Ranger, who is merely a low-level manager of capital rather than an owner. But this is precisely the problem: the "we" I am speaking of includes all oppressed people, including Mr. Ranger if he chooses to join. The Gitlin/Tomasky group makes the grave error of rendering movements struggling around issues of race, gender, and sexuality as inherently narrow and particularistic. The failure to conceive of these social movements as essential to the emancipation of the whole remains the fundamental stumbling block to building a deep and lasting class-based politics.

Part of their problem has to do with their perennial failure to take seriously the ideas coming out of these identity movements.

Their arguments rest less on what these movements espouse than in their racial, ethnic or gender makeup or their sexual orientation. "Choose a nonwhite ethnicity," Tomasky sneers, "combine it with a sexual practice or a physical condition, and there probably exists a movement to match." Let us take one of their favorite whipping girls: the black feminist, particularly of the lesbian variety. In a bizarre tautology, black feminists are narrowly concerned with their race and sex because they are black feminists. In fact, aside from Alice Walker and the statement issued by the Combahee River Collective (a radical black feminist group founded in the mid-1970s), black feminists in their texts have no names or organizations—they function as little more than signifiers (or, to put them in a more traditional context, as scapegoats). Tomasky was kind enough to quote one line from the Combahee River Collective's 1977 statement, though the line he quotes is intended to demonstrate how narrow identity politics can get. For him, the principles of black feminism are succinctly expressed in the following sentence: "We believe that the most profound and potentially most radical politics come directly out of our own identity." What he neglected to mention, however, is that the same statement proposed a clear socialist agenda, argued that emancipation for everyone could not take place until racism, homophobia, sexism, and capitalism are annihilated, and criticized mainstream feminist organizations for not being inclusive enough—for not dealing adequately with the needs of the poor or with racist oppression of men and women. Nor did Tomasky acknowledge the important line in the statement that "as Black women we find any type of biological determinism a particularly dangerous and reactionary basis upon which to build a politic."[8]

In other words, had Tomasky and Gitlin taken the time to read the material written by black feminists instead of simply reducing them to caricatures of their own imagination, they might have discovered some of the most sophisticated statements of the kind of radical humanism they claim to embrace. Anna Julia Cooper, whose writings continue to have a profound impact on black feminism, wrote in 1893:

> We take our stand on the solidarity of humanity, the oneness of life, and the unnaturalness and injustice of all special favoritisms, whether of sex, race, country or condition. . . . The colored woman feels that woman's cause is one and universal; and that . . . not till race, color, sex, and condition are seen as accidents, and not the substance of life; not till the universal title of humanity to life, liberty, and the pursuit of happiness is conceded to be inalienable to all; not till then is woman's lesson taught and woman's cause won—not the white woman's nor the black woman's, not the red woman's but the cause of every man and every woman who has writhed silently under a mighty wrong.[9]

This radical humanism, as theorist Patricia Hill Collins points out, has been a consistent principle of black feminist thought. Alice Walker insists that a "womanist" is "committed to the survival and wholeness of entire people, male and female," and is "not a separatist" but "traditionally a universalist."[10] Pauli Murray is even more explicit:

> The lesson of history that all human rights are indivisible and that the failure to adhere to this principle jeopardizes the rights of all is particularly applicable here. A built-in hazard of an aggressive ethnocentric movement which disregards the interests of other disadvantaged groups is that it will become parochial and ultimately self-defeating in the face of hostile reactions, dwindling allies, and mounting frustrations.

Audre Lorde's reflections on the politics of the 1960s go much further, illustrating the delicate balance between particular struggles and the interconnectedness of social movements: "There is no such thing as a single-issue struggle because we do not live single-issue lives. Malcolm knew this. Martin Luther King, Jr. knew this. Our struggles are particular, but we are not alone."[11] One can see this vision in the writings of many black feminists, including June Jordan, Barbara Christian, Angela Davis, Elsa Barkley Brown, Sonia Sanchez, Pat Parker, Barbara Smith, Cheryl Clarke, Julianne Malveaux, bell hooks, Margaret Simms, and Filomina Steady, to name a few.[12]

Of course, had Tomasky or Gitlin actually read these works, they might jump up in agreement and dismiss them as exceptions to the rule. (Whatever the rule is, however, always goes unnamed.) But a close reading reveals that they are not saying the same thing. "If all human rights are indivisible," then why privilege majoritarian concerns over all others and ridicule movements organized around sex, race, and gender? Why presume that such movements are necessarily narrow simply because black women and their concerns are central to them? Nothing could be further from the truth. One vital outgrowth of radical black feminism has been the black women's health care movement, its most notable manifestation being the National Black Women's Health Project.[13] Among other things, it has sought to create a healthier environment for poor and working-class women and reduce women's dependence on a health care system structured by capitalism and run primarily by men. If they succeeded, imagine how such a transformation might benefit all of us, irrespective of race or gender?

Unfortunately, these neo-Enlightenment leftists are blind to the radical humanist traditions that have undergirded black feminist movements, and this blindness has kept them from seeing how black feminism could contribute to their own emancipation. Similarly, they do not see how gay and lesbian movements might also contribute to our collective emancipation—a criticism made eloquently by Martin Duberman in his review of Tomasky's book in *The Nation*.[14] Some things are obvious: the continuing struggle of gays and lesbians against discrimination in public and private life has important implications for national civil rights law; the work of ACT UP and other movements has made AIDS visible—a disease that is now killing many more heterosexual people, especially poor black women. Less obvious is the role of scholarship coming out of gay and lesbian studies programs as well as women's studies programs—grist for the anti–identity politics mill. Queer theory, for example, begins with the premise that sexuality is a vital part of human existence, and that how sexual identities get defined (and policed) has to do with social relations of power, the role of the state, public institutions, and social movements. The best work understands that sexual identities and practices are lived through race and class and can only be understood historically. What does this scholarship have to do with the rest of us? What are the implications for the "universal"? For one, we know now that there is no universal masculinity or femininity. The idea of "normal" behavior is a social construction, which means that there is nothing natural or inevitable about male dominance, the overrepresentation of men in positions of power, or the tendency of men to use violence as a means to resolve conflict.[15] These are all obvious points, to be sure. But how many heterosexual men and women stop to think about the emancipatory potential a more flexible sexual and gender identity could have on all of us? Besides reducing homophobic anxieties, freeing up self-expression, and enabling us all to reconstruct our relationships to one another (isn't that what revolution is all about?), I believe a less rigid definition of masculinity may actually reduce violence—from police brutality to domestic abuse.

While Gitlin tends to be slightly more sympathetic to feminism and gay and lesbian movements than Tomasky, both critics view them as prime examples of dead-end identity politics. On the other hand, when they proclaim a movement or issue "universal," they do not stop to analyze how race and gender shape various responses to issues. For example, Tomasky believes he hit on a common value/agenda when he writes: "Working people in this country need a movement that will put their interests and livelihoods first." Fair enough. But without an analysis that takes racism, sexism, and homophobia seriously, or considers deep historical differences, we won't know what "interests" mean. Let's take crime and the issue of neighborhood safety. It is an issue on which many people across race, gender, and even class lines can find common ground. Yet, racism—not narrow identity politics—persuaded many African Americans to oppose Clinton's $22 billion crime bill and the majority of white voters to support it. For many black people, the issue of neighborhood safety is not just about more police but what kind of police—where they live, how they relate to the community. Indeed, no matter what we might think of the Nation of Islam, many non-Muslims see the NOI's fight against drug dealers in black communities as more effective than the police.[16]

It is precisely this kind of economism that enables these critics to claim, without evidence, that declining wages are more important to most black people than police brutality or having to wait an hour for a seat at Denny's. One is hard economics, what unites people; the other is just narrow identity politics. Thus, when black gays and lesbians take to the streets to protest violence against them, that is "identity politics." When angry white males claim that affirmative action is taking jobs from them, that is class politics muffled beneath a racial blanket they themselves do not understand. When white people vote for David Duke and Pat Buchanan, that is class politics, not identity politics. Something is wrong with this picture.

WHOSE LEFT?

Central to the neo-Enlightenment Left's case against so-called identity politics is a nostalgia for the Old Left, back in the days before the sixties, when everyone who joined checked their race and gender identities at the door and embraced a radical universalism that transcended skin color, ethnic affiliations, and sex. Intense debates over the Negro Question or the Woman Question, not to mention charges of "chauvinism," simply vanish from this romantic narrative. Those were the days of "real" class struggle, the days of the Congress of Industrial Organization (CIO), the Knights of Labor, the IWW, the Reds, the rugged and manly Republican artisans in the Age of Jackson (Andrew, not Michael), the days before identity politics eroded the class struggle and we knew what the working class looked like. Then, around 1970, according to Tomasky, everything fell apart "when the American left cashiered traditional class-based politics for a new variant in which race and gender were preeminent. . . . For black activists, racism became more important than the exploitation of workers by capitalists; for women, sexism."[17]

Who is he talking about? Black Power and feminism had radical and conservative tendencies, and neither uniformly privileged race or sex or ignored class, for that matter. And what about the *black* Left? If these activists and the New Left more broadly abandoned "the exploitation of workers by capitalists," why did so many of these folks join Marxist-Leninist organizations in the early 1970s and begin working in factories to organize industrial workers? Workers became very important for the New Left, particularly for African American radicals. In 1968 and 1969, a fairly large contingent of black radical students at Duke University and the University of North Carolina at Chapel Hill helped organize key strikes of maintenance and dining hall workers. A few former Wayne State University students helped organize the Revolutionary Union Movement in Detroit's auto plants, which culminated in the League of Revolutionary Black Workers (LRBW). Some of the organizers who split from the League joined former Student Non-Violent Coordinating Committee (SNCC) leader James Forman and founded the Black Workers Congress. Not surprisingly, in his book Gitlin dismisses the industrial concentration movement coming out of the New Left in a sentence, probably because it contradicts his central thesis that the late sixties witnessed the flight from universal class struggle. Yet, some of these same people contributed substantially to labor struggles during the "dark ages" (the 1980s) and can take some credit for the current regeneration of the movement—from Eric Mann, who led the campaign to keep General Motors' Van Nuys plant open in the 1980s, to labor militants like Joe Alvarez, currently the political director for the Union of Needletrades, Industrial and Textile Employees (UNITE). Alvarez's presence is no small matter, for UNITE is one of the biggest unions in the country, formed in July 1995 as a result of a merger between the International Ladies' Garment Workers' Union (ILGWU) and the Amalgamated Clothing and Textile Workers Union (ACTWU). UNITE has also taken the lead in the fight against sweatshops throughout the Western hemisphere, building cross-border alliances from Latin America and the Caribbean to Canada.[18]

On the other hand, those white construction workers in the 1960s who battled antiwar protesters and supported Nixon—the folks Gitlin calls "the Common men"—were also notorious for having the most racist, exclusionary unions around. In Chicago, for example, racism ran so deep that in 1988, black pipe fitter Frank Daniels sued his union local and won a $331,000 settlement. Despite the Daniels case, the pipe fitters', electrical workers', plumbers', carpenters', and related building trades unions continued to discriminate against African Americans and women (in 1993 women made up only 2 percent of the construction workforce). In 1955 Black tradesmen in Chicago and throughout other parts of the country established the American Allied Workers Laborers International Union (AAWLIU), a black independent union, to challenge racism in the building trades unions. The situation for black construction workers has been so bad that AAWLIU held Labor Day rallies to protest union discrimination. With support from the Chicago-based Black United Communities (CBUC) and the Black Independent Political Organization (BIPO), the AAWLIU initiated training programs in 1996 to help African American workers get their journeymen cards, which will, one hopes, make it easier for them to find work throughout the nation.[19]

Now, compare these unions to the local, state, and federal employees' unions that supported black struggles for justice. Or compare them to, say, 1199 hospital workers union or Service Employees Industrial Union (SEIU)—unions that embraced the spirit (and the people) of the Civil Rights movement. Multiracial public sector unions were able to survive, even thrive, while construction workers belong to some of the most devastated unions in the country. Indeed, when unionization all around was on the decline, public sector unions rose by 37 percent.[20]

In other words, given black workers' commitment to organized labor, despite being overrepresented in the unemployment rolls and in occupations that have historically been difficult to unionize, it is ironic that African Americans bear so much of the burden for the decline of "class politics." Black workers, after all, have the highest union participation rate—in 1994, 21 percent of the African American workforce was unionized compared to 15 percent of whites. Furthermore, a 1989 AP/Media survey revealed that people of color had stronger union sympathies than whites. When nonunion workers were asked: "Would you join a union at your place of work?" 56 percent of African Americans answered yes, as did 46 percent of Latinos. Among white workers, only 35 percent responded affirmatively.[21]

If rebuilding class politics is the goal of the neo-Enlightenment Left, and the labor movement is one of the vehicles for doing so, then I do not understand why the neo-Enlightenment Left would invoke Enlightenment universalism to promote a version of *American nationalism* and support for "majoritarian" values which—it seems to me—is the very opposite of the cosmopolitanism they claim to be embracing. Gitlin derides the fact that the Republicans have seized the symbols of patriotism and progressives failed to promote "Democratic Americanism, an Americanism of constitutional faith strong enough to override the racism of American history." What an incredibly naive statement; it ignores actual historical context and presumes one can miraculously disentangle the language of "Americanism" from its roots in white supremacy, conquest, and xenophobia. Tomasky's chauvinism is even more strident:

> The United States alone, simply because its power and wealth are still so vast, can set the direction for the rest of the advanced world to follow. . . . An America that rises above its own particularisms and ethnic rivalries might be able to posit itself as an example for others, in Bosnia, in Macedonia, in Russia, in the Middle East and, with some credibility, lead a Western coalition that lays down principles that factions there must adhere to. And for the Third World, especially for those people making six dollars a day weaving those designer garments, an America devoted once again to working people will surely bear fruit.[22]

Can labor really afford to rally behind this sort of nationalist rhetoric in the age of global capital? Imagine if the AFL-CIO had been supporting progressive unions across the world rather than U.S. foreign policy driven by Cold War imperialism? It took the North American Free Trade Agreement to spur the AFL-CIO to take cross-border organizing more seriously, and though some campaigns are succeeding, labor leaders now have to break through a wall of suspicion and distrust following decades of AFL-CIO-supported Cold War policy. And yet Gitlin lampoons all Third World solidarity movements. The fact is, the South African divestment campaign as well as Central American solidarity movements opened doors to labor that might have otherwise been shut.

Rather than worry about offending "majoritarian sensibilities," the labor movement must make antiracism, antisexism, and antihomophobia foundational. This absurd argument that minority aggressiveness was responsible for white male backlash at the tail end of the 1960s masks the fact that the tragedy of most progressive movements in the United States has been white racism. As W. E. B. Du Bois, Dave Roediger, Alexander Saxton, Theodore Allen, Noel Ignatiev, Michael Goldfield, Eric Lott, David Wellman, and others have demonstrated, racism has been a noose around white work-ers' necks since the American Revolution. In the South during Re-construction, a misguided white majority sided with the wrong class and rejected the black workers and sharecroppers who pro-posed a Democratic South with massive land redistribution. De-spite the fact that the black freedom struggle, in alliance with the radical wing of the Republican Party, enfranchised poor whites who did not have the right to vote before the Fifteenth Amendment, the vast majority of exploited white labor still chose color over class. And in California, it was precisely anti-Chinese sentiment that galva-nized the multi-ethnic "white" working class and forged a dynamic union movement on the West Coast during the late nineteenth cen-tury. Of course, white workers were never uniformly racist and there are enough stories of interracial working-class solidarity to fill volumes. But we also must recognize the price these men and women had to pay: white workers willing to commit "race suicide" often faced the worst of state repression, ostracism, and sometimes criticism from within their own ranks. It is not an accident, for ex-ample, that the most militantly antiracist unions emerging out of the CIO campaigns of the 1930s and 1940s were the main targets of McCarthyite witch hunts.[23]

I can not stress enough how important the fight against racism is right now, especially with a growing backlash against affirmative action under the guise of supporting a "color-blind" society. Any-one seriously concerned about the labor movement and building multiracial unity must recognize the fundamental role racism has played in destroying internationalism. Anti-immigrant sentiment, for instance, is not just about class anger, because there really is no mobilization against Canadians or European immigrants taking what are essentially skilled jobs. It is about dark people, whether wetbacks or some invisible Pacific Rim empire run by sneaky Ori-entals. The history of conquest, repatriation in the Southwest, ste-reotypes of "Latin" hypersexuality, even racialized and gendered myths of the welfare mother, are fundamental to understanding anti-immigrant sentiment, the English-only movement, and pro–Proposition 187. They derive from a deep racism that conceals the structural relationship between the white middle class's standard of living and the exploitation of immigrant labor. As historian and social critic George Lipsitz explains,

> In their television and newspaper advertisements, in public pronouncements and privately circulated propaganda, supporters of Proposition 187 relied on racist and sexist stereotypes, on the "menace" posed by Mexican women coming to California to have babies at taxpayers' expense. This argument has little basis in fact; the amount of public funds spent on pre-natal care and childbirth for undocumented immigrants is both minimal and cost-effective. Yet by feminizing and infantilizing the enemy, by connecting the social transgression of non-white immigrants coming to California with the fear of unrestrained "Latin" sexuality and procreation, the advocates of Proposition 187 "played the race card," evoking powerful stereotypes that are especially well-suited toward concealing the real social relations between undocumented immigrants and California's white voters.[24]

Blanket support for "majoritarian" positions simply plays into American nationalism and chauvinism, reinforcing the very racist and sexist social policy that keeps poor people poor, the middle class relatively comfortable, men in positions to legislate women's lives, and whiteness on top. Besides, when have emancipatory politics ever reflected majoritarian principles? Activists of any kind have never been in the majority of any population, so what does this numbers crunching mean in terms of "majoritarian" ideology? As Jesse Lemisch makes clear, "many of our greatest successes have occurred when we have taken principled and unpopular stands and persuaded a majority. And the American left has contributed a good deal to the international left precisely because of its distinctive diversity."[25] The Labor Party, for example, was not created to represent the entire working class, but a vision of progressive class politics in which social justice and workers' empowerment are central to the broader agenda. As Tomasky himself admits, in the 1990 elections 40 percent of the union membership voted Republican.[26] Labor parties in most countries never claimed to represent all opinions expressed by the working class, or even the majority opinion, but a largely social democratic vision rooted (at least theoretically) in the working class.

So, how might people build class solidarity without suppressing or ignoring differences? How can we build on differences—by which I mean different kinds of oppressions as well as different identities—rather than in spite of them? One way to conceive of alliances across race and gender is as a set of "affiliations," of building unity by supporting and perhaps even participating in other peoples' struggles for social justice. Basically, that old-fashioned IWW slogan, "An injury to one is an injury to all!" After all, contrary to the neo-Enlightenment narratives, African American social movements have been practicing this principle for a very long time: black male abolitionists supported woman suffrage when few white men would; black radicals throughout the early part of the century supported the Irish struggle for self-determination; black soldiers and journalists shed tears at the sight of Nazi death camps; and after Roosevelt, we have been mainstays in the Democratic Party even to our own detriment. Black trade unions were never exclusionary; black labor leaders did not implement Jim Crow locals. And when the Chinese Exclusion Act seemed to have universal support among non-Asian workers, it was a black man, Frank Ferrell of the Knights of Labor, who told his comrades that they ought to organize the Chinese rather than attack them.[27]

In short, it is ludicrous to blame so-called identity politics of the 1960s for the collapse of the Left, the derailment of progressive social movements, or our inability to roll back poverty and unbridled corporate wealth. We have others to thank for that: Richard Nixon, Ronald Reagan, George Bush, Bill Clinton, white flight, red squads, redlining, Contra-backed crack dealers, economic restructuring, the NRA, right-wing think tanks, complacent labor leaders . . . and the list goes on. Of course, the Left—whatever that means now—is not blameless. The scars of sectarianism run deep and trace their roots to the glorious days when the Old Marxists were supposedly more "universal." Street fights erupted between socialists and anarchists; battles raged between the Trotskyists and Stalinists and a variety of sects claiming to be the true heirs of Lenin. And then China entered the picture, along with Albania. These battles within the Marxist world contributed more to the internal implosion and proliferation of left-wing parties than feminism and black nationalism.

Although identity politics sometimes works as a fetter on genuine multiracial/multicultural alliances, I believe it has also enriched our conception of class, not moved us away from it. Indeed, there are many serious scholars—I count myself among them—trying to understand how various forms of fellowship, racial solidarity, communion, the creation of sexual communities, and nationalisms shape class politics and cross-racial alliances. We are grappling with how self-love and solidarity in a hostile context of white supremacy, the embrace of certain vernaculars, and community institutions, can be expressions of racial *and* class solidarity, and how class and racial solidarity are gendered. Not to recognize this is to wonder why more West Indian workers participate in Carnival than in the Labor Day parade, or why 1199 had the foresight and vision to maintain an 1199 float and/or banner in the West Indian Day parade. Those who pine for the good old days before identity politics, when class struggle was simply rough guys who understood that simply fighting the bosses united us, forget that Yiddish was a source of solidarity within the International Ladies' Garment Workers' Union, to the point where union leaders were offering courses in Yiddish for Black and Puerto Rican workers in the late 1950s. *Identity politics, in other words, has always been central to working-class movements, from minstrelsy on up.*

More importantly, a careful examination of the movements dismissed as particularistic shows that they are often "radical humanist" at their core and potentially emancipatory for all of us. We need to seriously re-think some of these movements, shifting our perspective from the margins to the center. We must look beyond wedge issues or "minority issues" and begin to pay attention to what these movements are advocating, imagining, building. After all, the analyses, theories, and visions emerging out of the Black Liberation movements, the Chicano and Asian American movements, the gay and lesbian movements, and the women's movements, may just free us all. To extend the metaphor a bit, we simply can not afford to abandon the subway, with all of its multicultural messiness, to jump on board the Enlightenment train of pure, simple, color- and gender-blind class struggle. Neither Locke nor Jefferson offers a truly emancipatory vision—not then and certainly not now. Attempts to "transcend" (read: outgrow) our race and sex does not make for a unified working class. What does is recognition of the multiplicity of experiences and perspectives and a willingness to fight on all fronts—irrespective of what "the majority" thinks. We need to recognize the importance of environmental justice for the inner city; the critical role of antiracism for white workers' own survival; the necessity of men to fight for women's rights and heterosexuals to raise their voices against homophobia. It is in struggle that one learns about power and how it operates, and that one can imagine a different world. And it is in struggle, not in the resurrection of ideas that have also provided the intellectual justification for modern racism, imperialism, and the traffic of human beings, that we must begin to develop a new vision. It is to those contemporary struggles that I now turn.

CHAPTER FIVE

LOOKING FORWARD:

How the New Working Class
Can Transform Urban America

The people who dominate the inner cities numerically cannot possibly work out a plan or have any programme by which they can improve their own situation which does not take into consideration the city as a whole. A new situation has arisen for the urban black, for thinking in terms of the whole city means that you are automatically thinking in terms of the state and from the state you find yourself facing the whole nation.

—C. L. R. JAMES,
Black People in the Urban Areas of the United States, 1970

James's insights from over a quarter century ago still hold true. The predominantly black, Latino, and Asian American working classes who occupy our cities can win only if they are willing to challenge the problems of the whole city—together. Corporate downsizing, deindustrialization, racist and sexist social policy, and the erosion of the welfare state do not respect the boundaries between work and community, the household and public space. The battle for livable wages and fulfilling jobs is inseparable from the fight for decent housing and safe neighborhoods; the struggle to defuse cultural stereotypes of inner city residents cannot be easily removed from the intense fights for environmental justice. Moreover, the struggle to remake culture itself, to develop new ideas, new relationships, and new values that place mutuality over materialism and collective responsibility over "personal responsibility," and place greater emphasis on ending all forms of oppression rather than striving to become an oppressor, cannot be limited to either home or work.

Standing in the eye of the storm are the new multiracial, urban working classes. It is they, not the Democratic Party, not a bunch of smart policy analysts, not corporate benevolence, who hold the key to transforming the city and the nation. As I suggested in previous chapters, there is no doubt that progressive social policies must be implemented at the federal and state level, and that the terrain of electoral politics cannot be ceded to middle-class suburban voters. But my point is very, very simple. As C. L. R. James himself put it, "The rich are only defeated when running for their lives." I am suggesting that the only way to implement changes, whether at a policy level, a personal level, or a broad cultural level, is through collective struggle. And at the heart of this movement must be working people and the jobless poor.[1]

The purpose of this chapter is not to propose a utopian movement that does not yet exist. On the contrary, the following is a survey of movements in existence right now that are trying to develop a visionary strategy for change. I will examine labor or labor-based movements that have reached beyond workplace concerns to encompass the broader community and make issues of culture, race, gender, and sexuality fundamental to their agenda. These movements have pushed working-class politics beyond a defensive posture, beyond acceptance of the principle that profit, competition, and productivity are more important for both labor and capital than social justice. They are not perfect, nor are they all "mass movements" in terms of membership and resources, but together they represent the possible future of the labor movement and the future of the city.

MAKING OF THE NEW URBAN WORKING CLASS

As I suggested in chapter 1, the pervasive imagery of the "underclass" makes the very idea of a contemporary urban working class seem obsolete. Instead of hardworking urban residents, many of whom are Latino, Asian-Pacific Islanders, West Indian immigrants, and U.S.-born African Americans, the dominant image of the "ghetto" is of idle black men drinking forty-ounce bottles of malt liquor and young black women "with distended bellies, their youthful faces belying the fact that they are often close to delivering their second or third child."[2] And as I pointed out in chapter 4, white leftists nostalgic for the days before identity politics allegedly undermined the "class struggle" often have trouble seeing beyond the ruddy-faced hard hats or European immigrant factory workers who populate social history's images of the American working class. The ghetto is the last place to find American workers.

If you are looking for the American working class today, however, you will do just as well to look in hospitals and universities as in the sooty industrial suburbs and smokestack districts of days past. In Bethlehem, Pennsylvania, for example, once a stronghold of the steel industry, nursing homes have become the fastest growing source of employment, and the unions that set out to organize these workers have outgrown the steelworkers' union by leaps and bounds.[3] The new working class is also concentrated in food processing, food services, and various retail establishments. In the world of manufacturing, sweatshops are making a huge comeback, particularly in the garment industry and electronics assembling plants, and homework (telephone sales, for example) is growing. These workers are more likely to be brown and female than the old blue-collar white boys we are so accustomed to seeing in popular culture. While white male membership dropped from 55.8 percent in 1986 to 49.7 percent in 1995, women now make up 37 percent of organized labor's membership—a higher percentage than at any time in the U.S. labor movement's history.[4] Between 1976 and 1988, while the nation's overall labor force grew by 26 percent, the percentage of black workers rose by 38 percent, Asian American workers by 103 percent, and Latinos by 110 percent. According to the 1980 census, approximately one out of every three "Spanish origin persons" and three out of every five Asians in the United States were born in other countries.[5]

Organizing the new immigrant labor force is perhaps the fundamental challenge facing the labor movement. For one, a substantial proportion of immigrant workers is employed by small ethnic firms with little tolerance for labor unions. Besides obvious language and cultural barriers, union leaders are trying to tackle the herculean task of organizing thousands of tiny, independent, sometimes transient firms. Immigrants are also less represented in public sector jobs, which tend to have a much higher percentage of unionized employees. (Indeed, the heavy concentration of native-born black people in public sector jobs partly explains why African Americans have such a high unionization rate.) The most obvious barrier to organizing immigrant workers, however, has been discriminatory immigration policy. Even before Proposition 187 got on the ballot, the 1986 Immigration Reform and Control Act imposed legal sanctions against employers of "aliens" without proper documents. Thus, even when unions were willing to organize undocumented workers, fear of deportation kept many workers from joining the labor movement.[6]

Unions are also partly to blame for the state of labor organizing among immigrant workers. Until recently, union leaders too often assumed that Latino and Asian workers were unorganizable or difficult to organize—arguments that have been made about women and African American workers in the past. As we pointed out in the previous chapter, the American labor movement has a long and tragic history of xenophobia, racism, and anti-immigrant sentiment. Therefore, even when union organizers were willing to approach undocumented workers, they often operated on the assumption that immigrants were easily manipulated by employers, willing to undercut prevailing wages, or were "target workers" whose goal was to make enough money to return to their place of origin.[7]

The changing face of labor and the task of organizing workers of color turned out to be one of the most important issues in the bid for leadership of the AFL-CIO in 1995. In many ways, the victory of John Sweeney (president), Richard Trumka (secretary-treasurer), and Linda Chavez-Thompson (executive vice president)—the triumvirate that defeated the established old guard of Tom Donahue, heir apparent to Lane Kirkland and George Meany—depended to a large degree on their position vis-à-vis the so-called minority workers. As Sweeney himself put it, "The secret to our success, and the greatest potential for organizing, is among women, people of color, and young workers." It was not Sweeney's liberal good-heartedness that put the issue of women and workers of color on the agenda. Rather, it was the rank and file itself, particularly members of the public employees' unions, that for so long had been in the forefront of the battle to diversify the AFL-CIO and force it to recognize the pivotal role black, Latino, Asian-Pacific, and women workers irrespective of race and ethnicity, will play in the coming struggles. John Sturdivan, president of the American Federation of Government Employees and member of the AFL-CIO executive council, consistently challenged his colleagues to reach out to the most subordinate sectors of the working class. "As I tell my colleagues on the executive council," he explained, "if you can't promote diversity because it's the right thing to do, then look at the work force and recognize that you have to do it if you want to survive."[8]

Very early into their respective campaigns, however, neither Donahue nor Sweeney reached out to black workers. As William

Burrus, executive vice president of the American Postal Workers Union explained, "Decisions were made that Donahue and Sweeney would be the candidates ... and those decisions were made without including us. Now, after the fact, they are reaching out to hear our views." The Coalition of Black Trade Unionists (CBTU), along with several other key black union leaders, approached the candidates about diversifying the leadership of the union but remained skeptical of Sweeney and Donahue. CBTU leader William Lucy believed that, had black labor's position been fully represented in the upper echelons of the AFL-CIO before, some of the union's recent battles, such as their fight against the North American Free Trade Agreement, might have been more successful, or at least might have been posed more sharply. In Lucy's view, NAFTA was a civil rights issue as well as a labor issue, since the agreement enabled corporate interests to abandon urban communities where African Americans in particular were dependent on employment.[9]

After the historic election of Sweeney, Trumka, and Chavez-Thompson, the pressures on the AFL-CIO to diversify did not cease. At the first convention held three months after the elections, a coalition made up of the CBTU, the A. Philip Randolph Institute, the Asian-Pacific American Labor Alliance, the Labor Council for Latin American Advancement, and the Coalition of Labor Union Women came together and called for an expansion of the executive council to include more women and people of color. As a result, they gained some modest successes: the executive council was expanded and by the close of the convention included six women, nine African Americans, one Latino and one Asian American.[10]

As dramatic as these changes in national leadership might appear, they reflect several decades of grassroots, rank-and-file efforts on the part of workers of color to re-orient unions toward issues of social justice, racism, sexism, and cultural difference within their ranks. Indeed, one of the most significant labor-based social justice movements emerged out of the Service Employees International Union (SEIU), the union headed by John J. Sweeney before he took over the leadership of the AFL-CIO. Launched in 1985, Justice for Janitors sought to build a mass movement to win union recognition and to address the needs of a workforce made up primarily of people of color, mainly immigrants. As Sweeney explained, "The strategy of Justice for Janitors was to build a mass movement, with workers making clear that they wanted union representation and winning 'voluntary recognition' from employers. The campaigns addressed the special needs of an immigrant workforce, largely from Latin America. In many cities, the janitors' cause became a civil rights movement—and a cultural crusade." Throughout the mid- to late 1980s, Justice for Janitors waged several successful "crusades" in Pittsburgh, Denver, San Diego, Los Angeles, and Washington, D.C. With support from Latino leaders and local church officials, for example, their Denver campaign yielded a sudden growth in unionization among janitors and wage increases of about ninety cents an hour.[11]

From its inception, Justice for Janitors has been deeply committed to antiracism and mass mobilization through community-based organizing and civil disobedience. Heirs of the sit-down strikers of the 1930s and the Civil Rights movement of the 1950s and 1960s, they have waged militant, highly visible campaigns in major cities throughout the country.[12] In Los Angeles, for example, Justice for Janitors is largely responsible for the dramatic increase in unionized custodial employees, particularly among workers contracted out by big firms to clean high-rise buildings. The percentage of janitors belonging to unions rose from 10 percent of the workforce in 1987 to 90 percent in 1995.[13] Their success certainly did not come easily. Indeed, the turning point in their campaign began around 1990, when two hundred janitors struck International Service Systems (ISS), a Danish-owned company. A mass march in Century City, California, in support of the strikers generated enormous publicity after police viciously attacked the demonstrators. Overall, more than sixty people were hospitalized, including a pregnant woman who was beaten so severely she miscarried. An outpouring of sympathy for the strikers turned the tables, enabling them to win a contract with ISS covering some 2,500 janitors in Southern California.[14]

More recently, in April 1995 Justice for Janitors (SEIU Local 399) won a major victory over seven leading Los Angeles janitorial contractors. Their threat of a strike and mass civil disobedience persuaded the contractors and the Building Owners' Management Association to agree to practically all of the union's demands. Among other things, they won a uniform minimum wage rate of $6.80, to be implemented within five years in all buildings covered by the contract. It was a significant victory because many of the incoming janitors were making as little as $4.25 an hour. Moreover, the purpose of the agreement was to bring the lowest-paid workers closer to a living wage rather than to achieve an across-the-board percentage increase for all janitors. Higher-paid workers had to sacrifice a bit, but most agreed that a unified wage base would strengthen the union movement and thus put workers in a stronger position to bargain at a later date. Justice for Janitors also defeated a management proposal that would have forced workers to pay 25 percent of their health care premiums. Instead they successfully negotiated for a fully paid family health care plan for each member, to be phased in over five years.[15]

Justice for Janitors succeeded precisely because it was able to build links to community leaders, to forge an alliance with black and Latino organizations, churches, and progressive activists from all over the city. They built a powerful mass movement that went beyond the downtown luxury office buildings and the SEIU Local 399 headquarters into the streets and boardrooms. Their challenge is all the more remarkable when we consider the fact that Proposition 187, a California initiative denying basic rights to immigrants, had only recently been passed. After all, the SEIU in Los Angeles was primarily a union of immigrant workers—workers at whom Proposition 187 was directed. (I should add that Local 399 and Local 660 of the SEIU, the latter under the leadership of Gilbert Cedillo, waged a militant fight against Proposition 187.) Yet, what neither the contractors nor the conservative lawmakers nor many ordinary immigrant bashers realized was that, as L.A. activist Eric Mann put it, "Many of those workers began as militants in the shops and streets of El Salvador, Guatemala and Mexico. Their fight for a fair contract in Los Angeles was an 'in your face' answer to the immigrant-bashers of both political parties."[16]

In Washington, D.C., Justice for Janitors led the struggle of Local 82 of the SEIU in its fight against U.S. Service Industries (USSI)—a private janitorial company that used nonunion labor to clean downtown office buildings. But because they conceived of themselves as a social movement, they did not stop with the protection of union jobs. In March 1995, Justice for Janitors organized several demonstrations in the district that led to over 200 arrests. Blocking traffic and engaging in other forms of civil disobedience, the protesters demanded an end to tax breaks to real estate developers as well as cutbacks in social programs for the poor. As union spokesperson Manny Pastreich put it, "This isn't just about 5,000 janitors; it's about issues that concern all D.C. residents—what's happening to their schools, their streets, their neighborhoods." Many people who participated in the March demonstrations came from all over the country, and not all were janitors. Greg Ceci, a longshoreman from Baltimore, saw the struggle as a general revitalization of the labor movement and a recognition, finally, that the unions need to lead a larger fight for social justice. "We need to reach out to the workers who have been ignored by mainstream unions. We need to fight back, and I want to be a part of it."[17]

Indeed, D.C.'s Justice for Janitors is made up precisely of workers who have been ignored—poor women of color. Black and Latino women make up the majority of its membership, hold key leadership positions, and have put their bodies on the line for the SEIU as well as the larger cause of social justice. Twenty-four-year-old Dania Herring is an example of Justice for Janitors' new leadership cadre. A mother of four and resident of one of the poorest neighborhoods in the southeast section of the District, whose husband (at the time of the demonstrations) was an unemployed bricklayer, Herring had quit her job to become a full-time organizer for Local 82 and Justice for Janitors. Yet, these women were so militant that members of Washington's District Council dismissed them as "hooligans." "Essentially, they use anarchy as a means of organizing workers," stated African American councilman Harold Brazil. "And they do that under the mantle of justice—for janitors—or whoever else they want to organize."[18]

In the end, their challenge to the city and to USSI paid off. In December 1995, the National Labor Relations Board (NLRB) concluded that USSI had "a history of pervasive illegal conduct" by threatening, interrogating, and firing employees they deemed unacceptable, especially those committed to union organizing. African American workers, in particular, had suffered most from the wave of firings, in part because USSI, like other employers, believed immigrant workers were more malleable and less committed to unionization because of their tenuous status as residents. The pattern was clear to Amy Parker, a janitor who had worked under USSI for three years. "Before USSI got the contract to clean my building, there were 18 African-Americans. Now, I am the only one." After three steady years cleaning the same building, she earned only $5.50 an hour.[19] The NLRB's decision against USSI, therefore, was a substantial victory for Local 82 of the SEIU. It meant that USSI could no longer discriminate against the union and it generated at least a modicum of recognition for Justice for Janitors.

Such stories have been duplicated across the country. Justice for Janitors, in short, is more than a union. It is a dynamic social movement made up primarily of women and people of color, and it has the potential to redirect the entire labor movement. Unfortunately, much of the potential has yet to be realized. As Bob Fitch pointed out recently, the SEIU is beset with serious corruption problems and a lack of democracy at the level of national leadership. John J. Sweeney himself, former head of New York City Local 32B-32J, whose membership rolls count about 70,000 members, has been implicated in a number of scandals. When Sweeney took over the presidency of the SEIU International, he appointed "Greedy" Gus Bevona to head the Local 32B-32J. Bevona quickly became the highest-paid union official in the country, pulling in close to half a million dollars a year to run a union that protects the nation's lowest-paid workers. Equally suspect was Bevona's decision to hire Sweeney as an "executive advisor" and pay him an annual salary of $100,000 while he continued to draw his full SEIU presidential salary.[20]

The most dynamic unions are also turning increasingly to community-based organizing. In situations like Los Angeles, where Latino and Asian American garment workers are spread across many small plants and shops, organizing shop by shop would prove costly and time-consuming. The Union of Needletrades, Industrial and Textile Employees (UNITE) adopted a community-based strategy that has been quite successful. In the predominantly Latino community near MacArthur Park (downtown Los Angeles), UNITE runs a "justice center" that provides language and citizenship classes, as well as a support network to help workers resolve workplace disputes. By maintaining a major presence in these neighborhoods, providing services and working with neighborhood groups, organizers not only helped build the union but gained a better understanding of the community, its culture, and its leadership base.[21]

In Greensboro, North Carolina, UNITE's ability to build a strong base in the black community ensured the success of its three-year struggle against K-Mart, which finally ended in victory during the summer of 1996. Essentially, UNITE Local 2603 launched a campaign to win a union contract and protest racial inequities in wages: K-Mart workers at the nearly all-black facility were making a mere $4.60. In addition to filing a complaint with the Equal Employment Opportunity Commission (EEOC), UNITE enlisted all the key local black community leaders and were able to get over 10,000 signatures on a petition to K-Mart's chairman demanding an end to discrimination. As a result of intensive workplace and community-based organizing, K-Mart signed a contract with the union that included, among other things, "a grievance procedure protecting workers against unjust discipline and terminations, seniority rights in job bidding, a limit to the number of temporaries, two additional holidays," and wage increases of 50 cents an hour for the first year and 75 cents for subsequent years.[22]

The main force behind the boycott, besides the union, was a coalition of Greensboro black ministers called The Pulpit Forum, led by the Reverend William Wright. In addition to building communication networks through their congregations and speaking openly on behalf of the K-Mart workers, The Pulpit Forum organized mass civil disobedience campaigns in which several ministers were arrested. Wright, like his fellow workers in The Pulpit Forum, understood the campaign in terms of the Civil Rights movement—he characterized it as a crusade for justice with far-reaching implications. "K-Mart does not realize," he pointed out, "that what starts in Greensboro has a way of reaching the conscience of our nation." The Pulpit Forum leader the Reverend Nelson Johnson shared Williams's view and went further, recognizing UNITE's struggle as the beginning of a movement that could dismantle corporate power over the working class. A veteran activist with a long radical history in North Carolina, Johnson began in the Civil Rights movement and quickly moved to the Left, becoming one of the founders of the African Liberation Support Committee in 1972 and subsequently a leader of the Workers Viewpoint Organization (WVO; later called the Communist Workers Party). In fact, sixteen years before UNITE celebrated its victory over K-Mart, Johnson almost died on the same Greensboro streets when Klansmen and Nazis opened fire on a WVO-led anti-Klan demonstration.[23]

Rather than simply appeal to black workers as workers, UNITE appealed to the whole black community and tapped a deep tradition of resistance to racism and injustice. Mobilizing the entire black community was the key to their victory. Indeed, two years before the final contract with K-Mart, the Greensboro City Council passed a resolution requiring that all future employers moving into the city limits pay a minimum starting salary of $12.50 per hour before receiving any city tax incentives. It was a bold move, to be sure. Yet it represents a glimmer of what can happen when an entire community takes a stand against the rapaciousness of corporate capitalism and racial inequality.[24]

THE PROLETARIAT GOES TO COLLEGE

When we think of the contemporary labor movement, we often evoke images of overcrowded fly-by-night sweatshops, declining primary industries, huge retail conglomerates (i.e., K-Mart, Wal-Mart, and all the other multinational "marts" dotting the suburban/urban landscape). Many of my own colleagues in the groves of academe, for example, have always looked elsewhere for the working class rather than in our own campus cafes and hallways. The janitors, groundskeepers, cafeteria workers, and clerical workers are pretty much invisible on college campuses—at least until they raise their voices for better working conditions, dignity, and justice. The recent wave of campuswide strikes at places like Yale University and Barnard College, made even more pronounced by the struggles of graduate student teachers for union representation, compelled many observers to pay more attention to universities as sites of labor exploitation and corporatization. Of courses, these battles were not the first time workers on college campuses fought back, but for many labor activists these recent struggles certainly highlighted the changing character and position of the American working class.

Universities (as well as hospitals) stand among the largest and fastest growing sectors of the service economy. Universities, after all, employ a vast army of clerical workers, food service workers, janitors, and other employees whose job it is to maintain the physical plant, not to mention full- and part-time faculty and researchers. In 1991, for instance, colleges and universities directly employed 2,662,085 workers—a figure that does not include employees who work for other firms contracted out by universities and colleges.[25]

Public and private universities, like the rest of corporate America, are also undergoing major restructuring. Administrators claim that cutbacks in governmental and private support, compounded by political attacks on university affirmative action policies and multicultural curriculums, have created a major financial crisis. The past decade has witnessed massive downsizing in staff and even faculty while enrollments have remained steady or increased. These circumstances translate into layoffs, wage freezes, speed-ups, and the increased use of part-time and temporary labor without benefits or union protection.

Yale University officials have also declared a crisis, announcing major cuts to help reduce their $8 million deficit. Yet, just as the Fortune 500 companies are reaping some of the greatest profits in history, Yale University has earned a 15.7 percent return on its investments, bringing its endowment to almost $4 billion. Yale's proclaimed crisis is not only disingenuous, but it camouflages its real agenda: to bust existing unions—mainly Locals 34 and 35 of the Federation of University Employees—and nip any other organizing activity in the bud. Yale's treatment of its dining hall, custodial, and maintenance workers, represented by the predominantly black Local 35, can only be regarded as draconian. The proposed cuts would essentially create a permanent two-tiered system in which Local 35 workers would be unemployed during the summer months. The thirty-week schedule would reduce the typical full-time salary from $23,000 to about $10,000. Furthermore, Yale plans to increase subcontracting to bring nonunion labor to perform clerical, food, and maintenance work, and to massively reduce retirement and health benefits to these low-wage workers.

Clearly, the university is as much a part of the "real world" as Citibank and AT&T. Institutions of higher learning are by no means above exploitation or resistance, and the rules of the game are determined by the flow of capital. Thus unions are critical for defending university employees from corporate downsizing—a lesson few full-time faculty want to acknowledge. Beyond the obvious issues facing low-wage service workers at universities, few of my colleagues recognize that they are about to be caught in the crisis themselves, especially with the elimination of tenure just around the corner, the hiring of casual labor to teach undergrads, and the reliance on academic stardom as the first wedge in the creation of a two-tiered faculty. The only way to overturn these developments is by challenging the universities we work for and the administrators who carry out these corporate downsizing policies. We have to decide whose side we are on and realize that our base of support has already been established by the very black and brown workers who clean our offices, and to whom most faculty do not even speak.

But the question of unionization is not just a pragmatic issue. What kind of unions should university employees build, especially if their work brings them in contact with students? What should be the relationship between low-wage workers, faculty, students, and the larger community? After all, despite the resemblance universities are not exactly banks or investment firms. They have historically been places where alternatives to exploitation and oppression have been discussed and imagined in an institutional setting. They have been the sites of historic movements for social change precisely because the ostensible function of the university is to interrogate knowledge, society, and history. Students and some faculty at City

College of New York participated directly in the labor and unemployed movement of the 1930s; African American students at Fisk University and North Carolina Agricultural and Technical College helped launch the Civil Rights movement; the Free Speech and subsequent student movement got its start partly at the University of California at Berkeley. And even when important social movements emerged out of factory settings, such as the Dodge Revolutionary Union Movement in Detroit, students at Wayne State University played a key role.

Not surprisingly, unions that operate in the universities have not only been at the forefront of labor conflicts on campuses, but have also on occasion articulated a larger vision of social justice. Two important examples that are analogous to Local 35's struggle with Yale University took place almost three decades ago at Duke University and the University of North Carolina (UNC) at Chapel Hill. Because the struggles at Duke and UNC were as much a product of the Black Revolution in the South as the horrible working conditions of dining hall and maintenance workers, strikers made demands that extended far beyond basic bread-and-butter issues. On April 8, 1968, just four days after the assassination of Dr. King, students and faculty organized a massive sit-in in the quadrangle in front of Duke Chapel to demand $1.60 an hour minimum for nonacademic employees—primarily maintenance workers and food service employees organized in Local 77 of the American Federation of State, County, and Municipal Employees (AFSCME). They also demanded that Duke University president Douglas Knight form a grievance committee consisting of faculty, students, and employees; that he resign from the all-white Hope Valley Country Club; and that he sign a petition in support of open housing for African Americans. Despite militant opposition from workers and students, Duke University proved more powerful. When the food and maintenance workers finally returned to work, their union was in shambles.

In Chapel Hill, black food service workers at the University of North Carolina walked off their jobs in November 1969. It was the second strike that year—the first ending in success with the University paying $180,000 in back overtime. And their success depended on support from black students and faculty. The second UNC strike is remarkably similar to the struggles being waged by Yale's locals of the Federation of University Employees, in that they, too, were fighting the practice of subcontracting out work to firms that hire cheap nonunion labor. In Chapel Hill, the food service workers, members of AFSCME, fought the university's decision to contract out the running of dining halls by Saga Food Service. Saga had pretty much ignored the earlier contract between the university and strikers, and had apparently fired ten workers for alleged union membership. They also cut back UNC's staff from 147 to 100, despite protestations from workers. It turned out to be an extremely violent strike, with sixteen arrests and six people injured—most of whom were students in solidarity with striking workers.[26]

Both of these strikes anticipated the current situation university workers are facing, and they both point to the need to think critically about the unique opportunities universities offer as sites of working-class struggle. First, during the last quarter-century, at least, subcontracting has been part of a larger corporate strategy to reduce wages and benefits and to bring in casualized, temporary, nonunion labor. Of course, this general trend mirrors the rest of the corporate world, but within a university it also serves to take the administration off the hook by rendering even more invisible the exploitation of labor at the university. University officials work hard to project an image of their campuses as places of free exchange and intellectual inquiry. That universities are often the biggest exploiters of labor, not to mention the biggest landlords in some cities, is a fact their public relations people try to bury.

Second, the low-wage workforce at most major universities and colleges really reflects the American working class in general, and the renewed labor movement in particular. Workers of color, especially women, were at the forefront of the struggles at Duke and UNC in the late 1960s. The same holds true for Local 35 as well as similar locals across the country. Despite the fact that these workers tend to have relatively high union participation rates, they are nevertheless among the poorest paid and most exploited workers on campus. Indeed, Yale officials could justify such draconian policies toward dining hall and custodial workers precisely because these kinds of jobs have historically been associated with black labor (domestic servants, janitors, and the like). Racism and sexism largely explain the disparity in wages, as well as the labeling of these jobs as unskilled. Clearly there is skill involved, but definitions of skill are raced, sexed, and historically determined. Hence, any union fighting for the rights of low-wage service workers, in the university or elsewhere, must make the struggle against racism and sexism fundamental.

Finally, the role of students and faculty in all of these strikes offers key lessons for future labor conflicts on college campuses. At both Duke and UNC, student and faculty support was pivotal. During the UNC strike, for example, student groups mobilized African American students from all over the state of North Carolina to descend on campus to observe "Black Monday" when the university failed to reach a settlement. Fear of unrest forced Chapel Hill Mayor Howard Lee to withdraw police from campus and compelled university officials to negotiate a settlement between the union and Saga Food Service. Students helped organize workers, joined picket lines, and incorporated tactics developed in the Civil Rights movement. Indeed, most student activists saw these campus strikes in much the same way Dr. Martin Luther King, Jr., viewed strikes by the Memphis sanitation workers and Charleston's hospital workers: they were part and parcel of the Civil Rights movement. Even when they lost, the strike gave birth to new movements for social justice. Several students in the college and medical school who actively supported the strike went on to be active in other labor movements, anti-Klan organizations, left-wing parties, and various Third World liberation movements. Owusu Sadaukai (Howard Fuller) became the business agent for Local 77 of AFSCME after the failed strike at Duke University. Soon thereafter, Sadaukai founded Malcolm X Liberation University in North Carolina, served as a leader in the African Liberation Support Committee, and developed a reputation as one of the leading black radicals in North Carolina.[27]

Unions at universities and elsewhere need to adopt a broad vision of social justice if they are to succeed. They cannot be business-as-usual unions. They need to embrace a far-reaching civil rights agenda and the struggle against class-based racism in addition to the basic bread-and-butter issues.[28] One sparkling example of a campus union that embraces such a broad-reaching, antiracist agenda is the Campaign to Organize Graduate Students (COGS) at the University of Iowa. An affiliate of the United Electrical Workers (UE), COGS insisted that the university administration agree to a "no discrimination" clause in their contract. Such a clause, consistent with the University of Iowa's own human rights policy, would enable graduate student employees to use a union grievance procedure to deal with workplace discrimination. When the administration refused, COGS activists decided to protest the university's position by disrupting a highly publicized campus lecture by visiting historian Taylor Branch, author of a Pulitzer Prize–winning biography of Dr. Martin Luther King, Jr., to honor King's birthday in January 1997. A group of about forty students marched into the auditorium ten minutes before Branch's talk carrying signs and leaflets that read "Respect the Memory: Support the No Discrimination Clause," and singing "This Little Light of Mine." Their presence won support of the crowd and revealed to many observers that discrimination was not a thing of the past. While the demonstration was a success, behind the scenes UE staff persons and their allies in COGS tried to block the event, arguing that it would upset delicate contract negotiations. Whereas the "veteran" labor organizers believed that basic "bread-and-butter" issues should take precedence over antiracism and antisexism, COGS activists such as John Scott, David Colman, Margaret Loose, and Paul Young recognized how inseparable these issues are. Fortunately, the militant wing of COGS prevailed, proving that it is possible to build a dynamic labor movement without subordinating race or gender. As COGS leader and veteran black radical John Scott put it in a moving speech to his fellow graduate students, never in his twenty-six years of movement work had he ever been involved with a predominantly white union willing to risk contract negotiations in support of racial justice. Perhaps a new day is on the horizon.[29]

Movements like these contain the seeds of a new political vision. A new vision is something progressives and labor organizers are sorely lacking, especially when it comes to dealing with the problems of a predominantly nonwhite urban working class relegated to low-wage service work, part-time work, or outright joblessness. Ironically, universities might ultimately be the source of a new radical vision, but instead of looking to the classroom and its attendant culture wars, we should pay more attention to the cafeteria.

LABOR/COMMUNITY STRATEGIES AGAINST CLASS-BASED RACISM

Of course, we cannot stop at the cafeteria or the classroom or workplaces in general. Urban working people spend much if not most of their lives in their neighborhoods, in their homes, in transit, in the public spaces of the city, in houses of worship, in bars, clubs, barbershops, hair and nail salons, in various retail outlets, in medical clinics, welfare offices, courtrooms, even jail cells. They create and maintain families, build communities, engage in local politics, and construct a sense of fellowship that is sometimes life sustaining. These community ties are crucial to the success of any labor movement, as the Greensboro workers' fight against K-Mart clearly illustrated. History has proven over and over again that in order to generate local support for union struggles, strikes, boycotts, and corporate responsibility campaigns, community-based organizations are key. Let us not forget that the intense class struggles that erupted across the country in the late nineteenth century, on the railroads in 1877, in the mines of the Rocky Mountains and the steel mills in the East and Midwest, and among black washerwomen in the urban South were *community* struggles. It was never a simple matter of labor unions versus employers. During some of those dramatic battles, the local police, families, and even some of the merchants sided with the union, which meant that the employers had to bring in state troops and private Pinkerton agents. The employers were forced to go outside precisely because communities were mobilized. During the 1930s the success of the sit-down strikes in Akron and Detroit, and the struggles of Latina and Asian-Pacific cannery workers in the West, depended on community support; families and friends and sympathetic organizations brought food and blankets, joined picket lines, got the word out, and pooled money to help struggling families survive the loss of a paycheck. Similarly, during the late 1960s and early 1970s, the League of Revolutionary Black Workers and the Revolutionary Union Movement made community organizing a central strategy.[30]

More importantly, working people live in communities that are as embattled as the workplace itself. Black and Latino workers, for example, must contend with issues of police brutality and a racist criminal justice system, housing discrimination, lack of city services, toxic waste, inadequate health care facilities, sexual assault and domestic violence, and crime and neighborhood safety. And at the forefront of these community-based movements have been women, usually struggling mothers of all ages dedicated to making life better for themselves and their children—mothers who, as we have seen, have become the scapegoats for virtually everything wrong with the "inner city." In cities across the United States, working-class black and Latina women built and sustained community organizations that registered voters, patrolled the streets, challenged neighborhood drug dealers, defended the rights of prisoners, and fought vigorously for improvements in housing, city services, health care, and public assistance. Of course, there was nothing new about women of color taking the lead in community-based organizing. A century earlier, black women's clubs not only helped the less fortunate but played a key role in the political life of the African American community. Over a half-century later, when militant, predominantly male organizations like the Black Panther Party and the Black Liberation Army received a great deal of press, black women carried on the tradition of community-based organizing. If one only looked at South Central Los Angeles in the mid-1960s, one would find well over a dozen such organizations, including the Watts Women's Association, the Avalon-Carver Community Center, the Mothers of Watts Community Action Council, Mothers Anonymous, the Welfare Recipients Union, the L. A. Chapter of the National Welfare Rights Organization, the Central City Community Mental Health Center, the Neighborhood Organizations of Watts, and the South Central Volunteer Bureau of Los Angeles.[31]

These movements were the precursors for contemporary groups such as Mothers ROC (Reclaiming Our Children) and Mothers of East Los Angeles (MELA). Mothers ROC was founded in 1992 by Theresa Allison, the mother of Dewayne Holmes, who helped engineer the historic gang truce in the aftermath of the L. A. rebellion but was falsely convicted on trumped-up charges soon thereafter. Her efforts to overturn his conviction convinced her to form a movement that could challenge the racist and sexist criminal justice system. "We formed Mothers ROC," Allison explained, "to ensure that our children would no longer face the lawyers, judges and courts alone. Our aim is to be the voice of the tens of thousands of young men and women who are locked away in the rapidly growing prison system." Among other things, Mothers ROC has called for an immediate end to the "war on drugs" (recognizing it for what it is: a war on black and Latino youth), the repeal of the "three strikes" law (meaning that three felony convictions, irrespective of the crime, lead to a mandatory life sentence); more funding for public defenders; an end to mandatory minimum laws; and an end to indiscriminate stops, warrantless searches, and the use of electronic databases to identify alleged gang members. In the five years since its founding, Mothers ROC has grown into a nationwide organization with over 100 chapters and a constantly expanding membership.[32]

Similarly, MELA got started as a result of a protracted battle with the prison-industrial complex. Founded in 1984 to fight efforts by the state of California to build a prison in East Los Angeles, MELA built a powerful coalition that not only blocked the prison but kept an oil pipeline and a hazardous waste incinerator from being built in their communities. In an age of deindustrialization and massive joblessness, MELA's resistance to these firms proved to be bold and visionary. While many community leaders were clamoring for jobs at any cost, the women of MELA understood that in the long run no job is worth sacrificing the health and well-being of the entire community. As MELA activist Aurora Castillo put it, "Because we are a poor and Hispanic community they think we will accept the destructive projects if they promise us jobs. But we don't want our children working as prison guards or in incinerators. We need constructive jobs—nurses, doctors, computer specialists, skilled workers, who can make a contribution to our community."[33]

MELA is one of many organizations involved in the struggle for environmental justice. All over the country, especially in the South, women of color are organizing against companies and government institutions responsible for placing landfills, hazardous waste sites, and chemical manufacturers dangerously close to low-income minority communities. The evidence that poor communities of color are singled out for toxic waste sites is overwhelming. One study released in 1987 estimated that three out of five African Americans live dangerously close to abandoned toxic waste sites and commercial hazardous waste landfills. The study also revealed that the largest hazardous waste landfill in the country is located in Emelle, Alabama, whose population is 78.9 percent black, and that the greatest concentration of hazardous waste sites is in the mostly black and Latino South Side of Chicago. A 1992 study concluded that polluters based in minority areas are treated less severely by government agencies than those in largely white communities. Also, federally sponsored toxic cleanup programs, according to the report, take longer and are less thorough in minority neighborhoods.[34]

The effects of these policies have been devastating. Cases of asthma and other respiratory diseases as well as cancer have been traced to toxic waste. Accidents involving the mishandling of hazardous chemicals have ravaged some poor black communities, often with little or no publicity. In July 1993, for example, a ruptured railroad car at General Chemical's plant in Richmond, California, caused a disaster for this overwhelmingly poor black city located just north of Oakland. As journalist and activist Ruth Rosen explained it, the damaged car "spewed a fifteen-mile-long toxic plume of sulfuric acid through surrounding residential communities. People wheezed and coughed, their eyes and lungs scorched by the toxic cloud. Three hours passed before the explosion could be capped. Over the next few days, more than twenty thousand residents sought medical treatment from nearby hospitals." Sadly, the city of Richmond had endured nauseating fumes a few years earlier when fires broke out in a neighboring warehouse owned by Safeway supermarkets.[35]

The environmental justice movement's roots apparently go back to 1982, when black and Native American residents tried to block state authorities from building a chemical disposal site in Warren County, North Carolina. Since then, dozens of local movements have followed suit, including the Concerned Citizens of South Central (Los Angeles), and the North Richmond West County Toxics Coalition. By demonstrating, holding hearings and public workshops, conducting research, and filing suits against local and state governments, these groups have tried to draw attention to the racial and class biases that determine how hazardous waste sites are selected.

One of the pioneers of the movement for environmental justice was Patsy Ruth Oliver, founder and leader of the Carver Terrace Community Action Group. When an investigation revealed that Carver Terrace, a black suburb outside of Texarkana, Texas, had been built on an old toxic waste site and sold to unsuspecting black home buyers, Texas officials asked that the federal government add it to its Superfund cleanup program (a $1.3 billion trust that Congress created to clean up toxic waste dumps). When the Environmental Protection Agency (EPA) came to investigate, they concluded that the soil was contaminated but it posed no danger to the residents. Oliver and her neighbors were outraged, especially after they discovered that the EPA had withheld information suggesting that the residents were, in fact, at risk. Through persistence and protest, Oliver and the Community Action Group were able to force the government to buy them out and help them relocate. Although the people of Carver Terrace lost their homes, it was a significant victory for the movement because they forced the government to acknowledge the seriousness of toxic dumping. Oliver continued to speak out against environmental racism until her death in 1993.[36]

The struggle against environmental racism is integrally tied to workplace struggles, the criminal justice system, the welfare state, and the movements of global capital. Whereas most community- and labor-based organizations limit their focus to an issue or set of issues, even when they are able to see the bigger picture, once in a while there are movements that attempt to fight on all fronts. Such organizations, where they do exist, are often products of the best elements of Third World, feminist, and Black Liberation movements. Rather than see race, gender, and sexuality as "problems," they are, instead, pushing working-class politics in new directions. The exemplary movements include the Center for Third World Organizing, the Southern Organizing Committee for Economic Justice, New Directions, and Labor Notes, to name a few.

One of the most visible and successful examples of such a broad-based radical movement is the Labor/Community Strategy Center based in Los Angeles. The leaders of the Strategy Center have deep roots in social movements that go back to Black Liberation and student activism of the 1960s, urban antipoverty programs, farmworkers' movements, organized labor, and popular left movements in El Salvador and Mexico. They have been at the forefront of the struggle for clean air in the Harbor area of Los Angeles—a region with a high concentration of poor communities of color. They have worked closely with Justice for Janitors, providing crucial support to Local 660 of the SEIU. They fought President Bush's proposed "Weed and Seed" program (an urban policy developed in response to the L. A. Rebellion that would provide big tax breaks to entrepreneurs willing to invest in inner cities, and a massive buildup of the police and criminal justice system). They mobilized against Proposition 187, waged a campaign to protect immigrants' rights, and have even engaged in cross-border organizing with Mexican transit workers.[37]

The Strategy Center's most important campaign during the last few years has been the Bus Riders Union (BRU), a multiracial organization of transit-dependent working people who have declared war on race and class inequality in public transportation. The BRU is not a single-issue advocacy group, however. The struggle for equity in public services, particularly in urban transit which is so essential to the economic and physical well-being of cities battered by capital flight and deindustrialization, is a working-class movement made up of people of color whose very survival is in question in an age of downsizing, cutbacks, rising racism, xenophobia, and sheer callousness toward the poor. Public transportation is one of the few issues that touches the lives of many urban working people across race, ethnic, and gender lines. And ultimately, equal access to affordable transportation is tied to equal access to employment opportunities, especially now that manufacturing and other medium- to high-wage jobs have migrated to suburban rings or industrial parks. The combination of rising fares and limits on services has sharply curtailed the ability of workers to get to work. The cost of transportation for many families is a major part of their monthly budget. The average working-class commuter in Los Angeles rides the bus between sixty and eighty times a month, including for work, family visits, medical care, and shopping. For transit-dependent wage earners, bus fare could potentially comprise up to one-fourth or more of their total income! For many poor people even a small increase makes riding prohibitive. They might visit family less often, skip grocery shopping, or even miss work if they do not have bus fare. Forcing low-income riders off the buses with higher fares moves the Los Angeles County Metropolitan Transit Authority (MTA) out of the business of transporting the urban poor.

After three years of conducting research and riding the buses to recruit members, in 1994 the Strategy Center and the Bus Riders Union, along with the Southern Christian Leadership Conference and the Korean Immigrant Workers' Advocates as coplaintiffs, filed a class action suit against the MTA on behalf of 350,000 bus riders, the vast majority of whom are poor people of color. Represented by the National Association for the Advancement of Colored People's Legal Defense and Educational Fund, the plaintiffs challenged proposals to raise bus fares from $1.10 to $1.35; eliminate monthly bus passes, which cost $42 for unlimited use; and introduce a zone system on the blue line commuter rail that would increase fares by more than 100 percent for half of the passengers. A temporary restraining order issued by federal Judge Terry Hatter kept fares frozen for six months until a pretrial compromise was reached: the MTA agreed to retain monthly passes at $49 in exchange for the full 25-cent fare hike.

As veteran activist and Strategy Center director Eric Mann points out, the suit challenged "transportation racism and the creation of racist, separate and unequal public transportation systems in the way that *Brown v. Board of Education* did for challenging racist structures of public education." The analogy to *Brown* is quite apt and its implications reach far beyond Los Angeles. The plaintiffs argued that the MTA's policies violate Title VI of the Civil Rights Act of 1964, which provides that no person "shall on the ground of race, color, or national origin, be excluded from participation in, be denied the benefits of, or be subjected to discrimination under any program or activity receiving Federal financial assistance."[38]

The evidence that the MTA *has* created a separate and unequal transit system is overwhelming. On one side is the underfunded, overcrowded bus system which carries 94 percent of the MTA's passengers (80 percent of whom are African American, Latino, Asian-Pacific Islander, and Native American) yet receives less than one-third of the MTA's total expenditures. As a result, riders of color experience greater peak-hour overcrowding and tend to wait at neighborhood bus stops that are benchless and unsheltered. On the other side is the lavish commuter rail system connecting (or planning to connect) the predominantly white suburbs to the L.A. downtown business district. Although commuter line passengers make up 6 percent of the ridership, the system receives 70.9 percent of the MTA's resources. To make matters worse, the fare hike and proposed elimination of the monthly bus passes were to be accompanied by massive cutbacks in bus service.[38]

Such massive inequities in public transit access not only violate the equal protection clause of the Fourteenth Amendment. The MTA's policies might have served as a test case for *Plessy v. Ferguson*, for the proposed rail system has already created a two-tiered riding public—luxury trains for the white middle class, buses for the colored poor. Furthermore, the MTA paid for its Metrolink (train) lines with revenues earned from poor and working-class bus riders. Monies that should have been earmarked to improve bus service instead went to a partially finished, impractical rail system that will cost approximately $183 billion and only serve 11 percent of the population. It doesn't take a high IQ to realize that poor black and brown riders who have to crowd onto South Central, Inglewood, and East Los Angeles buses have been subsidizing the commuter rail. The average commuter rail rider is a white male professional with a household income of $64,450, who receives a $58 transportation subsidy from his employer and owns a car. By contrast, a typical bus rider is a person of color with no car and whose household income falls below $15,000. Put another way, the MTA's subsidy for bus #204, which runs through predominantly black and Latino neighborhoods along Vermont Avenue, will remain 34 cents per passenger, while the projected subsidy for the proposed Azusa and Torrance rail lines will be $55.64 and $52.87, respectively. Of course, the MTA will use revenues from sales tax and fare-box receipts to pay for this, but it is also dependent on federal funding: hence the violation of Title VI of the Civil Rights Act.

Like the Student Non-Violent Coordinating Committee in the 1960s, Strategy Center and BRU organizers take litigation *and* mass organizing seriously, but they are very clear which component drives the process. They have held legal workshops for members, conducted hours and hours of background research, prepared the initial strategy document on which the case is based, and carefully examined and re-examined all legal documentation pertaining to the suit. At the same time, they have worked hard to ensure that "the class" has a voice in the class action suit. In addition to collecting detailed declarations from riders, their main core of organizers are also plaintiffs—that is, bus riders. Leaders such as Della Bonner (a paralegal from Watts), Pearl Daniels (a hotel worker), and Ricardo and Noemi Zelada (garment workers originally from El Salvador), came to the movement as victims of discrimination. Now they are actively working to challenge the MTA's policies, using their knowledge and experience to strengthen both the legal case and day-to-day organizing strategies. Della Bonner sees the union's work as an extension of the militant struggles of thirty years ago. In fact, she constantly reminds fellow riders that a social movement put blacks and Latinos in office, and a social movement will hold them accountable. "We have to remind them. 'The policies that you help create and implement are not meeting the needs of the people who did the protesting. We are still around. We still have our needs. It is not acceptable for you to sell out!'" In other words, making "class action" meaningful is not just a legal strategy. "If we lose in court," Eric Mann points out,

> we want the class to know that it was a racist legal system that validates even more the urgency of our organizing work, and if we win it will take a mass movement to move the courts from "liability"—finding the MTA guilty of racism, to "remedy"—actually moving hundreds of millions of dollars per year from rail to bus to dramatically improve the conditions of the urban poor of color. In either case, it is the bus riders who must be the bus drivers of their own history."[40]

Eric Mann, Liann Hurst Mann, Della Bonner, Rita Burgos, Martin Hernandez, Kikanza Ramsey, Ricardo Zelada, Chris Mathis, and the many others who have built this dynamic movement have consistently made connections between civil rights, environmental justice, labor struggles, privatization, and the problems of capitalism. BRU organizers see their constituency in all of its "identities"—as workers, consumers, largely people of color, and city dwellers tired of toxic living. The union's demands—more resources devoted to buses, a moratorium on an overpriced rail service, lower fares, better service, safety, no-emissions electric buses, MTA policies that create jobs in inner city communities—genuinely reflect a range of issues beyond the problem of transportation. The BRU is forging a new social movement, not by appeals to color blindness but by rethinking class politics in a multicultural context. The growth of black elected officials and the integration of corporate boardrooms has sharpened the class dimension of the Civil Rights movement and complicated the racial politics. Now the battle lines are drawn between a multiracial class that is primarily African American, Latino, and Asian American, and a multiracial class that is predominantly white. Union organizers know that politicians and MTA board members of color who support the status quo play a critical part in the perpetuation of class-based racism. They also know that the remaining 20 percent of poor and working-class white riders are their friends. (The only reason they are not part of the suit is because class oppression in this country is still legal.) But rather than see race as a problem for working-class unity, the BRU argues that the struggle against racism is in the interest of the class.

BRU organizers also recognize the fundamental importance of culture and identity for mobilizing working people. The cultural work of the Strategy Center, from its creative use of graphics to attract members, to its dance-a-thons and related cultural events, sets an example for political movements that understand that "cultural politics" is more than an analytical category or political escapism under a different name. It is a practice. Lian Hurst Mann, founding member of the Strategy Center and editor of its new bilingual publication *Ahora Now!*, is an architect and designer who has drawn on her experience as a political organizer to develop new ways to "visualize" multiracial, working-class struggles. *Ahora Now!* consistently carries articles and interviews exploring cultural work, language, and identity, which offer important lessons about "art making" in a political context.[41]

The BRU and the Strategy Center have also collaborated with various performance groups, including the San Francisco Mime Troupe and the multiracial, predominantly female collective Street

Arts. Calling themselves the AgitProps, the Strategy Center's cultural activists created "props"—moving pieces of architecture, fifteen-foot scrolls emblazoned with BRU demands, and other works that help organizers create "counter-spaces" that enable people to engage more fully in mass meetings and rallies and allow "poor people to reclaim public space for the public good." Lian Hurst Mann describes one very powerful performative act of reclamation:

> AgitProps' action piece, *L. A. Lethal Air Kills the Dada-Puppen*...
> makes reference to Hannah Hoch's 1920 dada dolls, Walter Benjamin's charge to ask the position of work within the relations of production and unhinge its bourgeois aura through its technical reproduction, and the longtime Mexican costuming tradition of *cadavera* (dressing up like the living skeleton that honors the memory of the dead), in an action montage of one hundred dolls donning the shriveled-lung bodies and faces of child cadavers (challenging the humanist presumption that dolls are alive). At a board meeting of the Air Quality Management District, [AQMD] during which the board voted on how many cancers per million they would allow in the Latino Wilmington community (a community surrounded by five oil refineries), the corpses were piled in a mass "grave" before the board in an act of collective rage and public mourning through civil disobedience. As board members left the podium and the community activists seized the board seats, claiming community control of the "space" until being removed from the room by the county sheriffs, the AQMD audiovisual personnel repeatedly flashed on the big-screen video monitor the "representation" of the board's consent to the "allowable cancer deaths"—that is, the presentation of the corpses and the camera panning the death and focusing in close frame on the individual faces of the amassed dead dolls.[42]

Furthermore, the BRU, in collaboration with the L.A.-based Cornerstone Theater, plans to transform the interiors of buses into spaces for guerrilla theater. As an extension of the BRU's longstanding and successful organizing campaign, the bilingual performances will address complicated issues of race and ethnic identity, citizenship, gender, immigration, language, and capitalism more broadly, while building a multiracial, multiethnic social movement.[43]

The Bus Riders Union has been incredibly successful. Besides building a truly multicultural, multiracial mass movement, the BRU recently wrested a settlement from the MTA that imposed a two-year freeze on bus fares, a substantial reduction in the price of monthly and biweekly bus passes, a 5-percent increase in the number of buses in the MTA fleet in order to reduce overcrowding, the creation of new bus lines with the intention of eradicating "transportation segregation," and the creation of a joint working group in which the BRU would play a major role in drafting a five-year plan to improve bus service for all.[44] Hence a solidly antiracist movement resulted in a victory for all riders, including transit-dependent white workers, the disabled, the elderly, and students.

While the settlement marks a critical landmark in the history of civil rights struggle, Strategy Center organizers understand that the specific legal challenge is less important than the social movement that grows out of it and the political direction it provides for rebuilding a progressive alternative to the right-wing drift. Through their own struggles, in the courts and city council chambers, on the streets and buses of Los Angeles, the Bus Riders Union has advanced a radical vision of social justice. What they are offering is precisely the vision of social justice progressives tragically seem to have lost. Lacking such a vision, many of us have not been able to see why the struggle over public transportation is so important for working people, or how antiracism benefits the entire working class. And given what sociologist Stephen Steinberg rightly calls the "liberal retreat from racial justice," white progressives have a poor record when it comes to recognizing the fundamentally racist character of the class war being waged against the urban poor. The bus campaigns powerfully demonstrate that the issues facing the vast majority of people of color, for the most part, are working-class issues. Thus, unless we understand the significance of the "billions for buses" campaign or the historic class action suit against the MTA, we will never understand the deeper connections between welfare, workfare, warfare, and bus fare . . . or bus riders and unions, for that matter.

In this tragic era of pessimism and defeat, these grassroots, working-class radical movements go forward as if they might win. While some holier-than-thou leftists might view these movements, and my interpretation of them, as another example of misplaced optimism, I would venture to say that the women and men who have built and sustained these organizations do not have the luxury *not* to fight back. In most cases, they are battling over issues basic to their own survival—decent wages, healthy environment, essential public services. At the heart of these movements are folks like my mother and the many other working-class women of color, women like Patsy Oliver and Della Bonner, Dania Herring and Theresa Allison, women who have borne the brunt of the material and ideological war against the poor. They understand, better than anyone, the necessity of fighting back. And they also understand that change does not come on its own. As Dr. Martin Luther King, Jr., so eloquently explained:

> A solution of the present crisis will not take place unless men and women work for it. Human progress is neither automatic nor inevitable. Even a superficial look at history reveals that no social advance rolls in on the wheels of inevitability. Every step toward the goal of justice requires sacrifice, suffering, and struggle; the tireless exertions and passionate concern of dedicated individuals. Without persistent effort, time itself becomes an ally of the insurgent and primitive forces of irrational emotionalism and social destruction. This is no time for apathy or complacency. This is the time for vigorous and positive action.[45]

The time is now.

LOOKING B(L)ACKWARD:

2097–1997

*The tale you are about to read was inspired by Edward Bella-
my's utopian socialist novel* Looking Backward, *published in
1887. My apologies to the late Mr. Bellamy for shamelessly ap-
propriating the structure of his fascinating book. The ideas con-
tained in this essay, however, are my own and I take complete
responsibility for all of them—including the most retrograde.*

*Finally, many of the characters herein are fictitious and
are not intended to resemble real persons living or dead. If they
do, it is purely coincidental.*

"Don't try to speak. If you can hear me, blink your eyes." The voice
was faint but distinctive. Obviously a mature, learned man, though
in the flood of bright lights he was little more than a brown
silhouette.

"Where am I? Who are you?" I asked, trying desperately to
gather my bearings and sound intelligible.

"You're at University Hospital. How are you feeling?"

"I feel fine. What am I doing in a hospital? I'm perfectly healthy." It was true; I felt very well, indeed, as if I'd been vacationing in the Caribbean for three solid months. Given my usual pace, it had been a long time since I felt so rested and relaxed.

"The matter is quite complicated," the man replied. As my eyes adjusted to the light, the silhouette leaning over me became visible. He was an elegantly dressed black man, perhaps sixty years of age, with salt and pepper hair closely cropped around his ears. He had a kind face, though his expression was one of obvious concern laced with heavy doses of curiosity. "You've just been roused from a deep sleep, or, more properly, a coma. So much I can tell you. Do you recall when you fell asleep?"

"When?" I stammered, confused by the question. "When? Why just last evening, of course. I was attending a conference on Postraciality at the Crossroads of Signification—I think. I was on my way to a roundtable discussion on *The Bell Curve* but got turned around and couldn't find the room. I don't quite remember. In any case, there were two other sessions that caught my eye: one called "What's the 'Meta' For? Narrative, Metanarrative and Constructing the Sign in Postmodern America," the other titled "Deconstruct to Reconstruct, That's All We Do." I chose the latter, found a nice comfortable seat in the back of the room, and proceeded to doze off."

"I understand, Dr. Kelley. But if that's your story, it wasn't last night." As he uttered these eerily familiar words, I was suddenly overcome with anxiety; I felt an asthma attack coming on.

"How do you know my name, uh, Mr. . . . ."

"Legend. Ralph Legend. I'm a part-time instructor at the university and a part-time medical attendant—what they called in your day an 'orderly.' I know a great deal about your day because, like you, I'm a historian. My specialty is the mid- to late twentieth century, which isn't very popular these days since everyone wants to work on the twenty-first. . . ."

"Wait, hold on just a goddamn minute. I'm sure your life story is all that, but I need to know how long I've been sleeping. What day is it?"

"Thursday," he said. "Maybe you'd like to rest just a bit before we . . . "

"The conference was on a Saturday, so does that mean I've been sleeping for five days?"

"A bit longer than that, I'm afraid."

"More than a month?"

"Longer. Please, Dr. Kelley; you need to preserve your strength. If you calm down I'll tell you. Today is October 22 . . . 2097." Though his words fell somewhere between a whisper and a mumble, the final sentence felt like a gunshot in a dark, soundproof room. Silence stood between us for what felt like fifteen minutes but was probably more like thirty seconds.

"I know this is shocking and awkward, but I don't know how else to tell you. Perhaps you might want to rest a bit before . . ."

"Hell no," I shouted, surprised at the tone of my own voice and my use of profanity—something I've never been very good at, by the way. "Tell me everything—and I mean everything, right here and now."

"Well, I've been following your case for the past thirty years. For several months back in 1997 you were in the news. The headlines read: 'Promising Young Professor Falls into a Coma During Academic Conference.' Just when you were about to fall out of the media, Charles Murray—you remember him, right—used you as the basis for his book *The Negro Mind: A Case of National Distraction*, in which he argued that members of racial groups with lower average IQ scores who make it into the ranks of the cognitive elite are incapable of processing so much knowledge. Either they fake their way through their careers, suffer emotional breakdowns or severe nervous disorders, or fall into a coma. Granted, your case was his only evidence, but the man won a Pulitzer nonetheless.

"Anyway, you were eventually brought to the university and placed under observation. I discovered you because I wrote my thesis here at City Community University on race and the rise of the Right at the turn of the century—the twenty-first century. Since nobody wanted to publish the thing and I couldn't get a job, I ended up teaching one course a semester here at CCU and taking odd jobs to make ends meet. When I found out you had been relocated here, I took a position at the hospital so that I might be around if and when you woke up."

I couldn't believe my ears. At first I thought it was some kind of a joke—asleep for 100 years? Be real! But as I carefully studied the hospital room and took notice of all the new technology, it quickly became clear that things were different. Once I realized it was not a joke, I became angry and resentful. I missed seeing my daughter grow up or my wife's artistic career take off. I never had a chance to say good-bye to anyone in my family, not even my mother. And I never had the pleasure of seeing a book of mine reviewed in the *New York Times*. Nevertheless, my melancholy mood was quickly overtaken by curiosity: after all, I was, in essence, a 135-year-old time traveler with a rare opportunity to see the future.

The doctors checked me out and released me that afternoon under Dr. Legend's supervision. Legend kindly offered to show me around campus. At first I walked slowly, tentatively, across the sprawling urban campus; although modern technology had preserved my thirty-five-year-old frame, my legs were still weak. Once I got my stride, Dr. Legend started to fill me in:

"A lot has changed since your day," he warned. "Black college students make up about one tenth of one percent of the undergraduate students nationally and an even smaller proportion of the graduate population. With the exception of English, the number of black faculty have dropped to about a fifteenth of what it was 100 years ago. To make matters worse, the Afro-American Studies Program here at City Community, and elsewhere, is now balkanized into several different programs."

Dr. Legend gave me much more information than I could absorb. After a few minutes I began to fade out, hearing bits and pieces of his narrative—none of which sounded uplifting or positive. Fifteen minutes later, we entered a tiny gray building in bad need of repair. "This is Asante Hall, the home of the Center for Africological Thought and Practice. The director, Dr. Muhammad Khalid Mansa Musa, usually has office hours about this time. He is pretty well known around these parts, does a lot of media spots and holds the Distinguished Man of Kemet Chair in Africology. I should add, however, that all black faculty nowadays have chairs except for those of us who teach part-time."

Dr. Musa seemed genuinely pleased to see us. The place was dark and deserted and, besides himself, the only other live body in the building was his part-time secretary. And there were no students to be found anywhere.

"I heard on the radio that you had finally been jolted out of your deep sleep," he said as he extended his hand to greet me. "The ancestors work in mysterious ways." Without skipping a beat, he proceeded to tell me about the strength and vision of Africology generally, and his program in particular.

"We are out here in the community working with folks who buy our literature religiously. It's these outside funds that keep us going, not the university but the street vendors. Unlike those other Negroes, always talking about difference and diversity within blackness, we know that the man sees only one type—Nigger—and we've been fighting for him to see us as Africans, noble and proud. Any scholars not down for the struggle, not writing about the history or liberation of the Black Man, are worthless to us."

"With all due respect, Dr. Musa," I interrupted, "that's a very old debate. The pioneering black scholars practically had no choice but to devote their work to uplifting the race. But is that always the best place for them to be? Aren't there some negative consequences to allowing skin color and ethnic allegiances to drive one's scholarship?" I spoke with hesitation, surprised that people were still talking about such issues but cognizant of the fact that I hadn't a clue as to what transpired over the course of the past century.

"I beg to differ, my brother. You're either with us or against us. If you don't work on some aspect of our lives then you're selling out."

"I'm not too sure," I interjected. "I recall seeing something John Hope Franklin wrote a long time ago. An article titled 'The Dilemma of the American Negro Scholar.' I read it in a collection of his essays published a couple years after I finished grad school, but it's older—indeed, it predates Harold Cruse's *Crisis of the Negro Intellectual*."

"Now you're digging into some old-school shit!" blurted Dr. Legend, whose loss of composure surprised all of us. "I'm sorry, gentlemen. I don't know what came . . . uh. Anyway, please continue."

"Thank you. Franklin was pointing out how difficult it was for black scholars to carry the burden of the entire race on their shoulders and how that kept many from pursuing important work in the fields in which they were trained. Do you have a copy of that book around here?" I asked.

"Sure, we have everything on-line or on the ECD system. ECD stands for 'extremely compact disk.' Let me pull it up real quick." The new technology was fascinating. One subway-token-sized disk had the capacity to hold an entire university library. In addition to the printed words, we had the benefit of hearing the text read aloud in the author's voice, which had been digitally reconstructed through technology developed by a company called Da Lench Mob Electronics. Dr. Musa highlighted the text in question and pressed the return key. Magically, I was back in my own day listening to the eloquent voice of the Dean of Black History:

Imagine, if you can, what it meant to a competent Negro student of Greek literature, W. H. Crogman, to desert his chosen field and write a book entitled *The Progress of a Race*. Think of the frustration of the distinguished Negro physician C. V. Roman, who abandoned his medical research and practice, temporarily at least, to write *The Negro in American Civilization*. What must have been the feeling of the Negro student of English literature, Benjamin Brawley, who forsook his field to write *The Negro Genius* and other works that underscored the intellectual powers of the Negro? How much poorer is the field of the biological sciences because an extremely able and well-trained Negro scientist, Julian Lewis, felt compelled to spend years of his productive life writing a book entitled *The Biology of the Negro?*[1]

"I see your point, Dr. Kelley, but you completely misunderstand why these scholars made the decisions they did. Nobody held a gun to Benjamin Brawley's head and told him to abandon English lit. He was committed to black freedom and made the proper sacrifice. Besides, where could he have studied black studies? Harvard? Howard? Come on, man! He had to invent it first."

"Yes," I retorted, "but don't you think we ought to work in all fields? Perhaps our collective experience gives us a different perspective on science, technology, European literature, and art? Or maybe our experience *does not* give us any unique perspective on issues related to black people in the United States. After all, you're not suggesting that Africological insights are something we are born with or learn in our families and communities, right? If that were the case, why offer college classes and degrees?"

Dr. Musa, who looked visibly agitated, started to tug on his kente watchband. "You obviously missed a lot while you were sleeping. We're not the naive essentialists we've been made out to be. We insist that culture is learned, it isn't biological. If it were, we'd be out of business. We believe that the best culture, the most liberating culture, existed before the European invasion. We're trying to recover that and reconstruct it for the present generation. That has been our project over the past century plus. And you should know better than anyone that the work we do grows out of real deep historical scholarship, not guessing games or abstract theorizing. Go back and read the works of William Leo Hansberry or Cheikh Anta Diop or Frank Snowden."

I should have left it alone, but I couldn't. One hundred years is a long time without an argument. "But Dr. Musa," I interjected, "why does every useful thing have to always come out of Africa? What about the important contributions by black nationalist scholars who looked to the black experience in the United States, or the Americas more generally, for resistive and community-sustaining cultural values? I'm thinking about V. P. Franklin's book *Black Self-Determination* or John Langston Gwaltney's *Drylongso*.[2] Where do they fit in the paradigm you're constructing?"

Dr. Musa simply shrugged his shoulders and said, "I'm not familiar with those texts."

"Yea," Dr. Legend added, "they ought to be foundation texts but your predecessors couldn't see the sand for the pyramids. The lefties were no better, though. As soon as black folk start talking about 'us,' 'our people,' 'black aesthetic,' any of that, they start crying essentialism."

"Don't get me wrong," I added, trying to move our discussion to more institutional concerns. "I'm not arguing that the work Africologists do isn't important, politically or otherwise. There are obvious benefits to your approach; in the past black leaders have been able to mobilize folks by invoking a sense of community, a sense of nationhood, and in so doing they have made tremendous strides toward improving their condition and transforming America. But judging from the current situation, you all obviously didn't win. Why do you have such a small office, small staff, and from what I gather, an abysmal enrollment?"

"I admit, we've made mistakes in the past. A century ago we

were aware of declining enrollments and the assault on affirmative action, but we didn't have a very good strategy to deal with it. We thought building independent schools and independent institutions within established universities would be a base of support. But not many of our people responded; see, they're brainwashed and we need to set them straight. They need a trip to the East to see our heritage, to understand that we have a long tradition of learning dating back from Egyptian scientists to the Muslim clerics of West Africa. Modern Negroes are just . . . "

"Now hold on just a second, brother Musa," chimed in Dr. Legend. "Don't forget that black enrollment declined because we could no longer get into colleges; they dismantled all efforts to recruit people of color; used test scores against us; and cut out all financial aid. Now college is the preserve of the white minority."

"What happened to the black colleges" I inquired, "like Morehouse and Spelman and Morgan State?"

"You really want to know? Some became racially integrated colleges, the rest are behavior adjustment centers."

"Behavior adjustment?" The words struck me as both familiar and absurd. "Yes," Dr. Legend responded, "we'll talk about that later. At any rate, for the past three decades there have been fewer and fewer options for black high school grads. Even trade and technical schools have all but been abolished since there are no more trades to learn. Dr. Musa is right to say that the Africologists tried to establish independent schools for black folks, and it was a good strategy given the circumstances, but few could afford the tuition and those who could usually got their children into mainstream colleges."

"Running a school costs, you know," added Dr. Musa. "So does running a program—and time is money. I must bid you good day, sirs. Thanks for stopping by." Dr. Musa turned from us and stared coldly out the window. "You are quite fascinating," he murmured, "even if you are possessed with a limited late-twentieth-century understanding of the world. I wish you the best of luck readjusting to our society. Tuta o nana."

Dr. Legend gathered me up and together we walked next door to Stuart Hall, where the Program in Anti-Essentialist Black World Studies was housed. Instead of a single chair, the program was run by committee—each member representing a different voice, though the faculty was so small that certain individuals had to speak for multiple constituencies. Yet, everyone in the family of blackness was represented: Africans, West Indians, black Europeans, Afro-Canadians, black Pacific Islanders, women, men, gays, lesbians, ethnic and cultural hybrids, mulattoes, intellectuals, poor people, middle-class Negroes—you name it. Unfortunately, their vast and inclusive definition of blackness was not accompanied by vast office space. The program had one main office, four tiny faculty offices, and a copying machine which they shared with Africology. The walls were adorned with beautiful artwork and strikingly original posters. My favorite was from a conference titled, "She's a Bricolage House: Art, Desire, and Black Female Sexuality."

"Dr. Kelley, allow me to introduce you to Dr. Patricia Post; she's on faculty here in the program and holds the RuPaul Chair in Black Culture/Gender Studies." She was pleasant, though she looked tired and disheveled. As she explained to us, because of budget cuts, she and her colleagues had to teach overloads in order to cover the range of identities represented by the program. When I asked her if Dr. Musa's program offered some of these courses, she scoffed. "The Africologists have written off the majority of black folk, and they certainly have no interest in the less flattering and more complicated aspects of black life. Do you know their story? Let me tell you." She leaned toward me and began speaking in a low, conspiratorial tone.

"Those guys might be broke now, but during the turn of the century with the rise of the Gingrich regime, their predecessors, the

Afrocentrists, began getting huge government grants. Apparently, their militant defense of two-parent families, their judgments on homosexuality, their attacks on feminism, and their emphasis on tradition earned them support from the 'family values' conservatives. To be fair, not everyone under the banner of Afrocentrism advocated these conservative ideas, and the program directors felt rather uncomfortable taking money from an administration most African Americans opposed. Nevertheless, for a while there they were—as they used to say in the 1980s—'living large.' "

"Let's be honest," Dr. Legend interrupted. "Only a handful of Afrocentrists benefited back then, and most folks committed to an Afrocentric perspective—and there were many who did not always agree—bolted those government-funded programs in a hurry. Indeed, the institutions became a shell of their former selves, and once their faculty and student body left or started protesting, the money dried up. The state dropped them like a teenage welfare mother."

As Dr. Legend continued to speak, I recalled my own era, when the kind of scholarship Dr. Post promoted was hot and I, in my own way, was a part of it. "Things weren't so bad for the anti-essentialists in the nineties," I pointed out. "We had a real renaissance in black world studies: it was the age of diversity within black politics, representations, sexualities; the age when NBA referred to basketball *and* the New Black Aesthetic; the age of black snap queens and Clarence Thomas; the age when the Whitney Museum could organize an exhibit on black males and display Mapplethorpe's work and not invite hard-core black nationalist artists like the AfriCobra collective; the age of the black British invasion; when Paul Gilroy appeared in the *Chronicle of Higher Education*, Isaac Julien appeared on Black Entertainment Television's (BET) "Our Voices with Bev," and *The Black Atlantic* found a place on every hip person's bookshelf. It was an age when intellectuals and artists really exploded the cultural straitjacket that had been blackness in the past. Those were exciting times."

For a moment there, I was giddy with nostalgia; that is, until Dr. Post burst my bubble. "You are right; those were relatively good times if you never left the auditorium, conference room, or movie theaters where those issues were being discussed. And don't forget that, while black feminists were the wedge that opened up discussions of diversity within black communities, they were eased out real quick. Black males became the main subject and black male scholars became the primary voices. The issue of sexuality, for instance, which black women—lesbian and straight—put out on the table, became largely a black male issue. Even the black British invaders—they were men for the most part. O. K., except for Hazel Carby . . . but she is but one."

"I see. So what happened after that?" I asked.

"Like every other generation, black folks went out of style. The memoirs and films had become formulaic, and the really creative artists lost their foundation support with the new regime. Moreover, the really cutting-edge scholarship became less and less comprehensible to readers beyond a small circle of academics."

"That's true," added Dr. Legend, "but they also messed up by not drawing on and acknowledging earlier intellectual traditions. Sure, they were all into Du Bois and Hurston and the like—the usual suspects—but hardly anyone talked about Albert Murray. In the midst of the Black Power movement of the late sixties, Murray raised the issue of authenticity before some of the young lions of the 1980s and 1990s had sex for the first time. Dr. Post, can you bring up *The Omni-Americans* on the monitor? Yes, page ninety-seven."
Suddenly, a simulated voice of Albert Murray began to read:

> Being Black is not enough to make anybody an authority on U.S. Negroes, any more than being white has ever qualified anybody as an expert on the ways of U.S. white people. It simply does not follow that being white enables a Southern sheriff, for instance, even

a fairly literate one, to explain U.S. foreign policy, air power, automation, the atonality of Charles Ives, the imagery of Wallace Stevens, abstract expressionism, or even the love life of Marilyn Monroe.

If it did, then it would also follow that the oldest and blackest Negro around would be the most reliable source of information about Africa, slavery, Reconstruction politics, the pathological effects of oppression, the tactics and strategies of civil rights organizations, the blues, championship sports competition, and the symbolic function of the stud horse principle (and the quest for the earth-dark womb!) in interracial sexual relationships.[3]

"See what I'm saying!" shouted Dr. Legend. "You could go back further than that. How can anyone pick up a novel by Wallace Thurman or Countee Cullen or Zora and think black people had to wait till the 1980s to discover there was more than one way to be 'black.' Besides, if students had been steadily reading Benjamin Brawley, W. E. B. Du Bois, Amy Jacques Garvey, C. L. R. James, Eric Williams, Oliver Cox, or even Cedric Robinson, they would not have had to be told by Gilroy and others that black people—as labor, as thinkers, as bondsmen, as rebels—were central to the rise of the modern West. The difference between the work of your generation, Dr. Kelley, and that of, say, Du Bois and James, is that the former pretty much ignored political economy and reduced class to just another identity. It was as if scholars of your age wanted to study the construction of identities without exploring what these identities mean in terms of power and material access. As if identities have some kind of intrinsic meaning irrespective of specific structures of domination."

Dr. Legend's intervention struck a chord in me, evoking more memories of my own age and my own students. The growing interest in the politics of identity had contributed immensely to contemporary debates in black studies. It had successfully extended our analytical scope to overlooked or trivialized cultural spheres and had expanded our understanding of intellectual history. At the same time, the focus on identity had sometimes tended to leave discussions of power at the discursive level. Factors such as political economy, labor, and the state were too often missing from treatments of the African diaspora. More significantly, very few scholars of my era—exceptions being Cedric Robinson, John Higginson, Penny Von Eschen, Vincent Harding, Peter Linebaugh, perhaps others—situated black people in the larger world of revolutionary upheaval or paid attention to the role of black labor in both reproducing capitalism and destabilizing economies and regimes.

"You're quite right," I said to Dr. Legend. "In some respects it was liberal pluralism repackaged. While celebrating difference and hybridity, many of those same scholars chastised black people for believing in a core black culture or for insisting that there was such a thing as a single black community. Rather than examine why the notion of a black community continued to carry weight among lots of ordinary people, why appeals to racial solidarity continued to work, most anti-essentialists criticized black nationalists for being wrong and for trading in fictions. Not that I'm against criticism, but we need to begin where people are rather than where we'd like them to be."

"I don't disagree with either of you gentlemen," said Dr. Post. "We've learned a lot over the past century and we've made efforts to rectify the problems you've outlined. You especially know this, Dr. Legend, since you've taught in our program before. But it's been a hard row. Most of our grad students are still driven by identity politics and seem to always want to speak from his/her standpoint rather than see larger structures and transformations. See for yourself; drop in on Dr. Cannon's graduate seminar on the black body in servitude. In the meantime, I really must run. I have a meeting with the dean about getting our own copying machine."

We all walked out together; Dr. Post scurried down the hall and we headed upstairs to the seminar. Dr. Legend informed me that Dr. Cannon's course was once called "Slavery in the Antebellum

South" but students protested to have the name changed. Dr. Cannon, a crusty old historian who fought hard as a young scholar to break down disciplinary boundaries and to "invigorate" his discipline by promoting cultural studies, decided to throw his students off a bit by assigning an ancient text titled *Roll, Jordan, Roll: The World the Slaves Made.* (The students recognized the author as the late neoconservative theorist who served as top advisor for the Gingrich administration.) But Dr. Cannon didn't care about the author's politics; he still considered it a masterpiece of scholarly work on slavery—I mean, servitude.

"First of all," announced one of the first-year grads, "the book is too long. He could have said this in 150 pages. More importantly, the author says almost nothing about sexuality, and when he does he reveals his heterosexist biases. The master's obvious homoerotic desire for the black male body, for example, goes completely unexplored. After all, isn't this why they used chains and whips instead of other forms of punishment? They had other kinds of punitive technologies available to them—why chains and whips?"

"I don't know," added another young voice, "I think he's saying something about the interdependence of the slave and master—the construction of the master's identity is dependent on the slave and vice versa. I'm not too sure about that; they each have autonomous cultures, and within those cultures are a vast array of differences. If we just took the so-called slave community itself, how can we call it a community given distinctions by age, sex, sexual orientation, division of labor, skin color, etc. And when we take these factors into account, we can't talk about a uniform 'desire.' Desire is not only socially constructed but can only be understood through the individual psyche, for it manifests itself in a variety of different ways in different people."

"Hold on," interjected the aging professor. "I know this might sound absurd, but bear with me. Maybe the primary reason they enslaved these people was to work on the plantation. Maybe they're interdependent because the master's lifestyle depends on slaves picking cotton which is then sold on the market? Maybe the whips and chains were used to discipline the labor force?"

"What's with the crass economism, Dr. Cannon!? By emphasizing production over reproduction, you are privileging males and thus silencing black women's voices. . . ."

I had heard it all before; it reminded me so much of my own seminars past that I began to feel a bit homesick for 1997. Besides, for all the absurdity embodied in that exchange, from the ridiculously limited psychosexual reading of slavery to Dr. Cannon's unrestrained sarcasm, my students taught me that identity mattered. Scholarly discussions like these not only allowed them to grapple with their own multiple identities; in some respects they succeeded in humanizing the people they studied. By making slaves sexual beings, they cease to be just labor producing profits for the big house. Their interventions, then, were quite useful, so long as they avoided creating hierarchies among different identities and remained true to the historical moment of which they spoke.

Thinking about my students and colleagues made me a little queasy. Dr. Legend escorted me outside into the sunlit courtyard behind Stuart Hall, where I took a minute or two to rest. As it was already late afternoon and we had one last program to visit, we decided to get going as soon as possible. Unlike the programs in Africology and Anti-Essentialist Black World Studies, the Urban Underclass Institute had its own building and was located on the other side of campus. Indeed, W. J. Wilson Hall was spectacular—fifteen stories, red brick, huge picture windows in each office, lavish furniture. After the security guards frisked us, we proceeded to the main office on the twelfth floor where we were greeted by an army of secretaries and assistants.

"Dr. Thomas, there are two gentlemen here to see you. He'll be out in just a moment." A moment passed and out walked a clean-shaven, bespectacled man in his late forties, attired in an elegant tailor-made sharkskin gray suit. Dr. Legend stepped forward to make the formal introductions. "Dr. Kelley, this is the Institute's director, Dr. Souless Thomas; Dr. Thomas, meet Dr. Kelley."

"My pleasure, indeed. I read about you in Charles Murray's book. I don't agree with all of his assumptions, but he was a heck of a smart guy."

Suddenly, I felt very uncomfortable; I had an overwhelming desire to jump through the large bulletproof picture window behind his desk to see if it would lead me back to 1997. Dr. Legend probably sensed my discomfort but he did not make any gestures to leave. Instead he flashed a wide grin, letting me know that he found my suffering amusing.

"I have a million questions for you," announced Dr. Thomas. "What was it like in those days? Were you an affirmative action baby? Glad we got rid of that atrocious policy; too many of our people slid by in those days. Did Bill Clinton ever reveal his membership in the Republican Party? Did you ever run into the great thinkers of that era—Steele, Loury, Clarence Pendleton, Alan Keyes, Ken Hamblin? What was Clarence Thomas really like? You know I hold the Clarence Thomas chair in Economics, right?"

I thought I was going to throw up all over Dr. Thomas's $1500 wing tips. He not only brought out the worst in me, but he kept insisting on putting his arm around my shoulder as if we were old friends. I tried hard to be polite.

"I read about those people," I responded, "but never met any of them. Besides, that's all in the past. I'm very curious as to what you all do at the Urban Underclass Institute. When was it founded? Is it mainly a think tank, a research institution, do you teach classes here?"

"We train some graduate students, but we mainly conduct research on the underclass and develop government policy for dealing with this deviant population. We started out as a group of neoconservative black economists with similar research interests; the group then expanded into a full-fledged institute after we merged with the Department of Criminology and the School of Genetic Engineering. That, my friend, turned out to be a great move; we shifted from econometrics and regressions to applied technology."

"Applied technology? You mean in terms of actually creating jobs? Improving security? Providing better systems of transportation for urban residents? What do you mean?" I asked.

"Oh no!" He chuckled a bit, taken aback by the questions. "Nothing of the sort. By applied technology I'm speaking of behavior modification."

The way the words rolled out of his mouth . . . it was chilling, pure evil. When Dr. Legend first mentioned "behavior modification" centers, I thought he was half-joking, an inside reference to the ways historically black colleges emphasized deportment and manners. Or perhaps I had misunderstood him. Now it was all coming to light.

"You see," Dr. Thomas continued, "as we've been saying all along, what distinguishes the underclass from the rest of society is their behavior. By 'they,' however, I don't mean black people exclusively, though they are still in the majority; the underclass consists of Hispanics as well as whites, especially the growing number of refugees from the European ethnic wars. These people are dysfunctional in every respect—they're violent, nihilistic, grow up in deficient families, and have no desire to do an honest day's work. And before the abolition of welfare, they were addicted to the government dole. Soon after they were cut off, the crime rate skyrocketed. We turned to the most logical solution: since behavior was the problem we needed to figure out a way to change their behavior.

"At first, we tried compulsory national service. We sent young men and women from the inner cities (clearly the most criminal element) to work camps where specially trained staff tried to teach them the ways of civilization. It didn't work; they constantly complained and whined about the way they were treated, their pay, the food, the uniforms, the long hours, the discipline, the armed guards, the barbed wire. We then realized that true behavior modification requires some kind of physiological alteration. The answer was right in front of our eyes, locked away in the primitive simplicity of the frontal lobotomy. So, with the help of engineers and biochemists, we declared chemical warfare on the worst neighborhoods in the country. Through a combination of chemicals and high-frequency radio waves that the human ear cannot detect—you know how those people are; they have a thing for the low frequencies—we've discovered a method of altering the behavior of the poor. For the time being, the system is called Behavior Adjustment Technology, or BAT. Within minutes of experiencing BAT, they become kind, patient, forgiving, and passive. And their moral index has risen at least forty points. This method has turned the coldest homeboy into a model citizen—a better gentleman than myself, I might add. Ha, ha, ha! That's a good one. A better gentleman than myself. I must tell my wife that one."

I couldn't believe my ears. My anger turned to utter confusion; I became numb. "So, you've eliminated poverty?" I asked, searching desperately for some silver lining in this dark cloud of human manipulation.

"Eliminated poverty? What? Oh, no, Dr. Kelley. That was never our intent. If we solved the problem of poverty, what would we do for a living? But let's look on the bright side, my friend: they may be poor but they have wonderful dispositions. Right now, BAT is still experimental and has only been used in California. We're poised to implement BAT throughout the rest of the country, but our attorneys advised us to hold off for fear of being sued by the private security industry for taking away their livelihood."

Was this the world we helped create, either by our active participation or our silence? Were we so ill equipped politically and intellectually as to relinquish our basic right to humanity? What good are black studies, ethnic studies, cultural studies, any sort of humanistic studies in a world where our actions can be altered with the press of a button or a flip of a switch? If this was the fate of humanity, where were our scholars when it was time to respond?

My head began to tighten up, and the twelfth floor of Wilson Hall spun madly out of control. A dissonant cacophony of ringing cash registers and bloodcurdling screams grew louder and louder, becoming so unbearable it brought me to my knees, pulling me beneath the floorboards. Down, down, down I fell, into a vast, enveloping darkness, a pitch-black abyss . . .

"Robin, time to go. Wake up, it's show time. You don't want to disappoint the students." I knew that voice; it belonged to Wahneema Lubiano, the brilliant Duke University professor whose work on race and American culture has moved black studies to yet another level. Slowly I opened my eyes, afraid that I'd see nothing but darkness, or worse. To the contrary, I woke from my slumber to find that only a few minutes had passed, not the century of my nightmare. Before me stood the most beautiful sight I'd seen since the birth of my daughter. It was like the final scene in *Brother from Another Planet*. Dozens and dozens of men and women, intellectuals with the brilliance, vision, and political commitment to create a different future for black studies. Alongside Wahneema stood Patricia Williams, Kendall Thomas, Elizabeth Alexander, Nahum Chandler, Tera Hunter, Tricia Rose, Elsa Barkley Brown, Farah Jasmine Griffin, Craig Watkins—over there, Evelyn Hammonds and Evelyn Brooks Higginbotham, Earl Lewis, Kimberle Crenshaw, Sadiya Hartmann, Michael Eric Dyson, Rhonda Williams, Adam Green. Behind them stood Peter Linebaugh, Penny Von Eschen, Jerma Jackson, Philip Brian Harper, Guy Ramsey, George Lipsitz, Michael

Awkward, Charles Payne, Joe Trotter, Grant Farred; there was Gina Dent, and Brenda Stevenson, Tiffany Patterson, V. P. Franklin, Julie Saville, Michael Hanchard, Clarence Lusane, Denise Herd, Jerry Watts, bell hooks, Julius Scott, Kevin Gaines, Hazel Carby, Paul Gilroy, Dwight Andrews, Chana Kai Lee, Barbara Ransby, Sid Lemelle, Linda Reed, Adolph Reed, David Roediger, Tyler Stovall, David Anthony, Kobena Mercer; outside the Ivy walls stood Lisa Jones, Lisa Sullivan, James Spady, Greg Tate, Crystal Zook, Arthur Jafa, Joe Wood, Thelma Golden; poised in the background were dozens upon dozens of grad students bold enough to stand on the shoulders of our ancestors, elders, and mentors—Du Bois, Cox, Frazier, Herskovitz, Cayton, Drake, Allison Davis, Alaine Locke, Lorraine Wiliams, Charles Wesley, Dorothy Porter, Louise Kennedy, Anna Julia Cooper, John Hope Franklin, Carter Woodson, Walter Rodney, Baraka, Zora Neale Hurston, Leon Forrest, Gwendolyn Brooks, West, Morrison, Baker, Gates, Arnold Rampersad, Tom Holt, Darlene Clark Hine, Manning Marable, Mary Berry, Nell Painter, Nellie McKay, Robert Farris Thompson, Nathan Huggins, David Levering Lewis, Anthony Appiah, June Jordan, Hortense Spillers, Stuart Hall, ad infinitum. . . . Before me stood an endless sea of faces whose contributions to our work have been invaluable, faces gracious enough to forgive me for not mentioning their names and thoughtful enough to know that I am running out of space.

As I stand here, on the cusp of yesterday and tomorrow, looking out into the beautiful faces of my colleagues and future colleagues, I feel confident that the future of black studies African American studies/Africana studies, whatever we decide to call it, is secure and that there are enough sane, committed, brilliant intellectuals among us to put up a good fight against the right-wing, racist onslaught we now face. They will remain suspicious of liberal pluralism dressed up in postmodern garb, of analyses that completely ignore history or questions of power, of narrow identity politics that presumes people are the sum total of our academic categories, of the tendency to limit our critiques of people's actions to moral chastisement. And I know for a fact that these folks will continue to look b(l)ackward for sources of inspiration and insight, for it is only by looking back that we can make sense of where we are and how we got here. Knowing how we got here is essential if we ever hope to find the exit.

NOTES

INTRODUCTION

1 Quoted in Patricia Williams, *The Rooster's Egg: On the Persistence of Prejudice* (Cambridge: Harvard University Press, 1995), 6.

2 Dinesh D'Souza, *The End of Racism: Principles for a Multiracial Society* (New York: The Free Press, 1995), 24.

3 Richard Lynn, "Is Man Breeding Himself Back to the Age of the Apes?" *Times* (London), October 24, 1994, reprinted in *The Bell Curve: History, Documents, Opinions*, eds. Russell Jacoby and Naomi Glauberman (New York: Times Books, 1995), 356.

4 Peter N. Carroll, *It Seemed Like Nothing Happened: The Tragedy and Promise of America in the 1970s* (New York: Holt, Rinehart and Winston, 1982), 41.

5 Parliament, "Chocolate City," *Chocolate City*, Polygram Records, 1975.

6 Holly Sklar, *Chaos or Community? Seeking Solutions, Not Scapegoats for Bad Economics* (Boston: South End Press, 1995), 5–10, 55–56.

I: LOOKING FOR THE "REAL" NIGGA

1 John Langston Gwaltney, *Drylongso: A Self-Portrait of Black America* (New York: Random House, 1980), xix.

2 Mercer L. Sullivan, "Absent Fathers in the Inner City," *The Annals* 501 (January 1989): 49–50.

3 Recent proponents of a new "culture of poverty" thesis include Ken Auletta, *The Underclass* (New York: Random House, 1982); Nicholas Lemann, "The Origins of the Underclass: Part I," *Atlantic Monthly* 257 (June 1986): 31–61, and "The Origins of the Underclass: Part II," *Atlantic Monthly* 258 (July 1986): 54–68; Nicholas Lemann, *The Promised Land: The Great Black Migration and How It Changed America* (New York: Knopf, 1991); Charles Murray, *Losing Ground: American Social Policy, 1950–1980* (New York: Basic Books, 1984); and Lawrence Mead, *The New Dependency Politics: Non-Working Poverty in the U.S.* (New York: Basic Books, 1992). These works are quite distinct in scope, methods, and ideology from the pioneering studies of Oscar Lewis, who introduced the "culture of poverty" idea to American social science. Unlike the more recent works, he did not argue that poor people's behavior is the *cause* of their poverty. Rather, he insisted that capitalism impoverished segments of the working class, who were denied access to mainstream institutions. The culture they created to cope with poverty and disfranchisement was passed down through generations and thus led to passivity and undermined social organization. Lewis had no intention of using the culture-of-poverty thesis to distinguish the "deserving" from the "undeserving poor." See Oscar Lewis, *The Children of Sanchez* (New York: Random House, 1961)

and *La Vida: A Puerto Rican Family in the Culture of Poverty, San Juan and New York* (New York: Random House, 1966).

Critics of the culture-of-poverty thesis are many, and they do not all agree with each other as to the relative importance of culture or the causes of poverty. See especially Charles Valentine, *Culture and Poverty: Critique and Counter-Proposals* (Chicago: University of Chicago Press, 1968); Herbert J. Gans, "Culture and Class in the Study of Poverty: An Approach to Antipoverty Research," in *On Understanding Poverty: Perspectives from the Social Sciences*, ed. Daniel Patrick Moynihan (New York: Basic Books, 1968); Sheldon Danzinger and Peter Gottschalk, "The Poverty of *Losing Ground*," *Challenge* 28 (May–June 1985): 32–38; William Darity and Samuel L. Meyers, "Does Welfare Dependency Cause Female Headship? The Case of the Black Family," *Journal of Marriage and the Family* 46, no. 4 (1984): 765–79; and Mary Corcoran, Greg J. Duncan, Gerald Gurin, and Patricia Gurin, "Myth and Reality: The Causes and Persistence of Poverty," *Journal of Policy Analysis and Management* 4, no. 4 (1985): 516–36.

4 Michael Katz, "The Urban 'Underclass' as a Metaphor of Social Transformation," in *The Underclass Debate: Views from History*, ed. Michael Katz (Princeton, N.J.: Princeton University Press, 1993), 3–23.

5 The most prominent of the structuralists adopt some cultural explanation for urban poverty, suggesting that bad behavior is the outcome of a bad environment. William Julius Wilson's most recent work argues that the lack of employment has eroded the work ethic and discipline of the underclass, leading to behaviors that allow employers to justify not hiring them. See especially William Julius Wilson, *When Work Disappears: The World of the New Urban Poor* (New York: Knopf, 1996); William J. Wilson, *The Truly Disadvantaged: The Inner City, the Underclass, and Public Policy* (Chicago: University of Chicago Press, 1987); David T. Ellwood, *Poor Support: Poverty in the American Family* (New York: Basic Books, 1988); Elijah Anderson, *Streetwise: Race, Class, and Change in an Urban Community* (Chicago: University of Chicago Press, 1990); Elijah Anderson, "Sex Codes and Family Life among Poor Inner City Youth," *The Annals* 501 (January 1989): 59–78; Troy Duster, "Social Implications of the 'New' Black Underclass," *Black Scholar* 19 (May–June 1988): 2–9; Christopher Jencks, *Rethinking Social Policy: Race, Poverty, and the Underclass* (Cambridge: Harvard University Press, 1992); Mark S. Littman, "Poverty Areas and the Underclass: Untangling the Web," *Monthly Labor Review* 114 (March 1991): 19–32; Jacqueline Jones, *The Dispossessed: America's Underclasses from the Civil War to the Present* (New York: Basic Books, 1992); Douglas G. Glasgow, *The Black Underclass: Unemployment and Entrapment of Ghetto Youth* (New York: Random House, 1981); William Julius Wilson and Loic J. D. Wacquant, "The Cost of Racial and Class Exclusion in the Inner City," *The Annals* 501 (January 1989): 8–25; John D. Kasarda, "Caught in a Web of Change," *Society* 21 (November/December 1983): 41–47; John D. Kasarda, "Urban Industrial Transition and the Underclass," *The Annals* 501 (January 1989): 26–47; Maxine Baca Zinn, "Family, Race, and Poverty in the Eighties," *Signs* 14, no. 4 (1989): 856–74; Mary Corcoran, Greg J. Duncan, and Martha S. Hill, "The Economic Fortunes of Women and Children: Les-

sons from the Panel Study of Income Dynamics," *Signs* 10, no. 2 (1984): 232–48; Mary Jo Bane, "Household Composition and Poverty," in *Fighting Poverty: What Works and What Doesn't*, eds. Sheldon Danzinger and Daniel Weinberg (Cambridge: Harvard University Press, 1986); David Ellwood, *Poor Support* (New York: Basic Books, 1988); Barry Bluestone and Bennett Harrison, *The Deindustrialization of America* (New York: Basic Books, 1982); Richard Child Hill and Cynthia Negrey, "Deindustrialization and Racial Minorities in the Great Lakes Region, USA," in *The Reshaping of America: Social Consequences of the Changing Economy*, eds. D. Stanley Eitzen and Maxine Baca Zinn (Englewood Cliffs, N.J.: Prentice-Hall, 1989); Elliot Currie and Jerome H. Skolnick, *America's Problems: Social Issues and Public Policy* (Boston: Little, Brown and Co., 1984); Carl Nightingale, *On the Edge: A History of Poor Black Children and Their American Dreams* (New York: Basic Books, 1993); and Staff of *Chicago Tribune*, *The American Millstone: An Examination of the Nation's Permanent Underclass* (Chicago: Contemporary Books, 1986). While most of these authors focus on deindustrialization and the effects of concentrated poverty, Douglas S. Massey and Nancy A. Denton have argued that racial segregation is the key to explaining the persistence of black urban poverty. See their *American Apartheid: Segregation and the Making of the Underclass* (Cambridge: Harvard University Press, 1993).

6 Kathryn Edin, "Surviving the Welfare System: How AFDC Recipients Make Ends Meet in Chicago," *Social Problems* 38 (November 1991): 462–74.

7 Charles P. Henry, *Culture and African-American Politics* (Bloomington, Ind.: Indiana University Press, 1990), 12–13. Likewise, social philosopher Leonard Harris asks us to imagine what would happen if we used the same indices to study the "urban rich": "Suppose that their behavior was unduly helpful to themselves; say they rarely married, had more one-child families, were more likely than previous rich to be sexual libertines practicing safe sex, were health conscious, and were shrewd investors in corporate and ghetto property without moral reflection." Leonard Harris, "Agency and the Concept of the Underclass," in *The Underclass Question*, ed. Bill E. Lawson (Philadelphia: Temple University Press, 1992), 37.

8 Lee Rainwater, *Behind Ghetto Walls: Black Families in a Federal Slum* (Chicago: Aldine Publishing Co., 1970); Elliot Liebow, *Tally's Corner: A Study of Negro Streetcorner Men* (Boston: Little, Brown and Co., 1967); Ulf Hannerz, *Soulside: Inquiries into Ghetto Culture and Community* (New York: Columbia University Press, 1969); Carol B. Stack, *All Our Kin: Strategies for Survival in a Black Community* (New York: Harper and Row, 1974); Betty Lou Valentine, *Hustling and Other Hard Work: Life Styles in the Ghetto* (New York: Free Press, 1978); Joyce Ladner, *Tommorrow's Tommorrow: The Black Woman* (Garden City, N.Y.: Anchor, 1971); David Schulz, *Coming Up Black: Patterns of Ghetto Socialization* (Englewood Cliffs, N.J.: Prentice-Hall, 1969).

9 Stephen M. Joseph, ed., *The Me Nobody Knows: Children's Voices from the Ghetto* (New York: Avon Books, 1969); Caroline Mirthes and the Children of P.S. 15, *Can't You Hear Me Talking to You?* (New York: Bantam Books, 1971).

10 These typologies are drawn from Hannerz, *Soulside*; William McCord, John

Howard, Bernard Friedberg, Edwin Harwood, *Life Styles in the Black Ghetto* (New York: W. W. Norton, 1969).

11 Gwaltney, *Drylongso*, xxiv, xxxii.

12 James Clifford, "On Collecting Art and Culture," in *The Predicament of Culture: Twentieth-Century Ethnography, Literature, and Art* (Cambridge: Harvard University Press, 1988), 246. Don't get me wrong. The vast and rich ethnographic documentation collected by these scholars is extremely valuable because it captures the responses and survival strategies hidden from economic indices and illuminates the human aspects of poverty. Of course, these materials must be used with caution since most ethnographies do not pay much attention to historical and structural transformations. Instead, they describe and interpret a particular community during a brief moment in time. The practice of giving many of these communities fictitious names only compounds the problem and presumes that region, political economy, and history have no bearing on opportunity structures, oppositional strategies, or culture. For an extended critique, see Andrew H. Maxwell, "The Anthropology of Poverty in Black Communities: A Critique and Systems Alternative," *Urban Anthropology* 17, nos. 2 and 3 (1988): 171–92.

13 Charles Keil, *Urban Blues* (Chicago: University of Chicago Press, 1966), 1–12, 23.

14 Stack, *All Our Kin*; Ladner, *Tommorrow's Tommorrow*. This dichotomy also prevails in Anderson's more recent *Streetwise*.

15 Lee Rainwater, ed., *Soul* (Trans-Action Books, 1970), 9.

16 Rainwater, *Soul* (especially essays by John Horton, Thomas Kochman, and David Wellman); Ulf Hannerz, "The Significance of Soul" in *ibid.*, 15–30; Hannerz, *Soulside*, 144–58. For other interpretations of soul, see Keil, *Urban Blues*, 164–90; William L. Van Deburg, *New Day in Babylon: The Black Power Movement and American Culture, 1965–1975* (Chicago: University of Chicago Press, 1992), 194–97; Claude Brown, "The Language of Soul," in *Mother Wit from the Laughing Barrel: Readings in the Interpretation of Afro-American Folklore*, ed. Alan Dundes (New York: Garland Publishing Co., 1981), 232–43; and Roger D. Abrahams, *Positively Black* (Englewood Cliffs, N.J.: Prentice-Hall, 1970), 136–50.

17 Hannerz, "The Significance of Soul," 21.

18 Schulz, *Coming Up Black*, 78, 103; Rainwater, *Behind Ghetto Walls*, 372. See also John Horton, "Time and Cool People," in Rainwater, *Soul*, 31–50.

19 Hannerz, "The Significance of Soul," 22–23.

20 Robert L. Allen, *Black Awakening in Capitalist America: An Analytic History* (Garden City, N.Y.: Doubleday, 1969), 163; Van Deburg, *New Day in Babylon*, 201–2.

21 Van Deburg, *New Day in Babylon*, 201–2.

22 Lois Liberty Jones and John Henry Jones, *All about the Natural* (New York: Clairol, 1971).

23 Andrea Benton Rushing, "Hair-Raising," *Feminist Studies* 14, no. 2 (1988): 334; Jones and Jones, *All about the Natural*; Helen Hayes King and Theresa Ogunbiyi, "Should Negro Women Straighten Their Hair?" *Negro Digest* (August 1963): 68.

24 King and Ogunbiyi, "Should Negro Women Straighten Their Hair?" 69–70, 71.

25 Ibid., 67–68.

26 Rushing, "Hair-Raising," 334, 326.

27 Harold Cruse, *Rebellion or Revolution?* (New York: Morrow, 1968); Norman C. Weinstein, *A Night in Tunisia: Imaginings of Africa in Jazz (New York: Limelight Editions, 1993)*; Penny von Eschen, *Democracy or Empire: African Americans, Anti-Colonialism, and the Cold War* (Ithaca, N.Y.: Cornell University Press, 1997); Immanuel Geiss, *The Pan-African Movement* (London: Methuen and Co., 1974); Robert Weisbord, *Ebony Kinship: Africa, Africans, and the Afro-American* (Westport, Conn.: Greenwood Press, 1973); P. Olisanwuch Esedebe, *Pan-Africanism: The Idea and Movement, 1776–1963* (Washington, D.C.: Howard University Press, 1982).

28 Cruse, *Rebellion or Revolution?*, 73.

29 As Linda Roemere Wright's research reveals, ads and other images of Afrocoifed women in *Ebony* magazine declined around 1970, just as the number of images of black men with Afros was steadily rising. See Linda Roemere Wright, "Changes in Black American Hairstyles from 1964 through 1977, As Related to Themes in Feature Articles and Advertisements" (M.A. thesis, Michigan State University, 1982), 24–25.

30 Richard Majors and Janet Mancini Billson, *Cool Pose: The Dilemmas of Manhood in America* (New York: Lexington Books, 1992), 4.

31 Historian Roger Lane treats the dozens as a manifestation of a larger pathological culture: "Afro-American culture was marked by an aggressively competitive strain compounded of bold display, semiritualistic insult, and an admiration of violence in verbal form at least. 'Playing the dozens,' a contest involving the exchange of often sexual insults directed not only at the participants but at their families, especially their mothers, was one example of this strain." Lane, *Roots of Violence in Black Philadelphia, 1860–1900* (Cambridge: Harvard University Press, 1986), 146–47. See also Roger D. Abrahams, *Deep Down in the Jungle: Negro Narrative Folklore from the Streets of Philadelphia*, new ed. (Chicago: Aldine, 1970), 52–56; Herbert Foster, *Ribin', Jivin', and Playin' the Dozens* (Cambridge, Mass.: Ballinger, 1986); Thomas Kochman, *Black and White Styles in Conflict* (Chicago: University of Chicago Press, 1981), 51–58; Majors and Billson, *Cool Pose*, 91–101; and Nightingale, *On the Edge*, 26–28. There are some remarkable exceptions, such as the work of linguists, historians, literary scholars, and first-person practitioners, who treat the dozens as a larger set of signifying practices found in black vernacular culture or focus on the art and pleasures of verbal play. For these authors, the dozens is not merely a mirror of social relations. See Claudia Mitchell-Kernan, "Signifying, Loud-talking, and Marking," in *Rappin and Stylin' Out:*

Communication in Urban Black America, ed. Thomas Kochman (Urbana, Ill.: University of Illinois Press, 1972); H. Rap Brown, *Die, Nigger, Die* (New York: Dial, 1969); Geneva Smitherman, *Talkin' and Testifyin': The Language of Black America* (Boston: Houghton Mifflin Co., 1977), 128–33; Henry Louis Gates, Jr., *The Signifying Monkey: A Theory of African-American Literary Criticism* (New York: Oxford University Press, 1988), especially 64–88; and Houston Baker, *Long Black Song: Essays in Black American Literature and Culture* (Charlottesville, Va.: University Press of Virginia, 1972), 115. Despite disagreements between Baker and Gates, both try to make sense of black vernacular culture—including the dozens—as art rather than sociology. Although Lawrence Levine took issue with the functionalist approach to the dozens over fifteen years ago, he did not reject it altogether. He suggests that the dozens helped young black children develop verbal facility and learn self-discipline. See Lawrence Levine, *Black Culture and Black Consciousness: Afro-American Folk Thought from Slavery to Freedom* (New York: Oxford University Press, 1977), 345–58.

32 Levine, *Black Culture and Black Consciousness,* 357. A beginning is Marjorie Harness Goodwin, *He-Said-She-Said: Talk as Social Organization among Black Children* (Bloomington, Ind.: Indiana University Press, 1990), especially 222–23. However, Goodwin emphasizes "ritual insult" as a means of dealing with disputes rather than as an art form and thus is still squarely situated within social scientists' emphasis on function over style and pleasure.

33 Roger D. Abrahams, *Deep Down in the Jungle,* 60, 88–96; see also Roger D. Abrahams, *Talking Black* (Rowley, Mass.: Newbury House Publishers, 1976).

34 Schulz, *Coming Up Black,* 68. In McCord, et. al., *Life Styles in the Ghetto,* Edwin Harwood argues further that the lack of a father leads to violent uprisings and low self-esteem among black male youth: "Negro males who are brought up primarily by mothers and other female relatives pick up from them their hostility toward the males who are not there, or if they are, are not doing worth-while work in society. In such an environment it must be difficult to develop a constructive masculine self-image and the ambivalent self-image that does emerge can only be resolved in ways destructive both to the self and the society, through bold and violent activities that are only superficially masculine. If this analysis is correct, then the Negro youth who hurls a brick or an insult at the white cop is not just reacting in anger to white society, but on another level is discharging aggression toward the father who "let him down" and females whose hostility toward inadequate men raised doubts about his own sense of masculinity" (32–33).

35 Eugene Perkins, *Home Is a Dirty Street: The Social Oppression of Black Children* (Chicago: Third World Press, 1975), 32.

36 William Labov, *Language in the Inner City: Studies in the Black English Vernacular* (Philadelphia: University of Pennsylvania Press, 1972), 325. David Schulz, however, does not even trust the laughter of his subjects. He writes, "With careful listening one becomes suspicious of the laughter of the ghetto. So much apparent gaiety has a purpose all too often in the zero-sum contest

system of interpersonal manipulation for personal satisfaction and gain" (Schulz, *Coming Up Black*, 5).

37 See, for example, Venise T. Berry, "Rap Music, Self-Concept and Low Income Black Adolescents," *Popular Music and Society* 14, no. 3 (Fall 1990); Nightingale, *On the Edge*, 132–33, 162–63, 182–84; Wheeler Winston Dixon, "Urban Black American Music in the Late 1980s: The 'Word' as Cultural Signifier," *Midwest Quarterly* 30 (Winter 1989): 229–41; Mark Costello and David Foster Wallace, *Signifying Rappers: Rap and Race in the Urban Present* (New York: Ecco, 1990); and Andre Craddock-Willis, "Rap Music and the Black Musical Tradition: A Critical Assessment," *Radical America* 23, no. 4 (June 1991): 29–38. The case of Hip Hop might be unusual since social scientists working on the black urban poor have been conspicuously silent, leaving most of the discussion to music critics and cultural studies scholars. The result has been a fairly sophisticated body of work that takes into account both aesthetics and social and political contexts. See, for example, Tricia Rose, *Black Noise: Rap Music and Black Culture in Contemporary America* (Hanover, N.H.: Wesleyan University Press, 1994); Tricia Rose, "Black Texts/Black Contexts," in *Black Popular Culture*, ed. Gina Dent (Seattle: Bay Press, 1992), 223–27; Tate, *Flyboy in the Buttermilk*; Juan Flores, "Puerto Rican and Proud, Boy-ee!: Rap, Roots, and Amnesia," in *Microphone Fiends: Youth Music and Youth Culture*, ed. Tricia Rose and Andrew Ross (New York: Routledge, 1994), 89–98; William Eric Perkins, ed., *Droppin' Science: Critical Essays on Rap Music and Hip Hop Culture* (Philadelphia: Temple University Press, 1996); Joseph G. Eure and James G. Spady, *Nation Conscious Rap* (Brooklyn: P.C. International Press, 1991); James G. Spady, Stefan Dupree, and Charles G. Lee, *Twisted Tales in the Hip Hop Streets of Philadelphia* (Philadelphia: UMUM LOH Publishers, 1995); Brian Cross, *It's Not About a Salary . . . Rap, Race and Resistance in Los Angeles* (London: Verso, 1993); Michael Eric Dyson, *Reflecting Black: African-American Cultural Criticism* (Minneapolis: University of Minnesota Press, 1993); George Lipsitz, *Dangerous Crossroads: Popular Music, Postmodernism, and the Poetics of Place* (London: Verso, 1994); Jeffrey Louis Decker, "The State of Rap: Time and Place in Hip Hop Nationalism," *Social Text* 34 (1989): 53–84; Jonathan Scott, " 'Act Like You Know': A Theory of Hip Hop Aesthetics," (unpublished paper in author's possession, 1994); and S. H. Fernando, *The New Beats: Exploring the Music, Culture and Attitudes of Hip Hop* (New York: Anchor Books, 1994). Two good general histories are Steve Hager, *Hip Hop: The Illustrated History of Breakdancing, Rap Music, and Graffiti* (New York: St. Martin's Press, 1984); and David Toop, *Rap Attack 2* (London: Pluto Press, 1991).

38 Craddock-Willis, "Rap Music and the Black Musical Tradition," 37.

39 "Rockbeat," *Village Voice* 39, no. 4 (January 25, 1994): 76.

40 Tommy Lott, "Marooned in America: Black Urban Youth Culture and Social Pathology," in *The Underclass Question*, ed. Bill E. Lawson (Philadelphia: Temple University Press, 1992), 71, 72, 80–81.

41 Digital Underground's song "Good Thing We're Rappin,' " *Sons of the P*

(Tommy Boy Records, 1991) is nothing if not a tribute to the pimp narratives. One hears elements of classic toasts, including "The Pimp," "Dogass Pimp," "Pimping Sam," "Wicked Nell," "The Lame and the Whore," and perhaps others. Even the meter is very much in the toasting tradition. (For transcriptions of these toasts, see Bruce Jackson, *"Get Your Ass in the Water and Swim Like Me": Narrative Poetry from Black Oral Tradition* [Cambridge: Harvard University Press, 1974], 106–30.) Similar examples which resemble the more comical pimp narratives include Ice Cube, "I'm Only Out for One Thing," *AmeriKKKa's Most Wanted* (Priority Records, 1990) and Son of Bazerk, "Sex, Sex, and More Sex," *Son of Bazerk* (MCA Records, 1991).

42 Other examples include Capital Punishment Organization's aptly titled warning to other perpetrating rappers, "Homicide," *To Hell and Black* (Capitol Records, 1990); NWA's "Real Niggaz," *Efil4zaggin* (Priority Records, 1991); Dr. Dre's "Lyrical Gangbang," *The Chronic* (Deathrow/Interscope Records, 1992); Ice Cube's, "Now I Gotta Wet'cha," *The Predator* (Priority Records, 1992); Compton's Most Wanted's, "Wanted" and "Straight Check N' Em," *Straight Check N' Em* (Orpheus Records, 1991); as well as many of the songs on Ice Cube, *Kill at Will* (Priority Records, 1992); Ice T, *OG: Original Gangster* (Sire Records, 1991); Ice T, *Power* (Warner Bros., 1988); NWA, *100 Miles and Runnin'* (Ruthless Records, 1990). See also chapter 8 of my book *Race Rebels: Culture, Politics, and the Black Working Class* (New York: The Free Press, 1994).

43 Ice T [and the Rhyme Syndicate], "My Word is Bond," *The Iceberg/Freedom of Speech . . . Just Watch What You Say* (Sire Records, 1989); Ice Cube, "J. D.'s Gafflin,'" *AmeriKKKa's Most Wanted* (Priority Records, 1990). West Coast rappers also create humorous countercritiques of gangsterism, the most penetrating is perhaps Del tha Funkee Homosapien's hilarious, "Hoodz Come in Dozens," *I Wish My Brother George Was Here* (Priority Records, 1991).

44 See John Leland, "Rap: Can It Survive Self-Importance?" *Details* (July 1991): 108; Frank Owen, Hanging Tough," *Spin* 6, no. 1 (April 1990): 34; and James Bernard, "NWA [Interview]," *The Source* (December 1990): 34.

45 Quoted in Spady and Eure, *Nation Conscious Rap*, xiii, xxviii. On the early history of Hip Hop in New York, see Rose, *Black Noise*; Hager, *Hip Hop*; and Toop, *Rap Attack 2*.

46 Paul Willis, *Common Culture: Symbolic Work at Play in the Everyday Cultures of the Young* (Boulder, Colo.: Westview Press, 1990), 1–5, 65.

47 Cecil Brown, "James Brown, Hoodoo and Black Culture," *Black Review* 1 (1971): 184.

48 For insightful discussions of the way information technology in the late twentieth century opened up new spaces for building cultural links between black urban America and the African diaspora, see Lipsitz, *Dangerous Crossroads*; and Paul Gilroy, *The Black Atlantic: Modernity and Double-Consciousness* (Cambridge: Harvard University Press, 1993).

49 James Clifford, *The Predicament of Culture: Twentieth-Century Ethnography, Literature, and Art* (Cambridge: Harvard University Press, 1988), 246.

2: LOOKING TO GET PAID

1 Paul Gilroy, "One Nation under a Groove: The Culture Politics of 'Race' and Racism in Britain," in *Anatomy of Racism*, ed. David Theo Goldberg (Minneapolis: University of Minnesota Press, 1990), 274.

2 Nearly half of the unemployed in the 1980s were teenagers, and blacks and Latinos had the highest percentage. Terry Williams and William Kornblum, *Growing Up Poor* (Lexington, Mass.: D.C. Heath, 1985), 5–6.

3 Mike Davis, *City of Quartz: Excavating the Future of Los Angeles* (London: Verso, 1990), 304–7; Edward Soja, *Postmodern Geographies: The Reassertion of Space in Critical Social Theory* (London: Verso, 1989), 197, 201.

4 The idea that unemployed black youth turn to crime because it is more rewarding than minimum-wage, service-oriented work has been explored by a number of social scientists. See, for example, Richard B. Freeman, "The Relation of Criminal Activity to Black Youth Employment," in *The Economics of Race and Crime*, eds. Margaret C. Simms and Samuel L. Myers, Jr. (New Brunswick, N.J.: Transaction Books, 1988), 99–107; Llad Phillips and Harold Votey, Jr., "Rational Choice Models of Crimes by Youth," Ibid., pp. 129–87; Llad Phillips, H. L. Votey, Jr., and D. Maxwell, "Crime, Youth, and the Labor Market," *Journal of Political Economy* 80 (1972): 491–504; and Philip Moss and Chris Tilly, *Why Black Men Are Doing Worse in the Labor Market: A Review of Supply-Side and Demand-Side Explanations* (New York: Social Science Research Council Committee for Research on the Underclass, Working Paper, 1991), 90–93. For a discussion of the role of gangs in the illicit economy, see Martin Sanchez Jankowski, *Islands in the Street: Gangs and American Urban Society* (Berkeley, Calif.: University of California Press, 1991), 119–31. Despite the general perception that dealers make an enormous amount of money, at least one study suggests that the average crack peddler only makes about $700 per month. See Peter Reuter, Robert MacCoun, and Patrick Murphy, *Money for Crime: A Study of the Economics of Drug Dealing in Washington, D.C.* (Santa Monica, Calif.: Rand Drug Policy Research Center, 1990); and Davis, *City of Quartz*, 322.

5 Davis, *City of Quartz*, 244–51. For discussions of the ways in which the mass media depicts black youth gangs, violence, and the crack economy in inner city neighborhoods, see Jankowski, *Islands in the Street*, 284–302; Jimmie L. Reeves and Richard Campbell, *Cracked Coverage: Television News, the Anti-Cocaine Crusade, and the Reagan Legacy* (Durham, N.C.: Duke University Press, 1994); Herman Gray, "Race Relations As News: Content Analysis," *American Behavioral Scientist* 30, no. 4 (March-April, 1987): 381–96; Craig Reinarman and Harry G. Levine, "The Crack Attack: Politics and Media in America's Latest Drug Scare," in *Images of Issues: Typifying Contemporary Social Problems*, ed. Joel Best (New York: Aldine de Gruyter, 1989), 115–35; and Clarence Lusane, *Pipe Dream Blues: Racism and the War on Drugs* (Boston: South End Press, 1991).

6 Michael Gold, *Jews without Money* (New York: International, 1930), 42.

7 Cary Goodman, *Choosing, Sides: Playground and Street Life on the Lower East Side* (New York: Schocken Books, 1979), 9; and Nightingale, *On the Edge*, 15.

8 Jankowski, *Islands in the Street*, 119–31; Terry Williams, *Cocaine Kids: The Inside Story of a Teenage Drug Ring* (Reading, Mass.: Addison-Wesley, 1989); Jonathan Rieder, "Adventure Capitalism," *New Republic* 19 (November 1990): 36–40; and Philippe Bourgeois, "In Search of Horatio Alger: Culture and Ideology in the Crack Economy," *Contemporary Drug Problems* 16 (Winter 1989): 619–49.

9 Josh Sugarmann and Kristen Rand, "Cease Fire," *Rolling Stone Magazine* 677 (March 10, 1994): 31–42, quote on page 38. This is an excerpt from a report issued by the Violence Policy Center titled *Cease Fire: A Comprehensive Strategy to Reduce Firearms Violence* (Washington, D.C.: Violence Policy Center, 1994). See also Bruce C. Johnson, "Taking Care of Labor: The Police in American Politics," *Theory and Society* 3, no. 1 (1976): 106; Craig Wolff, "Guns Offer New York Teenagers a Commonplace Deadly Allure," *New York Times*, November 5, 1990; "Guns Take Ever Higher Toll among Young Blacks," *New York Times*, March 17, 1991; and Davis, *City of Quartz*, 240–48.

10 Davis, *City of Quartz*, chapter 4; Camilo José Vergara, "Our Fortified Ghettos," *The Nation* (January 31, 1994), 121, 122.

11 Jay S. Shivers and Joseph W. Halper, *The Crisis in Urban Recreational Services* (Rutherford, N.J.: Fairleigh Dickinson University Press, 1981), 77–79; Roy Rosenzweig and Elizabeth Blackmar, *The Park and the People: A History of Central Park* (New York: Henry Holt, 1994), 502. The increasing costs of policing public recreational facilities also contributed to the budget crisis (Shivers and Halper, *The Crisis*, 106, 248–61).

12 Much of this I learned by taking my four year old, Elleza, to these high-tech playgrounds. When we visited PlaySpace in December 1994, the employees refused to "buzz" me in at first, partly because they could not see Elleza through the window. When I picked her up and literally pointed to her, they allowed us to enter. For an interesting article about these pay-for-play spaces and the impact they are making on children's play in New York City, see Barbara Ensor, "Fun City," *New York Magazine* (October 24, 1994), 54–57. I should add that given the increasing workload of urban professionals, these "pay-for-play" spaces also offer inexpensive baby-sitting for older children.

13 Rosenzweig and Blackmar, *The Park and the People*, 508–9.

14 Goodman, *Choosing Sides*; David Nasaw, *Children of the City: At Work and at Play* (Garden City, N.Y.: Anchor Press, 1985); Amanda Dargan and Steve Zeitlin, *City Play* (New Brunswick, N.J.: Rutgers University Press, 1990), 136.

15 Houston Baker, *Black Studies, Rap, and the Academy* (Chicago: University of Chicago Press, 1993), 46–50; Robin D. G. Kelley, "Straight from Underground," *The Nation* 254, no. 22 (June 8, 1992): 793–96; Davis, *City of Quartz*, chapters 4 and 5; Rose, *Black Noise*, 106–14.

16 Nelson George, *Elevating the Game: Black Men and Basketball* (New York: HarperCollins, 1992), 200.

17 Spady and Eure, *Nation Conscious Rap*, 262; Michael A. Messner, *Power at Play: Sport and the Problem of Masculinity* (Boston: Beacon Press, 1992), 52;

see also Henry Louis Gates, Jr., "Delusions of Grandeur," *Sports Illustrated* (August 9, 1991): 78.

18 Steve James, Fred Marx, and Peter Gilbert, *Hoop Dreams* (New York: Kartemquit Films, 1994).

19 J. Hoberman, "Making It," *Village Voice* (October 18, 1994): 49; Messner, *Power at Play*, 45. Hoberman's essay is a review of *Hoop Dreams*.

20 Heidi Hartmann, "The Family as the Locus of Gender, Class, and Political Struggle: The Example of Housework," *Signs* 6 (Spring 1981): 366–94; Carolyn Steedman, *Landscape for a Good Woman: A Story of Two Lives* (New Brunswick, N.J.: Rutgers University Press, 1986), 13; Elizabeth Faue, "Reproducing the Class Struggle: Perspectives on the Writing of Working-Class History," paper presented at Social Science History Association Meeting, Minneapolis, October 19, 1990 (paper in author's possession), 8.

21 Dargan and Zeitlin, *City Play*, 157–61; Williams and Kornblum, *Growing Up Poor*, 77; June Goodwin, "Double Dutch, Double Dutch: All You Need is a Clothesline and Jet-Propelled Feet," *Christian Science Monitor*, October 7, 1980. See also Kyra Gaunt's brilliant dissertation, "The Games Black Girls Play: Music, Body, and 'Soul,'" (Ph.D. diss., University of Michigan, 1996).

22 As a boy "turner" in New York during the late 1960s and early 1970s, I remember vividly some of the accompanying songs and rhymes. My favorite was "Ain't your mama pretty / She got meatballs on her titties / She got scrambled eggs between her legs / Ain't your mama pretty." The most popular rhyme at that time went something like this: "——— and ——— sitting in a tree [any name will do] / K-I-S-S-I-N-G / First comes love / Then comes marriage / Here comes ——— with a baby carriage / How many babies did she have?" At that point the tempo would pick up and the other participants would count the number of times the jumper could skip without messing up. The final count, of course, equals the number of babies she and her boyfriend will have. For other examples, see Roger D. Abrahams, ed., *Jump-Rope Rhymes: A Dictionary* (Austin, Tex.: University of Texas Press, 1969); Gaunt, "The Games Black Girls Play"; Goodwin, *He-Said-She-Said*; and Bessie Lomax Hawes and Bessie Jones, ed., *Step It Down: Games, Plays, Songs, and Stories from Afro-American Heritage* (New York: Harper & Row, 1972).

23 Dargan and Zeitlin, *City Play*, 157, 160–61.

24 Willis, *Common Culture*, 1–5, 65.

25 On Larry Wright, see the film by Ari Marcopoulos and Maja Zrnic, *Larry Wright* (distributed by First Run Icarus Films, New York, 1990). I am basing some of my arguments here on my own observations in several U.S. cities. For a sensitive portrait of a young black homeless man in Washington, D.C. trying to make a living playing flute on the street, see Courtland Milloy, "Bittersweet Notes from the Street," *Washington Post*, October 3, 1985.

26 Unfortunately, there is very little written on Go-Go, so some of what I describe comes from my own observations and discussions with friends who grew up in Washington, D.C.—most notably, Marya McQuirter, a history graduate student at the University of Michigan. (I am grateful to Marya for

correcting a couple of errors in an earlier draft of this book.) Nevertheless, there are a few useful articles from the *Washington Post* which I consulted for this essay. See especially Richard Harrington, "Go-Go: A Musical Phenomenon, Bonding a Community," *Washington Post*, May 19, 1985; Michael Marriott, "Funky Sounds 'Bustin' Loose' in the District," *Washington Post*, October 5, 1984; and Courtland Milloy, "Go-Go Goes Across Town," *Washington Post*, July 15, 1985.

27 Harrington, "Go-Go."

28 Ibid.

29 Some important works on graffiti include Joe Austin, "Taking the Train: Youth Culture, Urban Crisis, and the 'Graffiti Problem' in New York City," (Ph.D. diss., University of Minnesota, 1996); Craig Castleman, *Getting Up: Subway Graffiti in New York* (Cambridge: MIT Press, 1982); Atlanta and Alexander, "Wild Style: Graffiti Painting," in *Zoot Suits and Second Hand Dresses: An Archaeology of Fashion and Music*, ed. Angela McRobbie (Boston: Unwin Hyman, 1988), 156–68; Martha Cooper and Henry Chalfant, *Subway Art* (New York: Holt, Rinehart, and Winston, 1984); Hager, *Hip Hop*; Ivor L. Miller, "Aerosol Kingdom: the Indigenous Culture of New York Subway Painters" (Ph.D. diss., Yale University, 1990); Rose, *Black Noise*, 41–47; and Jack Stewart, "Subway Graffiti: An Aesthetic Study of Graffiti on the Subway System of New York City, 1970–1978" (Ph.D. diss., New York University, 1989). On women aerosol artists, see especially Nancy Guevara, "Women Writin' Rappin' Breakin'" in *The Year Left 2*, ed., Mike Davis et al. (Verso Press: London, 1987), 160–75; and Rose, *Black Noise*, 43–44.

30 Austin, "Taking the Train," 118–75; Castleman, *Getting Up*, 117–25; Hugo Martinez, "A Brief Background of Graffiti," in *United Graffiti Artists Catalog* (n.p., 1975).

31 Quoted in Castleman, *Getting Up*, 131–32.

32 Ibid., 122–25; author conversation with St. Maurice, Staten Island, New York, January 1990.

33 Ivor Miller, "Guerrilla Artists of New York City," *Race & Class* 35, no. 1 (July–September 1993): 39; David Brendan Strasser, " 'It's the End of the World As We Know It (and I Feel Fine)': Keith Haring, Postmodern Hieroglyphics, Panic Hyperreality," (Ph.D., diss., Bowling Green State University, 1992); on the European art scene's fascination with graffiti, see Atlanta and Alexander, "Wild Style," 156–57; Kirk Varnedoe and Adam Gopnik, *High & Low: Modern Art, Popular Culture* (New York: Museum of Modern Art, New York, 1990), 337–82.

34 Austin, "Taking the Train," 186–327; Castleman, *Getting Up*, 126; author conversation with St. Maurice, Staten Island, New York, January 1990. I might add that because graffiti was one aspect of the larger Hip Hop culture, some writers, notably Freddy Brathwaite and Rammelzee, also produced and performed rap music. Brathwaite, known to the world as "Fab Five Freddy," did attend art school but went on to produce music videos, rap songs, and host the ever popular *Yo! MTV Raps*. Rammelzee rapped for a while (ap-

pearing in Charlie Ahearn's 1982 film *Wildstyle*) and eventually became a noted performance artist. See Atlanta and Alexander, "Wild Style," 158–62; and Rose, *Black Noise*, 194. The most extreme discussion of the transformation and commodification of graffiti can be found in Austin, "Taking the Train," chapter 6.

35 Quoted in Miller, "Guerrilla Artists," 39.

36 Joe Austin, "A Symbol that We Have Lost Control: Authority, Public Identity, and Graffiti Writing," (unpublished paper in author's possession).

37 On this last point, one need only look at the *New York Times Magazine*'s cover article on Basquiat in February 1985. As the physical embodiment of "primitivism" meets modernism, he appeared shoeless but with a shirt and tie. For other examples of Basquiat's body and lifestyle as spectacle, see Lorraine O'Grady, "A Day at the Races: On Basquiat and the Black Art World," *Artforum* 31 (April 1993): 10–12; "Jean-Michel Basquiat: Pop Life," *The Economist* 325 (November 21, 1992): 104–5; Martine Arnault, "Basquiat, from Brooklyn," *Cimaise* (November-December, 1989): 41–44; and Andrew Decker, "The Price of Fame," *Art News* 88 (January 1989): 96–101. On the problem of outsider/insider art and the question of boundaries, see the wonderful catalogue edited by Maurice Tuchman and Carol S. Eliel, *Parallel Visions: Modern Artists and Outsider Art* (Princeton, N.J.: Princeton University Press, 1992); and Michael D. Hall and Eugene W. Metcalf, Jr., *The Artist Outsider: Creativity and the Boundaries of Culture* (Washington, D.C.: The Smithsonian Institution Press, 1994).

38 On the early history of rap music, see Hager, *Hip Hop*; Rose, *Black Noise*; Bill Adler, *Rap: Portraits and Lyrics of a Generation of Black Rockers* (New York: St. Martin's Press, 1991); Nelson George et al., eds., *Fresh: Hip Hop Don't Stop* (New York: Random House, 1985); Spady and Eure, *Nation Conscious Rap*, xi-xxxi; Toop, *Rap Attack 2*; and Brian Cross, *It's Not about a Salary: Rap, Race, and Resistance in Los Angeles* (London: Verso, 1993). For more on the financial side of Hip Hop, see Clarence Lusane, "Rap, Race, and Politics," *Race & Class* 35, no. 1 (1993), 42–47; and Alan Light, "About a Salary or Reality?" *South Atlantic Quarterly* 90 (Fall 1991): 855–70.

39 Cross, *It's Not about a Salary*, 162–63, 145.

40 Ibid., 196–97. It is particularly interesting to contrast Dr. Dre's story with that of his former partner, Eazy E (aka Eric Wright). Easy's more publicized version of NWA's origins suggests that drug money was used to capitalize NWA's initial productions—a narrative that reinforces the idea that "authentic" gangsta rappers have criminal backgrounds. See David Mills, "The Gangsta Rapper: Violent Hero or Negative Role Model?" *The Source* (December 1990): 32; Dan Charnas, "A Gangsta's World View," *The Source* (Summer 1990): 21–22; "Niggers with Attitude," *Melody Maker* 65, no. 44 (November 4, 1989): 33; Frank Owen, "Hanging Tough," *Spin* 6, no. 1 (April 1990): 34.

41 Rose, *Black Noise*; Guevara, "Women Writin' Rappin' Breakin'"; Dan Cox, "Brooklyn's Furious Rockers: Break Dance Roots in a Breakneck Neighbor-

hood," *Dance Magazine* 58 (April 1984): 79–82; Hager, *Hip Hop*; Peter J. Rosenwald, "Breaking Away '80s Style," *Dance Magazine* 58, no. 4 (April 1984): 70.

42 Quoted in Cox, "Brooklyn's Furious Rockers," 81. Much has been written on injuries caused by break dancing. For a sample, see Ronald Wheeler and Rodney Appell, "Differential Diagnosis of Scrotal Pain After Break Dancing," *The Journal of the American Medical Association* 252 (December 28, 1984): 3336; Philip J. Goscienski and Louis Luevanos, "Injury Caused by Break Dancing," *The Journal of the American Medical Association* 252 (December 28, 1984): 3367; Robert A. Norman and Michael Grodin, "Injuries from Break Dancing," *American Family Physician* 30 (October 1984): 109–112; and Kui-Chung Lee, "Intracerebral Hemorrhage after Break Dancing," *The New England Journal of Medicine* 323 (August 30, 1990): 615–16.

43 Rose, *Black Noise*, 48, 50; Sally Banes, "Breaking Is Hard to Do," *Village Voice*, April 22–28, 1981: 31–33.

44 Dan Cox, "Brooklyn's Furious Rockers," 79.

45 Rosenwald, "Breaking Away '80s Style," 73–74.

46 Rose, *Black Noise*, 50; and on the training of professional dancers in break-dance techniques, see Joyce Mollov, "Getting the Breaks," *Ballet News* 6 (August 1984): 14–19; Margaret Pierpont, "Breaking in the Studio," *Dance Magazine* 58 (April 1984): 82.

47 The best discussion of women's involvement as Hip Hop artists can be found in Rose, *Black Noise*, especially chapter 5. See also Toop, *Rap Attack 2*, 93–95; and Guevara, "Women Writin' Rappin' Breakin,'" 160–75. Most of the work on women and rap focuses on representations of women or female rappers' representations of sexuality rather than their actual participation as artists or producers.

48 I am especially grateful to Wahneema Lubiano for helping me think through the valuing or devaluing of women's sexuality in relationship to the market. For examples of the celebration of the pimp in literature and popular culture, see Iceberg Slim [Robert Beck], *Pimp: The Story of My Life* (Los Angeles: Holloway House, 1969); Christina Milner and Richard Milner, *Black Players: The Secret World of Black Pimps* (New York: Little, Brown and Co., 1972). On the pimp in popular film, see Donald Bogle, *Toms, Coons, Mulattoes, Mammies and Bucks: An Interpretive History of Blacks in American Films*, new ed. (New York: Continuum, 1989), 234–42; Daniel Leab, *From Sambo to Superspade: The Black Experience in Motion Pictures* (Boston: Houghton Mifflin, 1975); David E. James, "Chained to Devilpictures: Cinema and Black Liberation in the Sixties," in Davis et al., *The Year Left 2*, 125–38; Brown, *Die, Nigger, Die*; Bobby Seale, *Seize the Time* (New York: Random House, 1970) and *Lonely Rage* (New York: Times Books, 1978) in which Seale himself takes on the characteristics of a pimp; and Eldridge Cleaver, *Soul on Ice* (New York: McGraw-Hill, 1968).

49 For a vivid and detailed description of black teenage prostitutes and pimps

during the 1970s and 1980s, see Williams and Kornblum, *Growing Up Poor*, 62–63.

50 My thinking here owes a great deal to Tera Hunter's *To 'Joy My Freedom: Southern Black Women's Lives and Labors After the Civil War* (Cambridge: Harvard University Press, 1997), esp. chapters 7 and 8; Kathy Peiss, *Cheap Amusements: Working Women and Leisure in Turn-of-the-Century New* (Philadelphia: Temple University Press, 1986); Hazel Carby, "Policing the Black Woman's Body in an Urban Context," *Critical Inquiry* 18 (Summer 1992): 738–55; Victoria Wollcott, "Remaking Respectability: African American Women and the Politics of Identity in Interwar Detroit" (Ph.D. diss., University of Michigan, 1995).

51 Williams and Kornblum, *Growing Up Poor*, 65–66.

52 Ibid., 66, 69.

53 Goodman, *Choosing Sides*, 28.

3 : LOOKING BACKWARD

1 "The Revolutionary Communist League (MLM) and the League of Revolutionary Struggle (M-L) Unite!" *Forward: Journal of Marxism-Leninism-Mao Zedong Thought* 3 (January 1980): 103.

2 "Minister Louis Farrakhan Calls for One Million Man March," *Final Call*, December 14, 1994; Dinesh D'Souza, *The End of Racism: Principles for a Multiracial Society* (New York: The Free Press, paperback edition), xxxi. A copy of the oath, which Farrakhan read at the march, is available through the Nation of Islam's home page on the World Wide Web. For more on the Million Man March and Farrakhan's conservative political agenda, see Patricia J. Williams, "Different Drummer Please, Marchers!" *The Nation* 261, no. 14 (October 30, 1995): 493; Hanes Walton, Jr., "Public Policy Responses to the Million Man March," *Black Scholar* 25 , no. 4 (1995): 17–25; Geneva Smitherman, "A Womanist Looks at the Million Man March," in *Million Man March Day of Atonement: A Commentary*, eds. Haki Madhubuti and Maulana Karenga (Chicago, Third World Press and University of Sankore Press, 1996), 104–7; and Sundiata Keita Cha-Jua and Clarence Lang, "Providence, Patriarchy, Pathology: Louis Farrakhan's Rise and Decline," *New Politics* 6, no. 2 (1997): 47–71.

3 Peter Schrag, "Backing off Bakke: The New Assault on Affirmative Action," *The Nation* 262, no. 16 (April 22, 1996): 11–14; Elaine R. Jones, "Race and the Supreme Court's 1994–95 Term," in *The Affirmative Action Debate*, ed. George E. Curry (Reading, Mass.: Addison-Wesley, 1996), 146–56; Stephen Steinberg, *Turning Back: The Retreat from Racial Justice in American Thought and Policy* (Boston: Beacon, 1995), 175.

4 Betty Reid Mandell, "Downsizing the Welfare State," *New Politics* 6, no. 2 (Winter 1997): 33–38; Ruth Coniff, "Welfare, Ground Zero: Michigan Tries to End It All," *The Nation* (May 27, 1996): 16–20; Rachel Melcer, "Elderly Immigrants Face Loss of Benefits," *Chicago Tribune*, March 2, 1997; Clifford Levy, "Welfare and the Working Poor," *New York Times*, November 17, 1996;

Carla Rivera, "Mothers Pressed into Battle for Child Support," *Los Angeles Times*, March 24, 1997; Jocelyn Stewart, "For Thousands of Children Aid Rides on a Definition," *Los Angeles Times*, October 17, 1996; Barbara Vobejda, "Cutoffs Start Today for Food Stamps: New Welfare Law Hits Jobless Adults," *Washington Post*, February 22, 1997; Robert A. Rosenblatt, "Welfare Law Will Exclude 135,000 Disabled Children," *Los Angeles Times*, February 7, 1997. For general background on the race and gender politics of welfare, see Mimi Abramowitz, *Regulating the Lives of Women: Social Welfare Policy from Colonial Times to the Present* (Boston: South End Press, 1988); Michael Katz, *In the Shadow of the Poorhouse: A Social History of Welfare in America* (New York: Basic Books, 1986); Michael Katz, *The Undeserving Poor: From the War on Poverty to the War on Welfare* (New York: Pantheon Books, 1990); Frances Fox Piven, *The New Class War: Reagan's Attack on the Welfare State and Its Consequences* (New York: Pantheon Books, 1982); Linda Gordon, ed., *Women, the State, and Welfare* (Madison, Wisc.: University of Wisconsin Press, 1990); Gwendolyn Mink, *The Wages of Motherhood: Inequality in the Welfare State, 1917–1942* (Ithaca, N.Y.: Cornell University Press, 1995); and James T. Patterson, *America's Struggle against Poverty, 1900–1985* (Cambridge: Harvard University Press, 1986).

5 Joe Sexton, "Discontented Workfare Laborers Murmur 'Union,'" *New York TImes*, September 27, 1996; Mandell, "Downsizing the Welfare State," 41; Coniff, "Welfare, Ground Zero," 16–20; Justin Blum, "Welfare Recipients Can't Survive on Wages in County: Social Services Chief Tells Board Poor Need to Move Up Pay Scale," *Washington Post*, March 5, 1997; Paul Freese, Jr., "Perspectives on Welfare: Mugging People Who Have Nothing; General Relief Recipients Are Mostly Unemployable But They Do Work for Their $212 a Month," *Los Angeles Times*, January 17, 1997. The fact is, most welfare recipients must supplement their transfer payments with either wage work or barter in order to survive. See Kathryn Edin, "Surviving the Welfare System: How AFDC Recipients Make Ends Meet in Chicago," *Social Problems* 38 (Nov. 1991): 462–74.

6 Bettina Boxall, "How Fair Is Workfare? Welfare: Rapid Expansion of Programs Raises New Questions about the Rights of Participants," *Los Angeles Times*, March 9, 1997; Sexton, "Discontented Workfare Laborers Murmur 'Union'"; and Mandell, "Downsizing the Welfare State," 41–43.

7 Sexton, "Discontented Workfare Laborers Murmur 'Union'"; and Mandell, "Downsizing the Welfare State," 41–43.

8 Dorothy Height, "Self-Help—A Black Tradition," *The Nation* (July 24/31, 1989): 136.

9 C. Eric Lincoln, *The Black Muslims in America*, 2d ed. (Boston: Beacon Press, 1973), 142.

10 Lincoln, *Black Muslims in America*, 26; see also Claude Andrew Clegg, III, *An Original Man: The Life and Times of Elijah Muhammad* (New York: St. Martin's Press, 1997), 110–19.

11 Ernest Allen, Jr., "Religious Heterodoxy and Nationalist Tradition: The Con-

tinuing Evolution of the Nation of Islam," in *New Movements and Trends in the World of Islam*, ed. Peter B. Clarke (London: Curzon, forthcoming); John Woodford, "Testing America's Promise of Free Speech: *Muhammad Speaks* in the 1960s, A Memoir," *Voices of the African Diaspora* 7 (Fall 1991): 3–16.

12 See Clegg, *Original Man*, 269–84; and Joseph D. Eure and Richard M. Jerome, eds., *Back Where We Belong: Selected Speeches by Minister Louis Farrakhan* (Philadelphia: P.C. International Press, 1989), 83–110. The NOI's conservatism runs even deeper than mere advocacy of family values and black capitalism. For several years now, the NOI has held joint rallies with Lyndon LaRouche, a former Trostskyist turned fascist whose ideas about the inferiority of Asians, Jews, Latinos, and African Americans are legion. LaRouche not only supported the apartheid regime in South Africa but his top security advisor, Roy Frankhauser, was closely linked with various white supremacist organizations. Yet, LaRouche has been able to forge alliances with conservative black leaders, including Farrakhan, Roy Innis of the Congress of Racial Equality, and Hulan Jack, ex-borough president of Manhattan and an important figure in the New York Democratic Party. Most recently, Farrakhan and Ben Chavis, Jr., invited LaRouche to address the National African American Leadership Summit meeting in St. Louis in September 1996. See Chip Berlet and Joel Bellman, "Lyndon Larouche: Fascism Wrapped in an American Flag," *A Political Research Associates Briefing Paper* (March 10, 1989); Clarence Lusane, *African Americans at the Crossroads: The Restructuring of Black Leadership and the 1992 Elections* (Boston: South End Press, 1994), 60–61; and Clarence Lusane, "The Far Right Goes after Black Support," *Covert Action Information Bulletin* (Spring 1987), 50–52.

13 Eure and Jerome, *Back Where We Belong*, 158.

14 Adolph Reed, Jr., "All for One and None for All," *The Nation* (January 28, 1991): 87.

15 Eure and Jerome, *Back Where We Belong*, 203; Stokely Carmichael and Charles V. Hamilton, *Black Power: The Politics of Liberation in America* (New York: Vintage Books, 1967).

16 David R. Francis, "A Black Economist Critiques Old-Style Affirmative Action," *Christian Science Monitor*, April 3, 1992.

16 While still unconvinced that affirmative action policies are an effective remedy to racial inequality, in a recent essay Loury admits that the state has a role to play in helping the black poor of the inner cities make up for the lack of social capital. Nevertheless, he still strongly advocates a "color blind" policy that eliminates any racial preferences and that would enable all people to compete on the basis of equal opportunity. See Glen C. Loury, "Performing Without a Net," in Curry, ed., *The Affirmative Action Debate*, 49–64.

17 For more on the conservative advocates of "personal responsibility," see Martin Carnoy, *Faded Dreams: The Politics and Economics of Race in America* (Cambridge: Cambridge University Press, 1994), 33–39; Lisa L. Jones-Granderson, "On the Right Side?" *Afro-American*, October 23, 1993; Playthell Benjamin, "GOP Goes the Weasel," *Village Voice* 36, no. 34 (August

20, 1991): 41–43; Doug Ireland, "The 'Black Conservative' Con: Alan Keyes Does the Hustle," *The Nation* 261, no. 14 (October 30, 1995): 500–503; Thomas Sowell, *Preferential Policies: An International Perspective* (New York: William Morrow, 1990); Shelby Steele, *Content of Our Character: A New Vision of Race in America* (New York: St. Martin Press, 1990); Joseph Perkins, ed. *A Conservative Agenda for Black Americans* (Washington, D.C.: Heritage Foundation, 1987).

18 Steven A. Holmes, "Propaganda Machine," *Emerge* 7, no. 10 (September 1996): 60. See also Annette Fuentes, "Behind the Lines," *Village Voice* 41, no. 43 (October 22, 1996): 28–29; Clint Bolick, *Changing Course: Civil Rights at the Crossroads* (New Brunswick, N.J.: Transaction Books, 1988); Clint Bolick, *Unfinished Business: A Civil Rights Strategy for America's Third Century* (San Francisco: Pacific Research Institute for Public Policy, 1990); Clint Bolick, *The Affirmative Action Fraud: Can We Restore the American Civil Rights Vision?* (Washington, D.C.: Cato Institute, 1996).

19 Robert L. Woodson, "Personal Responsibility," in Curry, ed., *The Affirmative Action Debate*, 111–19; Holmes, "Propaganda Machine," 61; Jean Stefancic and Richard Delgado, *No Mercy: How Conservative Think Tanks and Foundations Changed America's Social Agenda* (Philadelphia: Temple University Press, 1996), 54. The debate over "racial preferences" has produced an avalanche of literature in the past few years, most of it attacking affirmative action policies. For more recent examples, see Thomas Sowell, *Civil Rights: Rhetoric or Reality?* (New York: Quill, 1984); Steven Yates, *Civil Wrongs: What Went Wrong with Affirmative Action* (San Francisco: Institute for Contemporary Studies, 1994); Darien A. McWhirter, *The End of Affirmative Action: Where Do We Go from Here?* (New York: Carol Pub. Group, 1996); Terry Eastland, *Ending Affirmative Action: The Case For Colorblind Justice* (New York: Basic Books, 1996); Carl Cohen, *Naked Racial Preference* (Lanham, Md.: Madison Books, 1995); Paul Craig Roberts and Lawrence M. Stratton, *The New Color Line: How Quotas and Privilege Destroy Democracy* (Washington, D.C.: Regnery Pub., 1995). Recent defenders of affirmative action include Albert G. Mosley and Nicholas Capaldi, *Affirmative Action: Social Justice or Unfair Preference?* (Lanham, Md.: Rowman & Littlefield Publishers, 1996); Bryan K. Fair, *Notes of a Racial Caste Baby: Color Blindness and the End of Affirmative Action* (New York: New York University Press, 1997); Gertrude Ezorsky, *Racism and Justice: The Case for Affirmative Action* (Ithaca, N.Y.: Cornell University Press, 1991); Charles R. Lawrence III and Mari J. Matsuda, *We Won't Go Back: Making the Case for Affirmative Action* (Boston: Houghton Mifflin, 1997); Barbara R. Bergmann, *In Defense of Affirmative Action* (New York: Basic Books, 1996); and Ellis Cose, *Color-Blind: Seeing beyond Race in a Race-Obsessed World* (New York: HarperCollins Publishers, 1997).

20 Dorothy Roberts, "The Value of Black Mothers' Work," *Radical America* 26, no. 1 (August 1996): 10.

21 George Lipsitz, "The Possessive Investment in Whiteness: Racialized Social Democracy and the 'White' Problem in American Studies," *American Quarterly* 47, no. 3 (1995): 377; Douglas S. Massey and Nancy A. Denton, *American

Apartheid: Segregation and the Making of the Underclass (Cambridge: Harvard University Press, 1993), 54, 105–8; Kenneth T. Jackson, "Race, Ethnicity, and Real Estate Appraisal: The Home Owners' Loan Corporation and the Federal Housing Administration," *Journal of Urban History* 6 (1980): 419–52.

22 Melvin Oliver and Thomas Shapiro, *Black Wealth/White Wealth: A New Perspective on Racial Inequality* (New York: Routledge, 1995), 106, 109.

23 Ruth Rosen, "Who Gets Polluted?" *Dissent* 41, no. 2 (Spring 1994): 223–30; Robert Bullard, *Dumping in Dixie: Race, Class, and Environmental Quality* (Boulder, Colo.: Westview Press, 1990); Commission for Racial Justice, United Church of Christ, *Toxic Wastes and Race in the United States: A National Report on the Racial and Socio-Economic Characteristics of Communities with Hazardous Waste Sites* (New York: Public Data Access, 1987); Lipsitz, "Possessive Investment in Whiteness," 369–87.

24 Phillip Clay, "Housing Opportunity: A Dream Deferred," in *The State of Black America 1990*, ed. Janet Dewart (New York: National Urban League, 1990), 73–84; Carnoy, *Faded Dreams*, 150–171; Gerald Gill, *Meanness Mania: The Changed Mood* (Washington, D.C.: Howard University Press, 1980), 57–62; William Goldsmith and Edward Blakely, *Separate Societies* (Philadelphia: Temple University Press, 1992), 155. HUD has not fared much better under the Clinton administration. See James Ledbetter, "HUD's Demolition Man," *Village Voice* 40, no. 6 (February 7, 1995): 17; Anthony Freedman, "Clinton Dooms HUD," *National Law Journal* 17, no. 28 (March 13, 1995): A23–A24; Peter Valdes-Dapena, "Budget Cuts Will Have Devastating Effect on HUD and the Poor," *Crisis* 102, no. 4 (May 1995): 28–30.

25 Oliver and Shapiro, *Black Wealth/White Wealth*, 90.

26 Carnoy, *Faded Dreams*, 162–63.

27 Barry Bluestone and Bennett Harrison, *The Deindustrialization of America: Plant Closings, Community Abandonment, and the Dismantling of Basic Industry* (New York: Basic Books, 1982), 42, 25–48.

28 Mandell, "Downsizing the Welfare State," 40; see also David Corn, "The Fix Ain't In," *The Nation* (October 7, 1996): 5; Christopher D. Cook, "Texas Move to Privatize State Welfare Programs Draws Fire on Welfare Reform's Cusp," *Christian Science Monitor*, March 20, 1994; Ernest Holsendolph, "Lockheed and Others Eager to Run Welfare Programs," *Atlanta Journal Constitution*, February 9, 1997; Dave Lesher, "Privatization Emerges as New Welfare Option," *Los Angeles Times*, January 27, 1997.

29 Statistics are from Holly Sklar, *Chaos or Community?*, 119–21. On the rate and cost of incarceration, see Marc Mauer, *Americans Behind Bars: The International Use of Incarceration, 1992–1993* (Washington, D.C.: The Sentencing Project, 1994); James Jennings, "Race, Class, and Incarceration: The Political Economy of Prisons," *The NOBO Journal of African-American Dialogue (special issue: Black Prison Movements USA)* 2, no. 1 (Chicago: Africa World Press, 1995), 108–24.

30 Joseph Epstein, "Wackenhut and CCA: Convicts R Us," *Financial World*, March 25, 1996; "Prison Facilities Acquired for Close to $30 Million," *Wall*

Street Journal, August 22, 1995; "Wackenhut Gets Contract," *Wall Street Journal*, December 22, 1995; Linda Sandler, "Corrections Corp.'s Shares Are Causing a Stir: Are They Headed for Lockup or Breakout?" *Wall Street Journal*, June 3, 1996; "The Prison Boom," *The Nation* 260, no. 7 (February 20, 1995): 223–24; and Randy Gragg, "A High-Security, Low-Risk Investment: Private Prisons Make Crime Pay," *Harpers* 293 (August 1995); 51.

31 Michael Kroll quoted in Jennings, "Race, Class and Incarceration," 113; Gragg, "A High-Security, Low-Risk Investment," 50; see also Mike Davis, "A Prison-Industrial Complex: Hell Factories in the Field," *The Nation* 260, no. 7 (February 20, 1995); 229–33; Mick Ryan and Tony Ward, *Privatization and the Penal System: The American Experience and the Debate in Britain* (Philadelphia: Open University Press, 1989); Gary W. Bowman, Simon Hakim, Paul Seidenstat, eds., *Privatizing Correctional Institutions* (New Brunswick, N.J.: Transaction Publishers, 1993).

32 Gragg, "A High Security, Low-Risk Invetment," 50.

33 Michael Tonry, *Malign Neglect: Race, Crime, and Punishment in America* (New York: Oxford University Press, 1995); see also Elihu Rosenblatt, ed., *Criminal Injustice: Confronting the Prison Crisis* (Boston: South End Press, 1996); John Irwin and James Austin, *It's about Time: America's Imprisonment Binge* (Belmont, Calif.: Wadsworth Pub. Co., 1994); Franklin E. Zimring and Gordon Hawkins, *The Scale of Imprisonment* (Chicago: University of Chicago Press, 1992).

34 James Jennings, "Race, Class, and Incarceration," 111; Sklar, *Chaos or Community?*, 119–33; Jimmie L. Reeves and Richard Campbell, *Cracked Coverage: Television News, The Anticocaine Crusade, and The Reagan Legacy* (Durham, N.C.: Duke University, 1994); Herman Gray, "Race Relations as News: Content Analysis," *American Behavioral Scientist* 30, no. 4 (March–April, 1987): 381–96; Craig Reinarman and Harry G. Levine, "The Crack Attack: Politics and Media in America's Latest Drug Scare," in Joel Best, ed., *Images of Issues: Typifying Contemporary Social Problems* (New York: Aldine de Gruyter, 1989), 115–35; Clarence Lusane, *Pipe Dream Blues: Racism and the War on Drugs* (Boston: South End Press, 1991).

35 Jennings, "Race, Class, and Incarceration," 109.

36 Oliver and Shapiro, *Black Wealth/White Wealth*, 169.

37 Gwaltney, *Drylongso*, 123.

38 W. E. B. Du Bois, *Black Reconstruction in America: An Essay Toward a History of the Part Which Black Folk Played in the Attempt to Reconstruct Democracy, 1860–1880* (New York: Harcourt, Brace, 1935), 30.

39 Quoted in Holly Sklar, *Chaos or Community?*, 170.

4: LOOKING EXTREMELY BACKWARD

1 Todd Gitlin, *Twilight of Our Common Dreams: Why America is Wracked by Culture Wars* (New York: Metropolitan Books, 1995); Michael Tomasky, *Left for Dead: The Life, Death and Possible Resurrection of Progressive Politics in America*

(New York: The Free Press, 1996); Eric Hobsbawn, "Identity Politics and the Left," *New Left Review* (May/June, 1996); Jim Sleeper, *The Closest of Strangers: Liberalism and the Politics of Race in New York* (New York: W. W. Norton, 1990); Barbara Epstein, "Political Correctness and Collective Powerlessness," *Socialist Review* 21, nos. 3–4 (July–December 1991): 13–35 and "Postmodernism and the Left," *New Politics* 6, no. 2 (Winter 1997): 130–44; Barbara Epstein, Richard Flacks, and Marcy Darnovsky, eds. *Cultural Politics and Social Movements* (Philadelphia: Temple University Press, 1995); Jay Walljasper, "If Right Is Center, Where Is the Left?" *New York Times*, August 18, 1996; Robert Hughes, *Culture of Complaint: The Fraying of America* (New York: Oxford University Press, 1993); Richard Rorty, *Objectivity, Relativism, and Truth* (Cambridge: Cambridge University Press, 1991); Rorty, *Contingency, Irony, and Solidarity* (Cambridge: Cambridge University Press, 1989); and Rorty's address at the opening plenary session of "The Fight for America's Future: A Teach-In With Labor," Columbia University, October 3, 1996. See also Richard Shusterman's brilliant critique of Rorty, "Pragmatism and Liberalism between Dewey and Rorty," *Political Theory* 22, no. 3 (August 1994): 391–413.

2 To be fair, not all naysayers against identity politics are even concerned about finding commonalities around which we all might unite. Because I am particularly interested in how to build class-based alliances in a multiracial, multicultural society founded on racism and sexism, I will not address all of the literature critical of identity politics or what Walter Benn Michaels calls "identitarianism." Nonetheless, I am generally concerned with the way this anti-identitarian discourse, often in the name of pragmatism, presumes that individuals can just float above the structures of domination and see the world clearly, to choose our path and break the chains of tradition. It is not an accident that white men have led the charge against identity politics. The harshest critics do not even see how their own critique of identity politics is identity bound, issued from a site of racial, class, and gender privilege. Their universalist strategy is to dismiss Kwanzaa or look askance at dashikis and dreadlocks as "wearing identity," rather than *embrace these forms as their own.* And whenever Afrocentrists, for whatever reasons, claim the Greco-Roman civilization as *their own* (keep in mind that no book, not even George E. M. James's *Stolen Legacy,* has ever claimed that all of Greek culture was of African origin), these same "universalists" are quick to reduce Afrocentric claims to identity politics and do not see their rejection of these claims— their protection of European ownership of the emerging intellectual and cultural forms—as itself a form of identity politics. We might extend the analogy to language itself. According to Ross Posnock, intellectuals are a category unto themselves, transcendent of identity. Yet, curiously, they always seem to speak English or French or German, they always use the same rather complex languages and draw on similar sources—they rarely speak Spanish let alone Yao or Navajo. Europe always appears as the mediation point for their cosmopolitanism. Academic "intellectuals," the predominant social type, generally operate out of institutional structures with distinct cultural roots whose European origins are often taken for granted. The model of the modern university across the globe came from Italy, not Timbuktu, and yet

we accept this model as transcendent, universal. Moreover, for advocates of universalism, their practice as intellectuals tends to be surprisingly exclusionary. See Walter Benn Michaels's most recent calls for us to transcend "identitarianism" in his book *Our America: Nativism, Modernism, and Pluralism* (Durham, N.C.: Duke University Press, 1995); David Hollinger's *Postethnic America: Beyond Multiculturalism* (New York: Basic Books, 1995); Ross Posnock, "How It Feels to Be a Problem: Du Bois, Fanon, and the 'Impossible Life' of the Black Intellectual," *Critical Inquiry* 23 (Winter 1997): 323–49.

3 Gitlin, *Twilight of Our Common Dreams*, 150; David W. Harris, *From Class Struggle to the Politics of Pleasure: The Effects of Gramscianism on Cultural Studies* (London: Routledge, 1992), v.

4 Gitlin, *Twilight of Our Common Dreams*, 215.

5 George L. Mosse, *Toward the Final Solution: A History of European Racism* (Madison, Wisc.: University of Wisconsin Press, 1985); Cedric Robinson, *Black Marxism: The Making of the Black Radical Tradition* (London: Zed Press, 1983); David Theo Goldberg, *Racist Culture: Philosophy and the Politics of Meaning* (London: Basil Blackwell, 1993); and see Christian Delacampagne, "Racism and the West: From Praxis to Logis," in *Anatomy of Racism*, ed. David Theo Goldberg (Minneapolis: University of Minnesota Press, 1990), 83–88.

6 As I have argued elsewhere, and shall argue more forcefully in the next chapter, social movements rooted in race and gender do not necessarily elide or ignore class, but rather are often the ground upon which class conflicts are enacted. See my *Hammer and Hoe: Alabama Communists during the Great Depression* (Chapel Hill, N.C.: University of North Carolina Press, 1990) and *Race Rebels: Culture, Politics, and the Black Working Class* (New York: The Free Press, 1994), as well as several other scholars too numerous to name here. A few exemplary examples of writing that attempts to theorize how race, gender, and the politics of identity continually reshape class struggle include David Harvey, "Class Relations, Social Justice, and the Politics of Difference," in *Place and the Politics of Identity*, eds. Michael Keither and Steve Pile (New York: Routledge, 1993), 41–66; Hunter, *To 'Joy My Freedom*; George Lipsitz, *A Rainbow at Midnight: Labor and Culture in the 1940s* (Urbana, Ill.: University of Illinois Press, 1994); Eileen Boris, *Home to Work: Motherhood and the Politics of Industrial Homework in the United States* (Cambridge: Cambridge University Press, 1994); David Roediger, *The Wages of Whiteness: Race and the Making of the American Working Class* (London: Verso, 1991); Eric Lott, *Love and Theft: Blackface Minstrelsy and the American Working Class* (New York: Oxford University Press, 1993); George Chauncey, *Gay New York: Gender, Urban Culture, and the Making of the Gay Male World, 1890–1940* (New York: Basic Books, 1994); Dana Frank, *Purchasing Power: Consumer Organizing, Gender, and the Seattle Labor Movement, 1919–1929* (Cambridge: Cambridge University Press, 1994); George Sanchez, *Becoming Mexican-American: Ethnicity, Culture, and Identity in Chicano Los Angeles, 1890–1945* (New York: Oxford University Press, 1993); Earl Lewis, *In Their Own Interests: Race, Class, and Power in Twentieth-Century Norfolk* (Berkeley: University of California

Press, 1991); Michael K. Honey, *Southern Labor and Black Civil Rights: Organizing Memphis Workers* (Urbana, Ill.: University of Illinois Press, 1993); Joe William Trotter, *Coal, Class, and Color: Blacks in Southern West Virginia, 1915–1932* (Urbana, Ill.: University of Illinois Press, 1990); and just about anything by Stuart Hall. See, for example, Hall's "Subjects in History: Making Diasporic Identities," in *The House that Race Built: Black Americans, U.S. Terrain*, ed. Wahneema Lubiano (New York: Pantheon, 1997), 289–99.

7 As a participant of the Columbia University teach-in, I witnessed Friedan's and Rorty's remarks. See also Jesse Lemisch, "Angry White Men on the Left," *New Politics* 6, no. 2 (Winter 1997): 101–2; "Labor Goes to College," *The Nation* 263, no. 13 (October 28, 1996): 4–5.

8 Tomasky, *Left for Dead*, 89. The full text of the Combahee River Collective's statement can be found in Gloria T. Hull, Patricia Bell Scott, and Barbara Smith, eds., *But Some of Us Are Brave* (Old Westbury, N.Y.: Feminist Press, 1982), 13–22.

9 Anna Julia Cooper, "A Voice from the South," in *Black Women in Nineteenth-Century American Life: Their Words, Their Thoughts, Their Feelings*, ed. Bert James Loewenberg and Ruth Bogin (University Park, Penn.: Pennsylvania State University Press, 1976), 330–31.

10 Patricia Hill Collins, *Black Feminist Thought: Knowledge, Consciousness, and the Politics of Empowerment* (New York: Routledge, 1991), 38.

11 Pauli Murray, "The Liberation of Black Women," in *Voices of the New Feminism*, ed. Mary Lou Thompson (Boston: Beacon Press, 1970), 102; also quoted in Collins, *Black Feminist Thought*, 38; and Audre Lorde, "Learning from the 60s," in *The Woman that I Am: The Literature and Culture of Contemporary Women of Color*, ed. D. Soyini Madison (New York: St. Martin's Press, 1994), 457.

12 Collins, *Black Feminist Thought*, 37–39; Barbara Smith, ed., *Home Girls: A Black Feminist Anthology* (New York: Kitchen Table Press, 1983); bell hooks, *Ain't I a Woman: Black Women and Feminism* (Boston: South End Press, 1981); Audre Lorde, *Zami: A New Spelling of My Name* (Trumansberg, N.Y.: The Crossing Press, 1982); Elsa Barkley Brown, "Polyrhythms and Improvisation: Lessons for Women's History," *History Workshop Journal*, 31 (Spring 1991): 85–90; Hull, Bell Scott, and Smith, eds., *But Some of Us Are Brave*; Filomina Steady, ed., *The Black Woman Cross-Culturally* (Cambridge, Mass.: Schenkman, 1981); Alice Walker, *In Search of Our Mothers' Gardens* (New York: Harcourt Brace Jovanovich, 1983).

13 On the National Black Women's Healthcare movement, see Barbara Bair and Susan E. Cayleff, eds., *Wings of Gauze: Women of Color and the Experience of Health and Illness* (Detroit: Wayne State University Press, 1993); Gloria Naylor, "Power: Rx for Good Health," *Ms.* 14, no. 11 (May 1986): 56–62; Stephen Simurda, "Shooting Star," *American Health* 12, no. 2 (March 1993): 28–32; Trudy McLaurie, "Avery Speaks Out on Black Women's Health Issues," *Chicago Defender*, November 17, 1990; Renee Graham, "Activist Spotlights Black Women's Health," *Boston Globe*, October 21, 1991; Patricia Carr,

"Empowerment Begins with Health," *Atlanta Constitution*, October 10, 1991.

14 Martin Duberman, "Bring Back the Enlightenment," *The Nation* 263, no. 1 (July 1, 1996): 25–27.

15 See for example, Lisa Duggan, "Queering the State," *Social Text* 39 (Summer 1994): 1–14; Diana Fuss, "Lesbian and Gay Theory: The Question of Identity Politics," in her *Essentially Speaking: Feminism, Nature, and Difference* (New York: Routledge, 1989), 97–112; Phillip Brian Harper, *Are We Not Men? Masculine Anxiety and the Problem of African-American Identity* (New York: Oxford University Press, 1996); Michael Warner, ed., *Fear of a Queer Planet: Queer Politics and Social Theory* (Minneapolis: University of Minnesota Press, 1993); Bonnie Zimmerman, "Lesbians Like This and That: Some Notes on Lesbian Criticism for the Nineties," *New Lesbian Criticism*, ed. Sally Munt (New York: Columbia University Press, 1992), 1–16.

16 On the Nation of Islam's "war on drugs," see Fracassa Hawke, "In Detroit: March Targets Suspected Drug House," *Detroit News*, December 30, 1996; Vernon Loeb, "D.C. Hires Nation of Islam Guards for SE Complex," *Washington Post*, May 4, 1995; Beverly Muhammad, "Drugs and Public Housing," *Afro-American*, May 20, 1995; George Hackett, "Saying 'No' to Crack Gangs," *Newsweek* (March 28, 1988), 29; Sylvester Monroe, "Doing the Right Thing," *Time* (April 16, 1990): 22.

17 Tomasky, *Left for Dead*, 86–87.

18 For an extended discussion of these labor struggles, see chapter 5.

19 Stephen Franklin and Jerry Thomas, "Blacks Making Few Gains in Trades," *Chicago Tribune*, September 5, 1994; Brent Watters, "Black Union Members Air Demands in March and Rally," *Chicago Weekend*, September 10, 1995.

20 Michael Goldfield, *The Color of Politics* (New York: The New Press, 1997); Richard B. Freeman and Casey Ichniowski, "The Public Sector Look of American Unionism," in *When Public Sector Workers Unionize*, eds. R. B. Freeman and C. Ichniowski (Chicago: University of Chicago Press, 1988); Paul Johnston, *Success While Others Fail: Social Movement Unionism and the Public Workplace* (Ithaca, N.Y.: I.L.R. Press, 1994).

21 Bureau of Labor Statistics, "Union Members in 1994 (Press Release)," February 8, 1995; Gregory Defreitas, "Unionization among Racial and Ethnic Minorities," *Industrial & Labor Relations Review* 46 (January 1, 1993): 284–300.

22 Gitlin, *Twilight of Our Common Dreams*, 71; Tomasky, *Left for Dead*, 29.

23 Du Bois, *Black Reconstruction in America*; Theodore W. Allen, *The Invention of the White Race; Volume One: Racist Oppression and Social Control* (New York: Verso, 1994); Roediger, *The Wages of Whiteness* and *Toward the Abolition of Whiteness: Essays on Race, Politics, and Working-Class History* (London: Verso, 1994); Alexander Saxton, *The Rise and Fall of the White Republic: Class Politics and Mass Culture in Nineteenth-Century America* (London: Verso, 1990); Noel Ignatiev, *How the Irish Became White* (New York: Routledge, 1995); Eric Lott,

Love and Theft; David Wellman, *Portraits of White Racism*, 2d ed. (New York: Cambridge University Press, 1993); Goldfield, *Color of Politics*; and see also Alan Draper, *Conflict of Interests: Organized Labor and the Civil Rights Movement in the South, 1954–1968* (Ithaca, N.Y.: Cornell University Press, 1994). On anti-Chinese racism and labor in the West, see Alexander Saxton's brilliant *The Indispensable Enemy: Labor and the Anti-Chinese Movement in California* (Berkeley: University of California Press, 1971).

24 George Lipsitz, "Immigrant Labor and Identity Politics," in his *The Possessive Investment of Whiteness* (Jackson, Miss.: University Press of Mississippi, 1997). As usual, I am grateful to George for sharing his ideas and for permitting me to quote from his unpublished manuscript.

25 Lemisch, "Angry White Men on the Left," 103.

26 Tomasky, *Left for Dead*, 36.

27 Philip Foner, *Organized Labor and the Black Worker, 1619–1981* (New York: International Publishers, 1981), 47.

5: LOOKING FORWARD

1 C. L. R. James, *The Black Jacobins* (New York: Random House, 1963), 78. One glaring absence in this chapter is a discussion of the recently launched Labor Party, which began in 1991 as the Labor Party Advocates under the leadership of Tony Mazzocchi of the Oil, Chemical and Atomic Workers (OCAW). While I believe it is too early to tell what kind of impact it will have on working-class struggles in the future, I do think it is worth noting that the Labor Party's platform did take a relatively strong stand in defense of affirmative action and in support of several women's issues, from reproductive rights to child care. And it attacked Clinton for signing the welfare reform bill. However, as writer and union activist Jane Slaughter pointed out, the party's antibigotry plank avoids the word *racism*, focusing instead on hate crimes and obvious cases of discrimination, and it does not say anything specific about black workers (aside from condemning the church burnings).

On the other hand, on issues of race and gender the Labor Party is well ahead of most. For example, members of the Labor Party Advocates steering committee recognized that in order to have substantial representation of women and workers of color at the Labor Party's founding convention, they could not rely solely on established union contacts. So they made provisions in the convention rules for "designated workers' organizations—of women, workers of color and other workers' groups including those facing special discrimination"—to have voting power if they endorsed the Labor Party. As a result, groups like the Coalition of Labor Union Women, the Coalition of Black Trade Unionists, and Black Workers for Justice were able to participate and represent the interests of workers irrespective of union affiliation. See Jane Slaughter, "The Labor Party—Pressure on to Act Like One," *New Politics* 6, no. 2 (Winter 1997): 22–32; and Jane Slaughter, "History in the Making: Labor Party Founded in Cleveland," *Labor Notes* 208 (July 1996): 8–9; Ajamu Dillahunt, "Here Comes the Labor Party," *Independent Political Action Bulletin* 13 (Spring 1996): 8; Labor Party New York Metro Chapter, *A Call for Economic Justice: Labor Party Program* (pamphlet, 1996); and David Bacon, "For a Labor Economy," *The Nation* (April 1, 1996), 14.

2 This line is taken directly from D'Souza, *The End of Racism*, 516. He is actually describing scenes from Elijah Anderson's book *Streetwise: Race, Class, and Change in an Urban Community* (Chicago: University of Chicago Press, 1990).

3 Theo Emery, "Women Taking to Role in Unions," *Boston Globe*, July 20, 1996. On unions and the restructuring of universities and hospitals, see Cary Nelson, ed., *We Will Teach for Food: Academic Labor in Crisis* (Minneapolis: University of Minnesota Press, 1997); Toni Gilpin et al., *On Strike for Respect: The Clerical and Technical Workers' Strike at Yale University, 1984–85* (Urbana, Ill.: University of Illinois Press, 1995, reprint from 1987 booklet); Joel Denker, *Unions and Universities: The Rise of the New Labor Leader* (Montclair, N.J.: Allanheld, Osmun, 1981); Karen Sacks, *Caring by the Hour: Women, Work, and Organizing at Duke Medical Center* (Urbana, Ill.: University of Illinois Press, 1988); Leon Fink and Brian Greenberg, *Upheaval in the Quiet Zone: A History of Hospital Workers' Union, Local 1199* (Urbana, Ill.: University of Illinois Press, 1989); Susan Reverby, *Ordered to Care: The Dilemma of American Nursing, 1850–1945* (Cambridge: Cambridge University Press, 1987); Barbara Melosh, *"The Physicians Hand": Work Culture and Conflict in American Nursing* (Philadelphia: Temple University Press, 1982); and Darlene Clark Hine, *Black Women in White: Racial Conflict and Cooperation in the Nursing Profession, 1890–1950* (Bloomington, Ind.: Indiana University Press, 1989).

4 Alvin Peabody, "Black Women Win Brighter Futures With Unions," *Washington Informer*, June 22, 1995; James L. Tyson, "Labor Appeals to Minorities, Women in Turnaround Bid," *Christian Science Monitor*, Oct. 25, 1995; Kathy McCabe, "Trumka Says Revival of Labor Movement Hinges on Diversity," *Boston Globe*, January 23, 1996.

5 Gregory Defreitas, "Unionization among Racial and Ethnic Minorities," *Industrial & Labor Relations Review* 46 (January 1, 1993): 284–301.

6 Ibid.

7 Ibid.

8 Tyson, "Labor Appeals to Minorities"; see also John J. Sweeney, *America Needs a Raise: Fighting for Economic Security and Social Justice* (New York: Houghton Mifflin, 1996), 121–57.

9 Burrus quoted in Louis Uchitelle, "Blacks Seek Opening in AFL-CIO Leadership Fight," *New York Times*, July 15, 1995; Laura McClure, "AFL-CIO: A New Era?" *Labor Notes* 201 (December 1995): 10; Tyson, "Labor Appeals to Minorities" McCabe, "Trumka Says Revival."

10 McClure, "AFL-CIO"; McCabe, "Trumka Says Revival."

11 On Justice for Janitors and SEIU history, see Sweeney, *America Needs a Raise*, 26–27, 128–31; and Sharolyn A. Rosier, "Justice for Janitors Campaign Expands," *AFL-CIO News* (January 5, 1996).

12 Stephen Lerner, "Reviving Unions: A Call for Direct Action," *Boston Review* 21, no. 2 (April/May 1996).

13 Rosier, "Justice for Janitors Campaign"; Stuart Silverstein and Josh Meyer, "Fast-Growing Union Hits Obstacles in L.A.," *Los Angeles Times*, Sept. 18, 1995.

14 Sweeney, *America Needs a Raise*, 129–30; Silverstein and Meyer, "Fast-Growing Union"; Rosier, "Justice for Janitors Campaign"; Greg Goldin, "The New Surge in Latino Union Organizing," *Service Employees Union* 3, no. 3 (June/July 1989): 25–28.

15 Eric Mann, "Janitors Win a Measure of Justice," *Los Angeles Times*, April 11, 1995.

16 Ibid.

17 Pamela Constable, "Janitors Union Expands Its Campaign," *Washington Post*, March 23, 1995; Rosier, "Justice for Janitors Campaign."

18 Mary Ann French, "Taking It to the Streets," *Washington Post*, April 14, 1995.

19 Rosier, "Justice for Janitors Campaign."

20 Bob Fitch, "Sweeney among the Warlords," *New Politics* 6, no. 2 (Winter 1997): 152–58.

21 Stuart Silverstein, "Going to Work on L.A.: In Its Many Low-Paid Laborers, Unions See Big Potential for Organizing," *Los Angeles Times*, February 22, 1996.

22 "K-Mart Workers Declare Victory," *Justice Speaks* 14, no. 1 (September 1996): 5.

23 "K-Mart Workers Declare Victory," 1, 5. Williams quoted in "'Tis the Season to Pay Equal Wages," *UNITE!* 1, no. 4 (December 1995): 10. On Nelson Johnson, see Elizabeth Wheaton, *Codename Greenkil: The 1979 Greensboro Killings* (Athens, Ga.: University of Georgia Press, 1987); "The Revolutionary Communist League," 80–81.

24 "K-Mart Workers Declare Victory," 5.

25 U.S. Department of Education, National Center for Education Statistics, *Integrated Postsecondary Education Data System* (Washington, D.C.: GPO, 1995).

26 "Race and Pay Sit-in Shifts Site at Duke," *New York Times*, April 9, 1968; "Cafeteria Strike Nears Impasse," *New York Times*, December 7, 1969.

27 Wheaton, *Codename Greenkil*, especially 23–24. The struggle to improve the working conditions of black housekeepers at UNC continues to this day. On October 12, 1996, the UNC Housekeepers Association and the Coalition for Economic Justice organized a "March for Justice" demanding job security, no privatization, no retributions, a living wage, and better working conditions for service employees. They also filed a class action suit against the university that was scheduled to go to trial early in 1997. "Housekeepers March Disrupts UNC–Chapel Hill Homecoming," *Justice Speaks* 14, no. 3 (November 1996): 1.

28 Furthermore, as students and faculty in support of campus unionism, we must pay more attention to corporate campaigns and boycotts. Let us not forget the incredible success of the anti-apartheid divestment campaign, which required support from students, faculty, and staff.

29 Eric Neubauer, "Converting the Children," *Daily Iowan*, January 23, 1997; letter from Stephen Colman to author, January 25, 1997. I am grateful to Colman for sending me a package of material on the University of Iowa struggle, including miscellaneous leaflets.

30 My argument about the centrality of community for the labor movement is further developed in my book, *Race Rebels*. There is much available labor history that explores these strikes as well as the particular role communities have played in their success or failure. For an introduction, see Herbert Gutman, "Work, Culture, and Society in Industrializing America," in *Work, Culture, and Society in Industrializing America: Essays in American Working-Class and Social History* (New York: Knopf, 1976), 3–78; Hunter, *To 'Joy My Freedom*; Jacquelyn Dowd Hall et al., *Like a Family: The Making of a Southern Mill World* (Chapel Hill, N.C.: University of North Carolina Press, 1987); Michael Frisch and Daniel J. Walkowtiz, eds., *Working-Class America: Essays on Labor, Community, and American Society* (Urbana, Ill.: University of Illinois Press, 1983); Vicki Ruiz, *Cannery Women, Cannery Lives: Mexican Women, Unionization, and the California Food-Processing Industry, 1930–1950* (Albuquerque: University of New Mexico Press, 1987); Joe William Trotter, Jr., *Black Milwaukee: The Making of an Industrial Proletariat, 1915–1945* (Urbana, Ill.: University of Illinois Press, 1985) and *Coal, Class, and Color: Blacks in Southern West Virginia, 1915–1932* (Urbana, Ill.: University of Illinois Press, 1990); John C. Leggett, *Class, Race, and Labor: Working-Class Consciousness in Detroit* (New York: Oxford University Press, 1968); James A. Geschwender, *Class, Race, and Worker Insurgency: The League of Revolutionary Black Workers* (Cambridge: Cambridge University Press, 1977); Dan Georgakas and Marvin Surkin, *Detroit, I Do Mind Dying: A Study in Urban Revolution* (New York: St. Martin's Press, 1975); James Forman, *The Making of Black Revolutionaries* (Washington, D.C.: Open Hand Publishers, 1985); Clayborne Carson, *In Struggle: SNCC and the Black Awakening of the 1960s* (Cambridge: Harvard University Press, 1981); Eric Mann, *Taking On General Motors: A Case Study of the Campaign to Keep GM Van Nuys Open* (Los Angeles: Center for Labor Research and Education, Institute of Industrial Relations, University of California at Los Angeles, 1987).

31 James O'Toole, *Watts and Woodstock: Identity and Culture in the U.S. and South Africa* (New York: Holt, Rinehart and Winston, 1973).

32 Ruth Wilson Gilmore, "Public Enemies and Private Intellectuals," *Race and Class* 35, no. 1 (July–September 1993), 69–78; Mothers Reclaiming Our Children Web site: www.labridge.com/mroc/three.html

33 Eric Mann and the Labor Community Watchdog Committee, *L.A.'s Lethal Air: New Strategies for Policy, Organizing, and Action* (Los Angeles: Labor/Community Strategy Center, 1991), 18.

34 Bullard, *Dumping in Dixie*; Andrew Szasz, *Ecopopulism: Toxic Waste and the*

Movement for Environmental Justice (Minneapolis: University of Minnesota Press, 1994); Laura Pulido, *Environmentalism and Economic Justice: Two Chicano Struggles in the Southwest* (Tucson: University of Arizona Press, 1996).

35 Ruth Rosen, "Who Gets Polluted?" *Dissent* 41, no. 2 (Spring 1994): 223–30.

36 Bullard, *Dumping in Dixie*; Patsy Ruth Oliver, "West Dallas Versus the Lead Smelter," in *Unequal Protection: Environmental Justice and Communities of Color*, ed. Robert Bullard (San Francisco: Sierra Club Books, 1994).

37 See, for example, Eric Mann et al., *L.A.'s Lethal Air*; The Urban Strategies Group, *A Call to Reject the Federal Weed and Seed Program in Los Angeles* (Los Angeles: Labor/Community Strategy Center, 1992); Labor/Community Strategy Center, *Reconstructing Los Angeles from the Bottom Up* (Los Angeles: Labor/Community Strategy Center, 1993); Eric Mann, "Janitors Win a Measure of Justice"; "Sutaur 100: Lessons from Mexico City: An Interview with Jorge Cuellar Valdez conducted by Eric Mann," *Ahora Now!* 3 (Fall 1996): 6–9; Urban Strategies Group, *Derechos Humanos para los Inmigrantes/Immigrants Rights and Wrongs* (Los Angeles: Labor/Community Strategy Center, 1994).

38 Robin D. G. Kelley, "Freedom Riders (The Sequel)," *The Nation* (February 5, 1996): 19.

39 For background on the Metropolitan Transit Authority's unscrupulous dealings, see Mike Davis, "Runaway Train Crushes Buses," *The Nation*, September 18, 1995.

40 Kelley, "Freedom Riders," 18–20; Mann quote from interview with author, December 5, 1995.

41 See back issues of *Ahora Now!*, especially Lian Hurst Mann, "Left Culture in the Age of the Right," *Ahora Now!* 1 (Spring 1996): 1–3.

42 Lian Hurst Mann, "Subverting the Avant-Garde: Critical Theory's Real Strategy," in *Reconstruction Architecture: Critical Discourses and Social Practices*, eds. Lian Hurst Mann and Thomas A. Dutton (Minneapolis: University of Minnesota Press, 1996), 302–3.

43 L. H. Mann, "Subverting the Avant-Garde," 303–5; Staff of Labor/Community Strategy Center, "The Labor/Community Strategy Center: A Multiracial Regional Experiment in Grassroots Democracy" (unpublished report, 1996).

44 "A Historic Victory for Civil Rights," *Labor/Community Strategy Update* (undated flyer, ca. October 1996); Richard Simon, "Settlement of Bus Suit Approved," *Los Angeles Times*, October 29, 1996; *Los Angeles Daily News*, October 29, 1996.

45 Dr. Martin Luther King, Jr., *Stride Toward Freedom: The Montgomery Story* (New York: Harper, 1958), p. 197.

EPILOGUE: LOOKING B(L)ACKWARD

1 John Hope Franklin, *Race and History: Selected Essays, 1938–1988* (Baton Rouge, La.: Louisiana State University Press, 1989), 299.

2 V. P. Franklin, *Black Self-Determination: A Cultural History of African-American Resistance*, 2d ed. (Brooklyn, N.Y.: Lawrence Hill Books, 1992); and Gwaltney, *Drylongso*.

3 Albert Murray, *The Omni-Americans: Black Experience and American Culture* (New York: Vintage Books, 1983), 97–98.

PROPS, RESPECT, AND LOVE

First and foremost, I have to send extra phat props to Deb Chasman, my amazing editor at Beacon Press and the real brainchild behind this book; to Tisha Hooks for knowing everything and for laughing at my jokes; to Bruce Nichols of the Free Press for granting me a furlough; to Denise Stinson, agent extraordinaire, literary and otherwise; to the Africana Studies staff (New York University), especially Fatima LeGrand and Glenda Doyle; to the history department staff: Karin Burroughs, William Seward, Ben Maddox, and especially Delverlon Hall—she saved my life more than once and has remained a rock-steady friend throughout. Thanks to the good folks at the National Endowment for the Humanities for their generous support of the research and writing of this book.

Much love to Tera Hunter—brilliant historian, writer, critic, visionary—she's truly my role model. That all of these qualities can be found in such a warm, generous person is so rare I think she must be an alien. My other wonderful friends and colleagues at the University of Michigan—Elsa Barkley Brown, Earl Lewis, Jayne London, Michael Awkward, Lauren Rich, George Sanchez, Gina Morantz-Sanchez, and Julius Scott—have been like family to me. One cannot find better intellectual collaborators than Elsa and Earl. Much love and respect due to Michael Eric Dyson and Marcia Dyson for their unwavering support and ridiculous praises; to Sidney Lemelle, Salima Lemelle, and family for keeping me Black, Red, and honest; to Denise Greene and Emir Lewis for just letting me hang with their brilliant "New Niggerati" selves; and to Elenni Knight Davis, Michaela Angela Davis, (*the*) Graham Haynes, and Ezra Knight, for all their creativity and unothodox Afro-love.

Much respect due to George Lipsitz whose name should be listed in *Roget's Thesaurus* under "principled" and "generous"—his impact on this book should be evident to anyone who knows his

212 » YO' MAMA'S DISFUNKTIONAL!

work; to Nell Irvin Painter for continuing to mentor me and for proving to the world that cynicism and cash are not what black intellectuals are made of; to my homegirl Tricia Rose whose brilliant scholarship has been inspiring me to study urban culture for the past eleven years; and to my other colleagues at New York University, especially Thomas Bender, Manthia Diawara, Ada Ferrer, Steven Gregory, Philip Brian Harper, Martha Hodes, Walter Johnson, Andrew Ross, Jefferey T. Sammons, Nikhil Singh, and Daniel J. Walkowitz, for watching my back and helping me think in new ways; to Franklin and Penelope Rosemont, Ted Joans, Jayne Cortez, and James Spady for introducing me to the marvelous world below; to the scholars and activists who read the work, passed on ideas, and/or simply inspired me by their example: Elizabeth Alexander; Sam Anderson, Joel Washington, and the brothers and sisters in the Network of Black Organizers; Dana Baron; Rosalyn Baxandall; Eileen Boris; Wini Breines; Paul Buhle; MariJo Buhle; Rod and Melanie Bush; Hazel Carby; Sundiata Cha-Jua; Claude Clegg; Michael Denning; Nick Dirks; Geoff Eley; Grant Farred; Leon Forrest; Janet Francendese; Kevin Gaines; Kyra Gaunt; Gerald Gill; Herman Gray; Farah Jasmine Griffin; Michael Honey; (cousin) Ron Jackson; Geoffrey Jacques; Arthur Jafa; Gerald Jaynes, Nelson Lichtenstein; Peter Linebaugh; Wahneema Lubiano; Clarence Lusane; Eric Mann, Liann Hurst Mann, and the staff of the Labor/Community Strategy Center, Manning Marable, Leith Mullings, the entire Ida-Web Network of activist intellectuals and artists; Marya McQuirter; Cary Nelson; Carl Nightingale; Sherry B. Ortner; Tiffany R. L. Patterson; William Eric Perkins; Clement Price; Arnold Rampersad; Guthrie Ramsey; Pamela T. Reid; James Scott; Thomas Sugrue; Lisa Y. Sullivan and the other activists in the Children's Defense Fund; Greg Tate; Jeanne Theoharis; Jerry Tucker and the folks in New Directions; Akinyele Umoja; Penny von Eschen; Cornel West; Shane White; Joe Wood; Komozi Woodard; Gwendolyn Wright; Cynthia Young.

Deep gratitude to the many people who engaged me when I presented parts of this book as lectures and papers. I'm particularly indebted to those who attended the following seminars, conferences, or lectures: the Marion Wright Thompson Lecture (1997), Rutgers University, Newark Campus; the Martin Luther King, Jr., Distinguished Lecture (1996), Sarah Lawrence College; the Allison Davis Lecture (1995), Northwestern University; W. E. B. Du Bois Distinguished Lecture (1993), City University New York; the Institute for the Humanities (University of Michigan), "Race Matters: Black Americans/Urban Terrain," Princeton University; "The Negro Problem, 1895–1995," Princeton University (special thanks to Judith Jackson Fossett and Jeffrey A. Tucker); the Robert Penn Warren Center for the Humanities, Vanderbilt University; "Teach-In for the Labor Movement," Columbia University; African Educational Forum, Yonkers, New York; New Directions Socialist School, Stony Point, New Jersey; Committees of Correspondence, Labor Committee Forum; "Safe Communities: Toward A Comprehensive Urban Agenda," Penn Center, Helena Island, South Carolina; Black Student Leadership Network and Children's Defense Fund Retreat, Haley Farm, Tennessee; Bertolt Brecht Forum, New York; Labor Resource Center, Queens College; New York City Metro Labor Press Council; Labor Community Strategy Center, Organizers School, Los Angeles, California; Graduate Employees Organization Forum, Yale University; and various lectures given at Medgar Evers College, Brooklyn; Spelman College; Russell Sage Foundation; the National Humanities Center, Research Triangle, North Carolina; University of Michigan; Yale University; State University of New York at Binghamton; Georgia State University; Duke University; University of Maryland, College Park. Together, all of the criticisms and suggestions I received in these arenas made this a substantially better book.

Serious props to the many, many graduate students (much too numerous to name here) at the University of Michigan, New York

University, CUNY Graduate Center, Princeton University, Yale University, the University of Pennsylvania, Columbia University, and the New School for Social Research, who helped shaped my thinking on all of the questions this book attempts to address; crazy shout out to my crack research assistants Kim Gilmore, Betsy Esch, and Melina Pappademas. Much respect to the graduate student unions at Yale University and several other institutions across the country for leading the way to a brighter future; and to Stephen and David Colman, Paul Young, and John Scott for keeping me abreast of the University of Iowa struggle and for their unwavering commitment to antiracism.

A house full of love to my original mentors, Thelma Reyna and Jane Andrias (with a special shout out to Jane's husband, Richard, and their two brilliant daughters, Eve and Kate). A magic bag of love to Nichole! Rustin for giving her time, her brilliant (in)sight, her artistic vision, and for pulling me back when I was on the brink of insanity about to fall off the edge of the clef; and to Judith Macfarlane for reminding me that great poetry is not a mere representation but life itself.

Much, much love, respect, and straight-up deference to my brilliant big sister, Makani Themba, whose battle against the drug war being waged on poor black, Latino, and Native American communities by the alcohol and tobacco industry has irrevocably shaped parts of my argument. Indeed, her own frontline activism around urban issues was a primary source of inspiration for this book. Let me also give a loving shout out to my entire family: my mother-in-law Annette Rohan and all of the aunts—Evelyn, Nanette (rest in peace), Dorothe, Dolores, Marie, Betsy (Gloria), and Sheila; my father, Donald Kelley, and his wife, Mary Kay; my grandmothers, Carmen Chambers and Aileen Kelley; my late grandfather, the Reverend Rafe David Kelley (rest in peace); my other sisters and brothers—Meilan Carter (poet extraordinaire), Chris Kelley, Fujiko Kelley, Shannon Patrick Kelley, Benjamin Kelley, Craig Berrysmith, and all their children; Claudine and Stanley Allison, Irie Harris-Mitchell and Don Mitchell, Claudius Harris, Jr., and his wife Karen, and all of my wife's cousins (too numerous to name).

I must send infinite love to Diedra Harris-Kelley and Elleza Carmen Akilah Kelley for keeping me anchored. For sixteen years Diedra has been unwavering in support of our collective work, always finding ways to visualize things that mere words cannot express, always the selfless collaborator. Although her art did not find a place on the book jacket this time around, her paintings continue to be a constant source of inspiration. Her complex, surreal depictions of black women, masks, and architectural forms convey more "truth" than anything we might find in the writings of social policy analysts and conservative critics. Her work reminds me over and over again that she and I are essentially engaged in the same project: challenging racist/sexist representations of oppressed people, particularly black people. And as parents, we both recognize that, in many ways, Elleza drives our political activism. Yet, whenever Elleza and I read and write poetry together, share a cup of hot chocolate with whipped cream, or walk circles inside the Guggenheim Museum, I realize that my most important political project is at home.

Finally, much, much, much love to my mom, Ananda Sattwa, to whom this book is dedicated. She spent much of her life as a single parent (even when she was married!) and raised us to embrace the marvelous. She showed us where to look for beauty and art and love in the cracks and crevices of 157th and Amsterdam, up in Harlem. She taught us how to see past the profane in order to find the humanity and humor in the mundane. She taught us that pleasure is not always for sale. And she taught us that a sunset is a sunset no matter where you stand. So if my descriptions of the splendor and beauty of the contemporary "ghetto" and its inhabitants at times seem jarring to our modern senses, it is probably because I have my mother's eyes.

INDEX

Abrahams, Roger, 33–34
Account of the Regular Gradation in Man, An (White), 108
aerosol art. *See* graffiti
aesthetics, 41–42
AFDC. *See* Aid to Families with Dependent Children
affirmative action, 10–11; backlash against, 120–21; and color-blind society, 89–90; erosion of, 81–82; neoconservatives on, 89–90; public sector successes of, 95–96; for white Americans, 95
African Liberation Support Committee, 136
Afro (hairstyle), 26–31; history of, 27–28; political implications of, 30–31
Agee, Arthur, 54
AgitProps, 156
Ahora Now!, 155
Aid to Families with Dependent Children (AFDC), 82
Allison, Theresa, 158
Alvarez, Joe, 117
Amalgamated Clothing and Textile Workers Union (ACTWU), 117
American Allied Workers Laborers International Union (AAWLIU), 117
American Federation of State, County, and Municipal Employees (AFSCME), 140
antistatism, 80–81. *See also* government supports/entitlements
architecture, effects of fear of crime on, 50–53
artists: aerosol/graffiti, 44, 60–65; women, 30, 61, 69–71
arts: break dancing, 66–69; and community-based movements, 155–57; as employment, 57–71;

Go-Go music, 58–60; graffiti, 60–65; rap music, 65–66; vs. sports as financial opportunity, 69; street music, 57–58; and women, 69–71
authenticity/value: ethnography and, 20–21; Hip Hop and, 38–40; and marketplace participation, 26–27, 71–74

bagging. *See* dozens, the
Baker, Houston, 53
Baraka, Amiri (LeRoi Jones), 25, 79
Barnard College, 137
basketball: as career option, 53–54; compared with graffiti, 64–65
Basquiat, Jean Michel, 63, 65
B-boys/girls, 66. *See also* break dancing
behavior: as cause of poverty, 17–19; as culture, 9–10, 16–17, 22–23
Bell, Derrick, 78
Bellamy, Edward, 12
Bell Curve: Intelligence and Class Structure in American Life, The (Murray, Herrnstein), 3–4, 90
Bennett, Lerone, 25
Bevona, "Greedy" Gus, 135
Bilson, Jane Mancini, 31
Black Independent Political Organization (BIPO), 117
Black Muslims in America, The (Lincoln), 86
black nationalism, 30–31
Black Power movement, 6, 116; soul and, 25–26
Black Power: The Politics of Liberation in America (Carmichael, Hamilton), 88
black studies, future of, 12, 159–80
black urban culture: "authentic," 20–21; as coping mechanisms,